Don DeLillo, American Original

Don DeLillo, American Original

Drugs, Weapons, Erotica, and Other Literary Contraband

Michael Naas

BLOOMSBURY ACADEMIC
NEW YORK • LONDON • OXFORD • NEW DELHI • SYDNEY

BLOOMSBURY ACADEMIC
Bloomsbury Publishing Inc
1385 Broadway, New York, NY 10018, USA
50 Bedford Square, London, WC1B 3DP, UK

BLOOMSBURY, BLOOMSBURY ACADEMIC and the Diana logo
are trademarks of Bloomsbury Publishing Plc

First published in the United States of America 2020

Copyright © Michael Naas, 2020

Cover design: Eleanor Rose
Cover photograph: American flag painted on rusty door,
New York © Carlina Teteris / Moment / Getty Images

For legal purposes the Acknowledgments on pp. 226–227 constitute
an extension of this copyright page.

All rights reserved. No part of this publication may be reproduced
or transmitted in any form or by any means, electronic or mechanical,
including photocopying, recording, or any information storage or retrieval
system, without prior permission in writing from the publishers.

Bloomsbury Publishing Inc does not have any control over, or responsibility
for, any third-party websites referred to or in this book. All internet addresses
given in this book were correct at the time of going to press. The author and
publisher regret any inconvenience caused if addresses have changed or sites
have ceased to exist, but can accept no responsibility for any such changes.

Library of Congress Cataloging-in-Publication Data
Names: Naas, Michael, author.
Title: Don DeLillo, American original : drugs, weapons, erotica, and other
literary contraband / Michael Naas.
Description: New York, NY : Bloomsbury Academic, 2020. | Includes
bibliographical references. | Summary: "A radical reassessment of one of
our most important contemporary novelists"– Provided by publisher.
Identifiers: LCCN 2019052615 | ISBN 9781501361821 (hardback) | ISBN
9781501361814 (paperback) | ISBN 9781501361845 (pdf) | ISBN
9781501361838 (epub)
Subjects: LCSH: DeLillo, Don–Criticism and interpretation. | Deception in
literature.
Classification: LCC PS3554.E4425 Z757 2020 | DDC 813/.54–dc23
LC record available at https://lccn.loc.gov/2019052615

ISBN:	HB:	978-1-5013-6182-1
	PB:	978-1-5013-6181-4
	ePDF:	978-1-5013-6184-5
	eBook:	978-1-5013-6183-8

Typeset by Integra Software Services Pvt. Ltd.

To find out more about our authors and books visit www.bloomsbury.com
and sign up for our newsletters.

Contents

	List of Abbreviations	vii
	Preface: Don DeLillo's Contraband: Taking Stock, from *Americana* to *Zero K*	ix
1	Controlled and Uncontrolled Substances	1
	Drugs	1
	Alcohol	4
	Erotica and Stolen Art	6
	Weapons	7
	Knives	8
	Guns	10
	Nukes	18
2	Underworlds and Undercurrents	23
	Cults, Criminal Organizations, Spy Agencies	23
	Coincidences and Conspiracies	29
	Secrets and Rumors	33
	Undergrounds	39
3	Counterpoints and Counternarratives	45
	Bandwidths	45
	Battle of the Bands	55
4	Media and Mediatization	63
	Newspapers, Magazines, Tabloids	63
	Radio	65
	Television	70
	Telephone	76
	Tape Recorders and Answering Machines	78
	Internet	82
5	Arts of Duplicity	85
	Painting and Sculpture	85
	Theater, Performance Art, Graffiti	91

	Photography	100
	Film	105
	Videos, Home Movies, Newsreels	120
	Music	125
6	Double Takes	129
	Retrospection and Memory	129
	"Live" Perception	134
	White Noise, The World Hum	140
	Double Vision	142
	Repetitions and Mirror Images	145
7	Writing in Tongues	149
	Literature	149
	Numbers	164
	Writing	171
	Foreign Languages	181
	Glossolalia	188
	Linguistic Shrapnel	190
8	Words for Words	197
	Names	197
	Words	207
	Defining Words	211
	Simple Words	219
	Letters	221
	Punctuation	223
Countersignature		225
Acknowledgments		226

Abbreviations

Novels

A	*Americana*. Boston: Houghton Mifflin, 1971. Rev. Ed. New York: Penguin, 1989.
AZ	*Amazons: An Intimate Memoir by the First Woman Ever to Play in the National Hockey League*. Written under the pseudonym Cleo Birdwell. New York: Holt, Rinehart and Winston,1980.
BA	*The Body Artist*. New York: Scribner, 2001.
C	*Cosmopolis*. New York: Scribner, 2003.
EZ	*End Zone.* Boston: Houghton Mifflin, 1972. Paper: New York: Penguin, 1986.
FM	*Falling Man*. New York: Scribner, 2007.
GJ	*Great Jones Street*. Boston: Houghton Mifflin, 1973. Paper: New York: Vintage, 1989.
L	*Libra*. New York: Viking, 1988.
M	*Mao II*. New York: Viking, 1991.
N	*The Names*. New York: Knopf, 1982.
P	*Players*. New York: Knopf, 1977.
PO	*Point Omega*. New York: Scribner, 2010.
RD	*Running Dog*. New York: Knopf, 1978.
RS	*Ratner's Star*. New York: Knopf, 1976.
U	*Underworld*. New York: Scribner, 1997.
WN	*White Noise*. New York: Viking, 1985.
ZK	*Zero K*. New York: Scribner, 2016.

Short Stories

AE	*The Angel Esmeralda: Nine Stories*. New York: Scribner, 2011.
"AE"	"The Angel Esmeralda"
"BM"	"Baader Meinhof"
"C"	"Creation"
"HM"	"Human Moments in World War III"
"HS"	"Hammer and Sickle"
"IA"	"The Ivory Acrobat"
"MD"	"Midnight in Dostoevsky"
"R"	"The Runner"
"S"	"The Starveling"

Plays

EM	*The Engineer of Moonlight*. *Cornell Review* 5 (Winter 1979): 21–47.
LL	*Love-Lies-Bleeding*. New York: Scribner, 2006.
DR	*The Day Room*. New York: Knopf, 1987. Rpt. Viking/Penguin, 1989.
V	*Valparaiso*. New York: Scribner, 1999.

Essays

"PH"	"The Power of History"
"RF"	"In the Ruins of the Future," first published in *Harper's Magazine* (December 2001) and then republished in *The Guardian* on December 22, 2001.

Preface

Don DeLillo's Contraband: Taking Stock, from *Americana* to *Zero K*

Pause for a moment, you wretched weakling, and take stock of yourself.
U 295, from *The Cloud of Unknowing*

A new month. Time to take stock.
Take stock of what?
AZ 373

Don DeLillo, American Original is not your typical work of literary criticism or academic scholarship. It is a reading of DeLillo's work, to be sure, with a theme and a thesis, but it is also a celebration and a retrospective, a taking stock, as it were, of the works of someone who has been, for over half a century now, one of America's most original, inventive, and prescient voices. The book attempts to give an account of Don DeLillo's unique voice and place in twentieth- and twenty-first-century American letters by following a single theme throughout his work, namely, *contraband*, at once literal contraband and literature as contraband. The book thus begins by exploring the many forms of illegal or semi-legal goods and substances that fill DeLillo's novels, everything from guns, drugs, and erotica to atomic weapons and nuclear waste, along with all the secret organizations, whether governmental (CIA, FBI) or extra-governmental (mafia, cults, terrorist networks) that traffic in them, in order then to argue that what is most interesting and innovative in DeLillo's work is its uniquely contrapuntal or contraband style, whether that be at the level of the entire narrative, the chapter, the paragraph, the sentence, the word, or the simple punctuation mark. This work shows that the extraordinary power, authority, insight, and inventiveness of DeLillo's fictions are thus the result of the way they traffic everywhere in contraband goods and narratives, in doubleness or duplicity of every kind, in multiple voices and story lines, multiple times, places, and media that at once interrupt and complement one another in a uniquely contrabanded fashion. It is through this doubleness or duplicity, this contrabanding at the level of both content and form, that DeLillo is able to show us, always with great insight and often with tremendous humor, that doubles, knockoffs, imitations, and repeats of all kinds are absolutely essential to anything that might be characterized as real, genuine, or authentic. The "thesis" here, then, is that it is nothing other than this ingenious exploitation of literary contraband, and, in the end, of literature as contraband, that has made Don DeLillo one of the most inventive and important writers in American literature, DeLillo's unique brand of contraband that, paradoxical as it may seem, has made him an American original.

"Contraband" is thus the single name under which I attempt to explore a series of motifs in DeLillo's writings from *Americana* (1971), DeLillo's first novel, to *Zero K* (2016), his latest, all his works from A to Z, therefore, on everything from alcohol (in *End Zone*), art (in *Underworld*), and the alphabet (in *The Names*) to the Zumwalt automatic (in *White Noise*), the Zero-One binary (in *Ratner's Star*), and the Zapruder film (in *Libra*). Instead, therefore, of developing a more academic argument about the modernism or postmodernism of DeLillo's work based on its ironic distance or its fragmented narratives, its penchant for pastiche or kitsch, or its radical rethinking of power, money, violence, religion, or what-have-you, this work attempts to read DeLillo's corpus through the single theme of contraband in order to explain both the topics he treats and the form his narratives have to take in order to treat them. For contraband is also, as we come to learn in the process, DeLillo's way of remaining true to the double- or multi-banded nature of contemporary society, which is itself irreducibly divided between these multiple voices, tracks, or bands, torn between high and low cultures, vast media networks and personal experience, massive corporate and governmental systems and individual desires, geopolitics and personal destinies, grand narratives and the everyday idiom.

This is thus a rather unconventional work of literary criticism, but then so is DeLillo's writing, which is what makes it so compelling. To pursue this theme of contraband in a full and systematic way and yet keep my argument as readable as possible, I have not engaged the many excellent commentaries and secondary sources on DeLillo's work. There was, I thought, no way to convey the pace, power, and humor of DeLillo's work in a more traditional work of literary criticism, no way to canvass DeLillo's corpus on all these motifs and also address, in the same work, even a fraction of the vast secondary literature on that corpus. Though I hope that DeLillo scholars will read and appreciate this work in the spirit in which it was written, I also hope that it will appeal to the average DeLillo reader, who is a committed, enthusiastic, and keenly perceptive reader, and so, in the end, anything but "average." While this is not, then, a typical academic or scholarly book about DeLillo's work or even about Don DeLillo the author, it is nonetheless a serious book about a very serious writer whose work reflects, perhaps like no other, the complexities of contemporary American society from the early 1970s right up to today.

In keeping with these aims, the book is organized not into traditional chapters (thirty to forty pages in length, say, with references and footnotes) but into brief five- to six-page sections, close to fifty of them in all, each devoted to a particular topic and each preceded (as a sort of contraband) by a few apposite epigraphs from DeLillo's work. Always insightful and often wickedly funny, these epigraphs are, I believe, a fitting counterpoint to the themes treated in each section. The work thus attempts to make a single, coherent argument that takes us from the notion of literal contraband to literary contraband, that is, from drugs, weapons, and erotica to words, letters, and punctuation marks. But by being divided up into so many short sections, the argument can be consumed, if the reader so wishes, in very manageable, bite-sized chunks. My aim, in the end, was to provide a different kind of reading experience, a work of literary criticism that might be read like a long essay, fast-paced, sometimes even rapid-fire, on everything from alcohol, guns, secrets, and nuclear waste to television, photography, video, and the internet. In short, I wanted there to be a *performative* element to this work, one that would try to reproduce or replicate at last some of the excitement and pleasure of reading a DeLillo work. For if DeLillo's writing is sophisticated and profound and thought-provoking, it is also extremely entertaining, often at once deeply disturbing and oddly pleasurable. I hope that this work conveys at least some of the pleasure that I myself as a reader have been taking in DeLillo's work for more than four decades now. One of my secret hopes, therefore, is that those who have never read DeLillo will be inspired by this book to begin reading him and that those who have read some of his work will be motivated to read more.

Finally, just a word about the writing of this work. I began thinking about this book in early 2016 but did not really turn to it in earnest until after the US presidential election in 2016 when I found myself reading DeLillo as something like a form of therapy, a countermeasure of sorts, a counternarrative to the grim narrative that seemed to be unfolding on the national scene. The idea behind this book was thus to steep myself in DeLillo's unique American language, voice, and vision while another, very different and a whole lot less humorous, open, and promising America was taking shape in politics and in American culture more generally. If this work can succeed in reminding us that visions or voices like DeLillo's are always necessary but are never more so than in times like our own, then it will have served some of its purpose. Let us hope there is still room in today's America for a contraband discourse that is this revealing and true, a work, a genuine work, capable of providing this much pleasure, insight, and wonder.

1

Controlled and Uncontrolled Substances

The customs men checked the cab for contraband and breezed through our bags and we were in our rented car in a matter of minutes.

U 589

Drugs

Thingness. If you're interested in things, either take dope or travel to an ancient country.

GJ 62

Hashish. Interesting, interesting word. Arabic. It's the source of the word assassin.

L 342

You know what's in my medicine chest. What secrets are left?

WN 62

In publishing a work with the proper name "Don DeLillo" coupled with "drugs," "weapons," "erotica," and, finally, "contraband" in its title, it was not at all my intention to try to tip off the TSA or Homeland Security or customs agents anywhere else in the world to anything Don DeLillo himself, Don DeLillo the author, may have hidden on his person or put in his luggage, whether in the bags he has checked in or those he has tried to fit under the seat in front of him or in the overhead compartment above. I was not trying to suggest that he or anyone associated with him is, will be, or ever should be placed on some no-fly list for smuggling illegal goods of any kind. In speaking of contraband, I was simply trying to encapsulate in a single and no doubt slightly illegitimate word DeLillo's unique narrative style or technique, his genius for smuggling into prose incongruous if not illicit items that contribute to both the poignancy and power of his work and its inimitable inventiveness and infectious humor.

In speaking of contraband, then, I was not referring to anything DeLillo or his characters could have gotten in trouble for by smuggling across state lines or international borders, things like pot, the kind Gary Harkness gets stoned on while playing football in *End Zone* (*EZ* 172; see *U* 397, 487)—not a good idea, by the way—or hashish, which Bucky Wunderlick has a hankering for in *Great Jones Street* (*GJ* 137) or that David Ferrie in *Libra* smokes with Lee Harvey Oswald one night as he is trying to get into Oswald's head and groom him for the assassination of JFK (*L* 331–332), or the microdot that appears later in *Great Jones Street* (*GJ* 155), or the drug Novo that is all the rage during "The Last Techno-Rave" in *Cosmopolis* (*C* 125), or, in *Ratner's Star*, Robert Hopper Softly's assortment of "stimulants, relaxants, euphoriants, deliriants, sedative-hypnotics, local anesthetics and animal tranquilizers" (*RS* 327) or his "most extreme deliriant," which he breaks out during a solar eclipse, "a sudsy composite of lighter fluid, paint thinner, airplane glue, nail polish remover and several types of aerosol propellant" (*RS* 436). Not any of those, then, and not "DMT, the quick-acting chemical superhigh devised by NASA to get us to the moon and back whether we want to go or not" (*U* 624), or crack cocaine, "supposedly the cravingest form of substance abuse" (*U* 268; see 264), or the drug that Matt Shay smokes one night with friends and colleagues involved in weapons research, "either a rogue strain of hashish or standard stuff laced with some psychotomimetic agent" (*U* 421; see 465), a drug that causes him to sit in a chair "studying someone's shoe" (*U* 422; see 465) and that makes him unable, despite his close study, to figure out whose foot the shoe—and shoes, as we will see, will be just as revealing as drugs in DeLillo—was on.

And I was especially not talking about heroin (see *WN* 60), which is all over *Underworld*, whether under the name "smack" (*U* 462), which dopster comic Lenny Bruce says "comes from the Yiddish *shmek*. ... Dig it, he's got a two hundred dollar *shmek* habit" (*U* 594), or the brand name "Wall Street" (*U* 231), or, "doojee," "one of the ninety-nine names of heroin" (*U* 502)—like "the ninety-nine names of God" in *The Names* (*N* 272)—whether that heroin is sucked through a straw (*U* 258), like Marian Shay, who feels pretty "lazy-daisy, you know" (*U* 261), afterward, or shot up with a needle, a high that comes with "the lure of critical risk, the little love bite of that dragonfly dagger" (*U* 242), the kind that soldiers got hooked on in Vietnam (*U* 462), or the kind that, already back in the 1950s, at once attracted and repelled Nick Shay, who was "scared of needles and drugs" (*U* 502) but fascinated when George the Waiter "reached into the drawer and came out with a box of kitchen matches and a spoon" and "a hypodermic needle" (*U* 725–726), the same George whom Nick finds sitting in the same shabby basement room on the day that would forever change both of their lives.

No, I wasn't talking about any of those illegal or non FDA-approved drugs or even about the use and abuse of prescription medications, which DeLillo also packs his novels with, all those drugs arranged, as they are described in *Falling Man*, in their little "mystic wheel, the ritualistic design of the hours and days in tablets and capsules, in colors, shapes and numbers" (*FM* 48), drugs that require the daily rituals of counting and dividing, coding and classifying, medications with "brand names … like science-fiction gods" (*M* 184; see 122–123), Eric Packer's "sedatives and hypnotics" for insomnia and who knows what else (*C* 6) or Bill Gray's "medications for ailments unknown to science" (*M* 52), or the three drugs for ailments well known to science that Albert Bronzini in *Underworld* sets out "next to his plate on the table, lined up for consumption. His heart pill, his fart pill and his liver pill" (*U* 230), or Jack Ruby's Predulin, the "obesity drug" (*L* 251, 351) he is popping obsessively in the days leading up to his murder of Oswald. And then there is, of course, in *White Noise*, the contrast—the contrabanding, to be more precise—between Jack Gladney's everyday medications, "blood pressure pills, stress pills, allergy pills, eye drops, aspirin. Run of the mill" (*WN* 62), and the new psychotropic his wife Babette is taking in the latest rogue clinical study by Big Pharma, the "super experimental and top secret drug, code-name Dylar," a drug that promises to cure our most ancient and deep-rooted fear, our fear of death (*WN* 193; see 62).

I wasn't talking about any of that, and not even about the language-inhibiting super-drug concocted by the Happy Valley Commune in *Great Jones Street*, an "extreme substance" that "attacks a particular region in the left hemisphere of the brain. … the verbal hemisphere," "where the words are kept" (*GJ* 171, 228), even though, as we will see, language, *words*, will be central to the kind of contraband I wish to highlight here. So not that and not even the little tab of acid that, in *Americana*, Bobby Brand—the first figure of a writer in DeLillo, and that is perhaps not a coincidence, though he is a failed writer, a fake writer, a contrabrand writer—gives to David Bell, that "ticket to unapproachable regions" that allows the twenty-eight-year-old Bell to catch sight of himself some thirty years later, "at the age of sixty, mangled larvae clinging to [his] bleak flesh" (*A* 114).

The contraband I wish to talk about is different than, though not unrelated to, all these substances that promise some kind of communion or forgetting, some sort of death or the forgetting of death, or else some insight into the nature of things. As someone says in *Great Jones Street*, "If you're interested in reading about *things*, you might as well take a little sniffy now and again. In the long run that's where thingness lies" (*GJ* 61). It's where thingness lies, but perhaps also, and especially, where *wordness* lies, or, better still, the relationship, the double-banded or contrabanded relationship, as we will see, between words and things.

Alcohol

Tod Morgan handed me what he called a real drink. It was scotch and water. It made me feel very warm and I didn't like the taste much. But I seemed to be having a good time.

A 188

I'm at that certain stage in a night of drinking and talking when I see things clearly through a small opening, a window in space. I know things. I know what we're going to say before we say it.

N 226

The important thing is to sit and wait, to be patient. The other important thing is not to vomit. You see a man every so often standing over a curbstone vomiting. He did not want to think of himself as that kind of man.

U 709–710

In speaking of contraband, then, I wasn't referring to any of DeLillo's drugs of choice, whether illegal, legal, or inventions of another kind, and I wasn't referring to drinking either, which is technically not contraband, at least not any more in the United States, but is also supposed to produce an altered or paranormal or counter-normal state and has always been, at least in American letters, part of the myth or the mystique of the writer. As Bill Gray says to his editor in *Mao II*, "Remember literature, Charlie? It involved getting drunk and getting laid" (*M* 122). That kind of literature may well be a thing of the past, as Gray suggests, but writers still drink and still write about drinking, and DeLillo is no exception, from the opening party in *Americana* to the drunken orgy of its closing pages, with David Bell's sloppy overindulgence at the Drake Hotel in Chicago sandwiched somewhere in between (*A* 265), and from the uproarious dormitory beer party in *End Zone* to Lyle with Rosemary in a series of New York bars in *Players* (*P* 58, 74) or Selvy with Moll in "Frankie's Tropical Bar" in *Running Dog* (*RD* 62), or, in the same novel, Selvy alone with Jim Beam in an Irish bar on Eighth Avenue (*RD* 115), or Nick Shay in *Underworld* not in the Red Rose or the White Rose or the Blarney Stone but, wouldn't you know it, back in Frankie's Tropical Bar, on the Lower East Side, where he says he'll drink whatever his old grammar school friend Jerry is drinking, which turns out to be a stinger, just before the lights go out on November 9, 1965 (*U* 617–623). Later in the novel, we find the same Nick drinking "vodka tonics" among managers at a business conference (*U* 281) and then, by the very end, it's the mid-1990s, "aged grappa" while listening to jazz at home in Phoenix (*U* 810), because these things tend to change over time.

But that is really just a taste of the many varieties of alcohol in *Underworld* alone, everything from potato vodka, brandy, tequila, Tanqueray martinis, and homemade wine from the Bronx (*U* 115, 357, 768; see 224, 484, 473) to Seagram's "in a short glass with a single ice cube" (*U* 356; see 649) and "Old Mr. Boston, a rye whiskey unknown to the Cabots and the Lodges" (*U* 708). For each drink there is, of course, a profile and an attitude, the Madison Avenue advertising type, for example, who drinks "gibsons straight up" and says "thanks much" (*U* 527) or who "inhales a Cutty on the rocks" before jumping on "the last express to Westport" (*U* 534–535; see *N* 261, *V* 34).

Or just in *Libra*, there's Laurence Parmenter's Beefeater martini on a flight from Dallas back to Washington after meeting with former CIA officials planning an attempt on the life of President Kennedy (*L* 30), David Ferrie's scotch and soda with mafia boss Carmine Latta (*L* 173), Wayne Elko in Little Havana in Miami, ready to train for the assassination of JFK but stopping off first for a "*cerveza* Schlitz" (*L* 176)—not his smartest move—and Guy Banister in New Orleans with his Early Times™ bourbon (*L* 61), or Oswald himself in a Moscow hospital, recovering from a feeble suicide attempt by drinking "vodka with cucumber bits" (*L* 153). Or in *Amazons*, not to be undone, the generous servings of Scotch (*AZ* 9, 58, 260, 275), Seagram's V.O. (*AZ* 212), Moët Champagne (*AZ* 319), red wine in gallon jugs (*AZ* 275), those drinks you get in Polynesian restaurants that are "so devastating the management limits the number you can order" (*AZ* 41), and those Tanqueray martinis again (*AZ* 170, 228, 236). *Amazons* also features a couple of truly novel forms of alcohol delivery, such as "a water pistol full of ouzo" (*AZ* 269) and, elderly take note, a hollow cane that can be filled with scotch and soda and emptied over the course of a long walk through the streets of Manhattan: "We finished the cane" (*AZ* 378).

There's thus sedentary drinking and then drinking on the run, drinking on the road—Eric Packer in *Cosmopolis* knocking back vodkas in his all-day limo ride across Manhattan (*C* 89)—even bicoastal or comparative drinking, if you will allow the expression, Jackie Gleason ordering an umpteenth beer for himself, Frank Sinatra, Toots Shor, and J. Edgar Hoover (who usually prefers "a tumbler of scotch" (*U* 556)) at the famous Giants-Dodgers game in 1951 at the Polo Grounds in New York (*U* 28, 34) and then, decades later, Nick Shay and his colleagues ordering rounds of sour mash whiskey—way more shi shi than beer—at Dodger Stadium in LA (*U* 91–92, 99). And then there's intercontinental drinking, James Axton in *The Names* drinking arak in Jerusalem (*N* 150), ouzo or red wine on the Greek island of Kouros (*N* 74), and another American, maybe CIA, maybe not, "inhaling short Scotches"

(*N* 261 *V* 34) in Athens, or Bill Gray from *Mao II* in Cyprus, after drinking Metaxa—"a medicine dating nobly to the nineteenth century" (*M* 196)—unable to recall how he got back to his hotel (*M* 211–212), or else, in *Underworld*, Nick and his colleague Brian Glassic sharing a bottle of Chivas Regal on their way to Kazakhstan, after all the vodka and warm beer during their layover in Semipalatinsk (*U* 789, 795, 799).

That's a decent amount of drinking, to be sure, though it could be worse. Indeed, there are American writers where it's a lot worse (think Hemingway, Kerouac, or Mailer), but there's still a lot of drinking, almost always related, and there should be no surprise here, to a kind of self-destructive, suicidal drive that is not unrelated to contraband. It could be worse, I say, but only a man who knows his drink could have concocted this sentence about a late-night glass of vodka and orange juice, commonly known as a screwdriver, in *Point Omega*: "The drink was at that stage in the life of a drink when you take the last bland sip and fade into rueful introspection, somewhere between self-pity and self-accusation" (*PO* 30–31). One would do well to keep an eye on all these alcohols in DeLillo, but also on that orange juice, which, in *Underworld*, will be not only a life-giving liquid but the ultimate contraband substance.

Erotica and Stolen Art

> *Do you want to read about Etruscan slave girls, Georgian rakes? I think we have some literature on flagellation brothels. What about the Middle Ages? We have incubi and succubi. Nuns galore.*
>
> WN 29

> *He wondered if he'd become too complex to look at naked bodies, as such, and be stirred.*
>
> P 17

Under the aegis or rubric of contraband I was thus not talking about drugs or alcohol or about any kind of stolen or contraband art, for example, the erotica that is secretly collected by both Senator Percival and Earl Mudger in *Running Dog*, erotic sculptures from the East, "the art of mystics and nomads. Old-fashioned contentments" (*RD* 222), or the rumored film of an orgy in Hitler's bunker during his last days, "the century's ultimate piece of decadence" (*RD* 20), the holy grail of collector contraband, with "hints, whispers of unnatural sexuality. Hush-hush even today" (*RD* 148). Because "if it's Nazis, it's automatically erotic. The violence, the rituals, the leather, the jackboots" (*RD* 52). It's the kind of material that can "help people upgrade their orgasms" (*RD* 53). And it couldn't get any juicier because the film supposedly features Hitler himself.

There's a black market for all this erotic contraband, you have to know someone to get it, but then there is, again in *Underworld*, a shop called Long Tall Sally in San Francisco, "Fantasy Enhancements … Books, movies, appliances" (*U* 320), just one slice of an infinitely divided niche market aimed at capturing today's "floating zones of desire." Born of "the dismantling of desire into a thousand subspecialties, into spin-offs and narrowings, edgewise whispers of self," it's the kind of fine-grained neoliberal specialization that can support "a dive with a back room where they showed sex movies involving people with missing limbs" (*U* 319).

If the internet has cornered a large segment of the twenty-first-century porn market, one must not forget the role played by the porn film or skin flick in the twentieth century:

> Movement, action, frames per second. This is the era we're in … a thing isn't fully erotic unless it has the capacity to move. A woman crossing her legs drives men mad. … Motion, activity, change of position. You need this today for eroticism to be total. (*RD* 15; see 18)

In *Amazons* we attend with half the New York Rangers on their off-day a showing of *The Open Kimono* with Seymour Hare, "the most amateurish … pornographic feature in the whole history of Cinematic Sleaze" (*AZ* 176; see 348). Less exotic but maybe no less erotic is the "locally crafted pornography" that, in *Players*, Lyle Wynant watches on his local cable channel (*P* 16).

Then there's all the other kinds of stolen art sold on the black market by people like Ernst Hechinger (aka Martin Ridnour) in *Falling Man*, an art dealer with a shadowy past who either "did or did not have a wife in Paris" (*FM* 42). But that's not the kind of contraband I am talking about either, even if the two Morandi paintings that Ridnour offers Lianne's mother will bring us closer—like the Hitler tape, or even just the rumor of the Hitler tape—to the sense of contraband I wish to underscore here.

Weapons

> *The comfort men found in the argot of weaponry. … Early man roaming the tundra. You have to name your weapon before you can use it to kill.*
>
> RD 208–209

> Why is the language of destruction so beautiful? ... stun grenades, parabellum ammo ... Kalashnikov ... Wehrmacht, Panzer, Blitzkrieg. He would have a patient theory to submit on the adductive force of such sounds, how they stir the chemistry of the early brain.
>
> N 115; see U 594

> If you think the name of the weapon is beautiful, are you implicated in the crime?
>
> N 118

In speaking of DeLillo's contraband I was thus not talking about drugs or alcohol or stolen art or erotica or anything else that might come under the watchful eye of US Customs, the Department of Homeland Security, or the Bureau of Alcohol, Tobacco, Firearms and Explosives—things like, precisely, firearms or weapons more generally, whether small or large, owned by individuals, groups, or governments, all of them surrounded by an aura of death and destruction, on the one hand, and religion and ritual, on the other. I wasn't talking about them, though they too are interesting, all those weapons that fill DeLillo's novels. Beginning with ...

Knives

> "I was opening my mail with a long thin instrument consisting of a flat-edged cutting surface terminating in a handle." "A knife?" "If you want to put it that way."
>
> RS 289

> Our Bibles are hand-glued and hand-stitched by refugees. ... Both testaments. Translated directly from the original tongues. ... Bulk orders get steak knives thrown in.
>
> RS 21

> She stabbed me in the shoulder with a steak knife. I was at the table eating the steak and she came up behind me and she stabbed me in the shoulder. Not a four-star restaurant steak knife with macho overtones but it hurt like hell anyway.
>
> ZK 100

In *Americana*, a sort of portrait of the artist as a young American man, David Bell recalls Stephen Dedalus's name from *Ulysses*, "Kinch. The knife-blade"

(*A* 143, 145). That is just the first in a long series of knives in DeLillo's work, from the knife that circumcises to the blade that threatens in *Ratner's Star* (*RS* 207, 255) to, in *Libra*, Lee Harvey Oswald's "penknife" (*L* 4)—his very first weapon, on his way to bigger and more lethal things—and Win Everett's "X-Acto knife" for cutting and fabricating false documents (*L* 147; see 361), as well as Wayne Elko's hunting knife, which he uses before the assassination, in a truly humanitarian gesture, to slit the throat of an old, suffering dog (*L* 292, 381; see *N* 105), and the bayonet whose use is described in the Marine manual with such stunning clarity: "'Principle number one.' 'Get the blade into the enemy.' 'Principle number two.' 'Be ruthless, vicious and fast in your attack'" (*L* 104). There are knives and, in *Underworld*, there is a knife grinder to sharpen them, someone from the same region in Italy as Nick Shay's father, "near a town called Campobasso, in the mountains, where boys were raised to sharpen knives" (*U* 696).

In *Running Dog* there is even a numbered list of seventeen different kinds of knives, all with precise, finely fashioned, almost poetic names, like the "gut-hook skinning knife" and the "combat knife with a double-edged point and an eight-inch blade," or else, this one, knife number seven, a hunting knife with "a dropped-point blade and a stag handle" (*RD* 129–130). They're such fine names that when Bill Gray cuts his medicine tablets with a knife in *Mao II* we know it's not going to be any old knife, some common pocket, paring, or Swiss army knife, but what looks like that very same knife number seven, the "old scarred stag-handle folding knife, undetected by security at three airports" (*M* 123). So there is it, a contraband knife smuggled across international and literary borders from one novel to another, since Bill Gray is, after all, one of DeLillo's own doubles or counter-characters.

But this last example already suggests that more important than the knife itself is the language surrounding it, and especially its name. In *Running Dog*, Earl Mudger, head of Radial Matrix and the person out to kill Selvy, makes his own weapons, and knives in particular, with the care and precision of a wordsmith, since what interests him about knives, says the narrator, is as much their wordness as their thingness:

> He liked the names of things. … He set to work on the handle. It would be burl maple. The names of things. Subtly gripping odors. Glues and resins. The names. Honing oil. Template. Brazing rod. The names of things in these two rooms constituted a near-secret knowledge. He felt obscure satisfaction, something akin to a freemason's pride, merely saying these names aloud … You couldn't use tools and materials well, he believed, unless you knew their proper names. (*RD* 119)

This same belief in the power of the names of things can be seen in Selvy, who, later in the novel, buys himself a "Filipino guerrilla bolo," "for the name," he says, "I like the name ... It's romantic" (*RD* 191). Like Mudger, then, Selvy respects both the thing and the name of the thing, at once the rigor needed to fashion such a thing, the discipline and knowledge needed to use it, and the precision of the words to name and describe it. When Selvy thus purchases a knife of his own, we know he is preparing for some kind of ritual slaughter or sacrifice out in the desert, a ritual death or a self-sacrifice (see *U* 247), as it will happen, out at Marathon Mines.

A knife in the desert: it is tempting to think that that knife from *Running Dog* (1978), which presumably gets left behind when Selvy is beheaded and buried, gets picked up some decades later in another novel, *Point Omega* (2010), during the search for Richard Elster's missing daughter in the desert, a knife found near "a former bombing range littered with unexploded shells" (*PO* 91). It's surely not the same knife—literature doesn't quite work like that—but it clearly belongs to the same DeLillo cache. The same could be said of the steak knife that a wife sticks in the shoulder of her husband in *Zero K*; it's no doubt from the same set of cutlery as the one with which another wife, another but similarly motivated, tries to cut up her husband in *Libra*, "swinging a knife across the kitchen table and catching the left side of his jaw, after a night of who knows what" (*L* 73). Again, they are not the same knife and a knife is not "a potato peeler," but when a wife goes after a husband in the kitchen with this latter we recognize a similar scene or ritual (*N* 256). It seems like wives are always giving their husbands knives in DeLillo's works: "[Murray] took a knife out of his inside jacket pocket. He called it has four-inch Wusthof. A utility knife. ... A gift from my ex-wife. She had excellent taste in cutlery" (*AZ* 258, 262).

The weapon thus always has a name (the X-acto, the Wusthof, the Filipino guerrilla bolo), which has to be learned and repeated, like a fetish. People give names to their weapons and, sometimes, as *The Names* recalls, they carve their names onto the handle of their weapons (*N* 291), or else the names or initials of those they've killed with them (*N* 169). A weapon is thus never just a weapon in DeLillo; it is always an instrument of ritual and that ritual always involves language, the ultimate contraband, as we will see.

Guns

Their bumper sticker read GUN CONTROL IS MIND CONTROL.
In situations like this, you want to stick close to people in right-wing fringe groups. They've practiced staying alive.

WN 157

They sat and talked about the guns. Wayne believed there was friendship in guns. This might or might not be a paradox.

L 295

Wayne's old man used to say, "God made big people. And God made little people. But Colt made the .45 to even things up."

L 379

There are thus knives everywhere in DeLillo, from *Americana* to *Point Omega*, but the DeLillo arsenal also includes, as it is stuttered out in *Players*, the "G-g-g-gun" (*P* 106), at once weapon, work of art, and quasi-religious object, a product of technology and consumer culture and fantasies of power and control. *Players* opens with an in-flight movie where terrorists attack golfers with semiautomatic rifles (*P* 7), and the novel is then nicely punctuated, at the midway point, by Moll buying a neon gun sculpture: "Guess I couldn't resist," she says, "More flash. Transience and flash. Story of my life" (*RD* 109; see 172). In America this is, of course, the story of all of our lives, all of us who live in the land of the political assassin, of "men firing from highway overpasses, attic rooms. Unconnected to the earth" (*N* 171), or of "the barricaded suspect ... exchanging gunfire with the police" in a "deserted commercial district" (*RS* 418). It is a violence that seems to be peculiar to America, a quintessentially American kind of violence. It is our story and none of us can escape it, which explains in part why there are so many guns, legal and illegal, registered and contraband, in DeLillo's novels, everything from the AR-18 that shoots up the bar where Selvy and Moll are drinking in *Running Dog* (*RD* 65–67) to sidearms on the various guards—"different soccer jerseys, same hip bulge" (*ZK* 5; see 3)—who are protecting the frozen bodies in the Convergence in *Zero K*. Even tennis stars are fascinated by guns: "He's extending the basement to build a shooting range. Seems he's discovered the handgun" (*AZ* 253).

As *Running Dog* puts it, "Everybody owns a gun of one kind or another, for one purpose or another." In a word, a single word without verb used by DeLillo in the following paragraph: "Cowboys" (*RD* 207). We remain cowboys, the kind we've seen only in Westerns, that is, in movies, which will also be, as we will see, central to DeLillo's unique brand of contraband. In *Underworld*, the narrator sees something approaching in the desert that makes him think "of a hundred movies in which something comes across the wavy plain, a horseman with scabbarded rifle" (*U* 64). Westerns, then, not to mention gangster films, which teach Americans like Lee Oswald such important life lessons as "the gut-shot man takes a long time dying" (*L* 47).

Americans and their guns: it is the gun that turns Benno Levin, a disgruntled employee turned community college professor, into an assassin, even though the gun hardly fits the profile. As Packer says to Levin: "All right. People like you can happen. I understand this. I believe it. But not the violence. Not the gun. The gun is all wrong. You're not a violent man" (*C* 193). But the gun makes him a violent man or at least makes for an atmosphere in which the gun will just have to go off. In *The Names* the murders committed by the strange cult *Ta Onómata* are carried out with primitive weapons—claw hammers, rocks, and an ax—but when the "Autonomous People's Initiative" (*N* 326) tries to kill an American banker living in Greece and making loans to Turkey, they use something a little more sophisticated, "a 9mm pistol called a CZ-75, made in Czechoslovakia" (*N* 326).

And then there is *Libra*, where Jack Ruby walks around Dallas with a loaded revolver (*L* 251), where Oswald's boss at the Book Depository, a certain Mr. Truly—no kidding, that was his name—looks in late November to buy guns for his son for Christmas, a deer rifle and a .22 (*L* 385), and then Raymo, one of two men behind the grassy knoll, with a "modified Winchester" (*L* 291), and the men with their AR-15s guarding the President (*L* 371). And then, of course, there's Guy Banister's detective agency in New Orleans, run by a former FBI agent involved in the JFK assassination, with "more guns than the Mexican army" (*L* 61), "rifle grenades, land mines, dynamite, antitank guns, mortar shells. ... canisters of napalm" (*L* 62). That doesn't even include Banister's associates, with their M-1s and M-4s, "a whole raft of Yugoslav Mausers with markings stamped in Russian if that impresses you" (*L* 64), or wacko David Ferrie with "land mines stacked in his kitchen" (*L* 140) and a rifle he calls with his signature homoeroticism "the Man-Licker" (*L* 337)—a homonym (pun intended) for the gun Oswald will use for the assassination. As for Guy Banister himself, he always carried "a blue-steel Colt under his jacket, chambered for the .357 magnum cartridge," because "Guy sincerely believed the old reliable .38 special with standard police loads was simply not enough gun for the type of situation a man of his standing might run into any time of day or night. Amen" (*L* 139).

Finally, there is Lee Harvey Oswald himself, as American as they come from this point of view, buying his first gun from David Ferrie, a "bolt-action .22, a varmint gun" (*L* 42), a "Marlin bolt-action .22" (*L* 43), and then, years later, when stationed in Japan in the service, "a pistol, small and silver-plated, a derringer, two-shot" (*L* 88). Then, upon his return to the United States, he buys two guns through the mail, using a false name, sending "$29.95 to Seaport Traders for a 38-caliber revolver with a shortened barrel," a gun "made by Smith & Wesson and known as the two-inch Commando" (*L* 273), and then "$21.45 to Klein's Sporting Goods in Chicago for a 6.5 millimeter

Italian military rifle, the Mannlicher-Carcano, equipped with a four-power scope," "a sniper's scope" (*L* 277, 136). It is with the former that Oswald would have killed Patrolman Tippet (*L* 410) and with the latter that he would have wounded—but certainly not killed, not from that distance or that angle—JFK.

DeLillo is never content simply to say that someone was killed with a "gun," "pistol," or "rifle." No lover of the lore and lexicon of the gun would be. For the power of guns, like that of knives, is in their names, even though that power extends, of course, far into the world and, as this passage from *Libra* suggests, can have all kinds of unimaginable consequences:

> Even after you think you've seen all the ways violence can surprise a man, along comes something you never imagined. How much force do bullets have to exert if they can hit a man in the chest and make his hat fly four feet in the air, straight up? It was a lesson in the laws of motion and a reminder to all men that nothing is assured. (*L* 188)

There are thus guns everywhere in DeLillo's novels, guns galore, because, hey, that's America for you. And just as with knives, there is always a discipline required to care for them, to handle them, to take them apart and put them back together, a routine that becomes a ritual and a form of renewal. "To Selvy," for example, "guns and their parts amounted to an inventory of personal worth" (*RD* 82). It is thus important to know both how to work a gun and how to fashion oneself when working one. "At the range he worked on stance, breath control, eye focus. The idea was to build almost a second self. Someone smarter and more detached" (*RD* 83).

It is, therefore, just as important to know how to speak of guns as it is to know how to fire them: "He found it reassuring to handle the parts, to know their names and understand their functions. Attention to detail is a form of vigilance" (*RD* 83). When Eric Packer confronts Benno Levin, his would-be assassin, with the question "What's the attachment that abuts the trigger guard? What is it called? What does it do?" Levin has to admit: "All right. I don't have the manhood to know these names. Men know these names. You have the experience of manhood. I can't think that far ahead. It's all I can do to be a person" (*C* 196). Here is yet another clue to the kind of contraband I wish to focus on here. It's not the manhood of these things, and not even the thinghood of them, the contraband itself, that most interests DeLillo but the language or words used to talk about the things, the linguistic contraband, so to speak, needed to speak of them: "Weapons were named, surnamed, slang-named, christened, titled and dubbed. Protective devices. Bearings of perfect performance. Reciting these names was the soldier's poetry, his counterjargon to death" (*RD* 209). Just as with knives, then, there is a whole language, a slang and a technical vocabulary, surrounding guns: "I took out the .38 and fired three times right into the breast pocket of his shirt. There was a war movie playing. ... It was like 20mm cannon fire. It was like hosing down an LZ with your 20 mike-mike. There's the slang again" (*A* 306). As we will see, the kind of contraband I wish to speak of here is essentially a thing of language, a counterjargon or counter-language to death and forgetting, a conjuring language and thus an instrument of writing.

It is, then, this care for weapons, precision with regard to the thing and the name, that makes weapons in DeLillo not just instruments of destruction that, because they are bound to go off, motivate the narrative but elements of ritual that bear language. There is, first of all, a bond created by these weapons, a cultish attachment to them. One of the leaders of a terrorist group says to Lyle in *Players*: "I want to show you something. It'll be your initiation. ... I have this fool notion that once you see this stuff, you're in for good. This nearly mystical notion" (*P* 101). He then goes on to show him "a stock of weapons" in the basement and, he's right, Lyle is in for good. Same thing goes for Hammad or Mohammed Atta, who gets a knife at the terrorist training camp in Afghanistan as a sort of graduation gift, a sign that he was ready for bigger things (*FM* 174). Weapons create a kind of kinship, like totems of a new religion, and the bigger the better, for size matters, not only for the "tumescent missiles" of *Americana* (*A* 55; see 66) but also for "the Phallic Master of the Levant," "a rocket-propelled grenade launcher that's about seven feet long," in *Mao II* (*M* 238), the same novel in which Rashid, the leader of the fringe Maoist group in Beirut, says, "Women carry babies, men carry guns. Weapons are man's beauty" (*M* 234).

Needless to say, though sometimes it needs to be pointed out, none of these views about weapons can be attributed to Don DeLillo himself. If anything, naming such a religion of guns, analyzing it, as he does, detailing the structure and the system, is the first step in disarming the entire apparatus, the whole network of murders, assassinations, suicides, and accidental shootings that makes up American society and history. Consider, for example, how the gun makes its appearance in *White Noise*. It all begins with random, innocent speculation, the kind we all engage in after every run-of-the-mill mass shooting:

> Six people. Did he care for his weapons obsessively? Did he have an arsenal stashed in his shabby little room off a six-story concrete car park? ... Some handguns and a bolt-action rifle with a scope. ... A telescopic sight. Did he fire from a highway overpass, a rented room? Did he walk into a bar, a washette, his former place of employment and start firing indiscriminately? (*WN* 44)

But then, some two hundred pages later, a Zumwalt automatic winds up in Jack Gladney's hand, a little gift from his father-in-law, and it changes everything:

> "Heft it around. Get the feel. It's loaded." ...
> A loaded weapon. How quickly it worked a change in me, numbing my hand even as I sat staring at the thing, not wishing to give it a name. ... This here is a 25-caliber Zumwalt automatic. German-made. (*WN* 253)

After getting the thing and learning the name, Jack begins leading another life, a secret life or counter-life, a contraband life animated by this concealed, contrabanded thing:

> What does it mean to a person, beyond his sense of competence and well-being and personal worth, to carry a lethal weapon, to handle it well, be ready and willing to use it? A concealed lethal weapon. It was a secret, it was a second life, a second self, a dream, a spell, a plot, a delirium.
>
> German-made. (*WN* 254)

We will return to this idea of a secret a bit later, but for the moment simply notice how this gun, once it enters a life, seems to take on a life of its own.

> Whenever I remembered the gun, lurking in a stack of undershirts like a tropical insect, I felt a small intense sensation pass through me. ... I knew it mainly as a childhood moment, the profound stir of secret-keeping. (*WN* 274)

Once the gun then actually comes out of hiding, out of the drawer or closet and into one's pocket, it begins to suggest its own plotlines, its own narratives; it begins to build its own realities around itself: "The next day I started carrying the Zumwalt automatic to school. ... The gun created a second reality for me to inhabit" (*WN* 297). Soon one begins thinking, like Jack in his office at the College-on-the-Hill—and it's funny until you really think about it—"How stupid these people were, coming into my office unarmed" (*WN* 297).

Jack thus gets the gun, then talks about the gun, then takes the gun around with him, on his person, and then begins plotting exactly how to use it. "Four Dylar tablets, three Zumwalt bullets," he thinks to himself (*WN* 297), and then, five pages later.

> I reached into my pocket, rubbed my knuckles across the grainy stainless steel of the Zumwalt barrel. The man on the radio said: "Void where prohibited." (*WN* 303)

We will come back to the radio a bit later, to this counterband voice on the radio at this climatic moment, but the sheer momentum or logic of the narrative seems to bring us, just nine pages later, to this, as if we were on automatic: "I fired the gun, the weapon, the pistol, the firearm, the automatic" (*WN* 312).

Gun control is indeed mind control; as soon as one has it under one's control one begins to think differently and so is no longer quite in control. That's because there is another force behind guns, a force of attraction that no amount of training, or discipline, or legislation can control. It is posed as a question in *White Noise*, but the question is pretty much settled by the narrative itself: "Does a gun draw violence to it, attract other guns to its surrounding field of force?" (*WN* 298).

All this is never more clear than when it comes to what might be called the mother of all guns, the ur-gun, as it were, in DeLillo, the sawed-off shotgun with a "pistol grip arrangement" (*U* 779)—and don't forget that pistol grip—that Nick Shay was holding in his hands when George Manza got shot, a legal gun, this time, made into an illegal, contraband one, when it made its way into the hands of a seventeen-year-old boy, on the threshold of legal age. There are other guns in *Underworld*—like the one used by the Texas Highway Killer, his "father's old .38," a gun that "did not have massive knockdown power and it did not shoot through concrete blocks or make fist-size holes in silhouette targets. It just killed people" (*U* 269; see also 694)—but this is the gun at the center of the novel, the gun whose shot will be heard all 'round Nick Shay's world.

Nick begins his recollection of that fateful event with what sounds like a dream or a memory or an echo of *White Noise*, "I hefted the weapon and pointed it and saw an interested smile fall across his face, the slyest kind of shit-eating grin. / Maybe that was the dream—I wasn't sure" (*U* 132). Like the gun that Jack's father-in-law suddenly introduces into Jack's life, this gun simply comes into Nick's life, destined to go off. George the Waiter had found it a couple of days earlier as he was parking someone's car, "a shotgun, sawed-off, the barrel extending only a couple of inches from the forearm part and the stock cut down to a pistol grip arrangement" (*U* 779). It was a legal weapon, George reminds us, but "once you cut the thing down it's a concealed weapon" (*U* 780). George thus gives the gun to Nick, who—in a long American tradition that runs from the pioneer days up to Oswald, as we will have occasion to recall later when we look at some photographs—"posed with it, Nick did, a pirate's pistol or an old Kentucky flintlock if that's the word" (*U* 780). Six hundred and fifty pages after the first recollection of that "hefted" gun and that "shit-eating grin" on the face of George the Waiter, a heroin addict who scared the shit out of Nick some weeks before with his spoon and needle, Nick recounts his ensuing conversation with George, an exchange that really does a number on all our notions of "guilt" or "intention" or even "action":

> "Is it loaded?" "No," George said. ... Nick pulled the trigger. / In the extended interval of the trigger pull, the long quarter second, with the action of the trigger sluggish and rough, Nick saw into the smile on the other man's face. ... Then he felt the trigger pull and heard the gun go off and the man and chair went different ways. ... Why would the man say no if it was loaded? / But first why would he point the gun at the man's head? (*U* 780–781)

Here is how the event gets told earlier in the novel, in a sort of confession scene in a hotel room between Nick and a woman he has just met from a swingers gathering:

> I was seventeen when it happened and to this day I'm not sure whether the intent was express or implied or howsoever the law reads. Or was it all a desperate accident? ... Well at some point, with my finger already moving the trigger, at some micropoint in the action of the mind and the action of the finger and the trigger-action itself, I may have basically said, So what. I'm not really sure. Or, Why not do it and see what happens. (*U* 299)

Or again, later: "I was only seventeen at the time and I agreed with their reasoning, that there was a cold-blooded element in this crime whatever the shadings" (*U* 510).

So, what was it, negligence, maliciousness, fear, curiosity, all of the above? There are no definitive answers to these questions. What is said in *Libra* in a wholly other context describes well what can be known about why Nick pulled the trigger: "He believed that nothing can be finally known that involves human motive and need. There is always another level, another secret, a way in which the heart breeds a deception so mysterious and complex it can only be taken for a deeper kind of truth" (*L* 260). Every decision is indeed split second, taking place in a moment that is never simply one but always divided, complex, multiple (see *U* 149–150). Benno Levin says in *Cosmopolis*, "All through the day I became more convinced I could not do it. Then I did it. Now I have to remember why" (*C* 61).

We cannot know why Nick pulled the trigger, but we can know, DeLillo seems to suggest, that once we design such a thing, such contraband, it cannot but go off, somewhere, at some point, for some reason and despite all intentions to the contrary. It's not an encouraging thought when it comes to guns, and it's so much less so when it comes to the next item on the contraband list. Because "once they imagine the bomb ..." (*U* 801).

Nukes

All technology refers to the bomb.

U 467

There is the secret of the bomb and there are the secrets that the bomb inspires ... the genius of the bomb is printed not only in its physics of particles and rays but in the occasion it creates for new secrets.

U 50–51

There's a little thing you might have had occasion to hear of, called the Nuclear Accident Readiness Foundation. Basically a legal defense fund for the industry. Just in case kind of thing.

WN 56

In proposing a topic like Don DeLillo's contraband, then, it was not those weapons I had in mind, all those knives and guns, or rocket-launchers, missiles, and heavy artillery, or the Soviet tank at the head of the wedding procession in Beirut at the end of *Mao II*—"an old Soviet T-34," "sold and stolen two dozen times, changing sides and systems and religions" (*M* 239)—or even all those bombs or bombers, the "tailored man with a suitcase bomb" in *Cosmopolis* (*C* 42), the terrorist or fringe group suicide bombers in *Mao II* (*M* 227), or even all those atomic bombs or nuclear weapons with Uranium-238 cores the size of baseballs in *Underworld*, weapons developed and tested underground but then dropped from above in order to rise up magic mushroom-like from the earth. Though we read in the opening pages of *Running Dog* that "weapons have become godless," that they have "lost their religion" (*RD* 4), they seem to have gotten it back by *Underworld*, where the mushroom cloud seems to replace the cross as the emblem of twentieth-century religion.

As a Cold War and early post-Cold War novelist, DeLillo writes about the fears and fantasies of the bomb and its aftermath, the thrill of watching the whole thing go up and the fantasy of surviving for a while to see the fallout. Here is what David Ferrie, who is looking to build and equip a bomb shelter, thinks of it in 1963:

It was heart-lifting in a way to think about the Bomb. How satisfying, he thought, to live alone in a hole. Not because he resembled a mutant form of life but just to eke out extra time while all hell thundered on the surface. (*L* 29; see 173, 392)

There are nukes and talk of nuclear weapons and wars throughout many DeLillo novels, but it all comes to a head, as it were, in *Underworld*. The first mention of the nuclear threat occurs already in the Prologue, entitled "The Triumph of Death," when J. Edgar Hoover, attending the infamous baseball game in the Polo Grounds, learns that "the Soviet Union has conducted an atomic test at a secret location somewhere inside its own borders" (*U* 23). This is the central conceit, the core, as it were, of the novel, the shot heard 'round the world, the home run by Bobby Thomson coinciding with this nuclear test, because "when they make an atomic bomb, listen to this, they make the radioactive core the exact same size as a baseball" (*U* 172). It's October 3, 1951, and Hoover thinks, "now this," "the sun's own heat that swallows cities" (*U* 24). That test blast in the Kazakhstan desert was just one of many Soviet rejoinders to the United States' own tests in the 1940s and 1950s in the American desert, the desert being, in DeLillo, a contraband place par excellence, a place not only of nuclear weapons tests but also of art and religion, replete with the "awe and terror" that tends to accompany both (*U* 70–71). We are no longer talking about the terrible but still somehow imaginable terror and violence of knives and guns. Since August 1945 something else has entered human history, something unimaginable or unsayable. *Underworld* would be an attempt to imagine or give voice to that unimaginable, unsayable something:

They had brought something into the world that out-imagined the mind. They didn't even know what to call the early bomb. The thing or the gadget or something. And Oppenheimer said, It is merde. I will use the French. J. Robert Oppenheimer. It is merde. He meant something that eludes naming is automatically relegated, he is saying, to the status of shit. You can't name it. It's too big or evil or outside your experience. (*U* 76–77)

With the bomb comes a capacity and a fear that are, quite simply, and literally, apocalyptic. As a New York City (NYC) street preacher says later in the novel—putting the day's news together with Matthew 24:36: "No one knows the day or the hour. Seems there's been the Russians exploding an A-bomb" (*U* 140). "They say that only insects survive. … All the creatures god put on earth, only insects survive the radiation" (*U* 352). It is this preacher whom Lenny Bruce hears and begins channeling during a concert at Carnegie Hall in New York more than a decade later (*U* 626), after engagements in LA, San Francisco, Chicago, and Miami. It's October 1962 this time, the Cuban Missile Crisis, and Lenny is feeling the threat of a nuclear showdown between the two superpowers. It is, as David Ferrie, a nut case but far from crazy, calls it in *Libra*, "the purest existential moment in the history of mankind" (*L* 316). Suddenly there is the realization that life and death, survival and destruction, to say nothing of the fate of the world itself, are completely out of our hands, or, worse, completely in our hands, for "the mushroom cloud was the godhead of Annihilation and Ruin" and "the state controlled the means of apocalypse" (*U* 563).

But this control over the apocalypse by the state, this seemingly rational "arms control," is every bit as nebulous or tenuous as the "gun control" we saw earlier. It requires constant research and development, as it's called, to produce more and more powerful and effective weapons, the kind of research Nick Shay's brother Matt did in the 1970s in an underground weapons research facility, one of those "mountains hollowed out in New Mexico" (*U* 457) designed to protect us from our enemies, to help us "match our weapons to theirs" (*U* 419). It all sounds perfectly reasonable or rational—mutually assured destruction and all that—but when Matt's girlfriend Janet hears him speak about his work she hears echoes of another discourse: "You make it sound like God." Like God or, continues the narrator's voice, "some starker variation thereof. Go to the desert or tundra and wait for the visionary flash of light, the critical mass that will call down the Hindu heavens, Kali and Shiva and all the grimacing lesser gods" (*U* 458).

It's not just nukes, of course, because "if you knew anything about modern war, you knew that weapons utilizing pathogenic bacteria could be every bit as destructive as megaton bombs" (*U* 557). But nukes are central to *Underworld*, and, because they are not going away anytime soon, they remain central to our collective well-being and anxiety. With nuclear weapons technology come threats of future wars as well as incidents from the past that the public has never been told, like "the thing that fell to earth on Albuquerque in 1957, a thermonuclear bomb of jumbo tonnage mistakenly released from a B-36—*nobody's perfect, okay*—and landing in a field within the city limits"; fortunately "the conventional explosives detonated, the nuclear package did not" (*U* 401–402). Or tests that were not so accidental—in both the United States and Russia—with fallout that was not as unforeseeable as all that. Here are four passages, two for each side:

> Nobody's supposed to know this. It's something that's more or less out in the open but at the same time. ... Secret. Untalked about. Hushed up. ...
> Multiple myelomas. Kidney failures. Or you wake up one morning and

you're three inches shorter. ... Old Testament outbreaks of great red boils. Great big splotches and rashes. And coughing up handfuls of blood. (*U* 405–406)

They did this deliberately, without telling people what the risks were. They exposed troops to the atomic flash and some of them were given protective eye filters and some were not. They experimented on children, infants, fetuses and mental patients. (*U* 417–418)

It [the "Museum of Misshapens" in Semipalatinsk] is part of the Medical Institute ... The fetuses, some of them, are preserved in Heinz pickle jars. There is the two-headed specimen. There is the single head that is twice the size of the body. There is the normal head that is located in the wrong place, perched on the right shoulder. ... Then there is the cyclops. The eye centered, the ears below the chin, the mouth completely missing. (*U* 799)

It is the people who were downwind, the villagers who are patients now, and their children and grandchildren ... It is the victims who are blind. It is the boy with skin where his eyes ought to be, a bolus of spongy flesh, oddly like a mushroom cap, springing from each brow. ... It is the man with the growth beneath his chin, a thing with a life of its own, embryonic and pulsing. It is the dwarf girl who wears a T-shirt advertising a Gay and Lesbian festival in Hamburg, Germany ... There are unknown diseases here. And words that are also unknown, or used to be. For many years the word radiation was banned. (*U* 800–801)

There are, throughout *Underworld*, first published in 1997, constant reminders of the nuclear weapons that were then and are still today housed in silos beneath the ground, as well as reminders of those B-52s flying 24/7 around the earth with those weapons at the ready to serve and protect (*U* 75). There are memories of trips to fallout shelters (*U* 411) and nuclear readiness drills in school (*U* 715, 728), but then, in the present, "fighter jets ... in tight formation" (*U* 284), "F-4 Phantoms in silver skin" flying over the desert, reminders that while the Cold War may be officially over the arms race is doing just fine.

The Convergence of *Zero K* appears to be located not all that far from former Soviet nuclear bomb test sites (*ZK* 35), or from the nuclear waste disposal sites of *Underworld*, yet another indication that, in DeLillo, waste is always the counterband of weaponry. More than seventy years after they were first invented and tested, nuclear weapons continue to threaten the living and, in the Convergence, the semi-living, those living a kind of counter- or contraband life. Someone wonders:

Are we safe here in our subterrane? And whatever the megatonage, how will the shock register continent to continent, the blow to world consciousness? How post-Hiroshima and post-Nagasaki? ... Or am I lost in the hazy memory of old film footage? (*ZK* 244; see *EZ* 83)

It all depends on what you can believe—or hope for or, perhaps, can try not to imagine:

> Once they imagine the bomb, write down equations, they see it's possible to build, they build, they test in the American desert, they drop on the Japanese, but once they imagine in the beginning, it makes everything true. ... Nothing you can believe is not coming true. (*U* 801–802)

And so it happens that the unimaginable and unthinkable becomes suddenly imaginable and inevitable, having already happened, repeatable and replayable—YouTube-able—on the World Wide Web: "Then the world lights up. A glow enters the body that's like the touch of God" (*U* 613). Like the radiance of a star, the mushroom cloud makes its own light and consumes everything around it—a cloud of unknowing that makes everything imaginably, unimaginably true:

> First a dawnlight, a great aurora glory massing on the color monitor. Every thermonuclear bomb ever tested, all the data gathered from each shot ... She sees the flash, the thermal pulse. She hears the rumble building, the great gathering force rolling off the 16-bit soundboard. She stands in the flash and feels the power. She sees the spray plume. She sees the fireball climbing, the superheated sphere of burning gas that can blind a person with its beauty ... and then the mushroom cloud spreads around her, the pulverized mass of radioactive debris, eight miles high, ten miles, twenty, with skirted stem and smoking platinum cap. (*U* 825)

Nuclear weapons are thus central to DeLillo's work, as they are to the latter half of the twentieth century. But then there is also, as we recall from *Falling Man*, on the cusp of the twenty-first century, the simple box-cutter that wreaked such damage on 9/11: million dollar weapons, therefore, and weapons sold for a dollar twenty-nine at Home Depot, the most sophisticated and the most primitive side-by-side, contrabanded, in the twentieth and twenty-first centuries, all of them associated with a kind of rigor or reverence if not exactly religion and so accompanied, almost always, by some ritual act, some contrabanding of word and thing.

2

Underworlds and Undercurrents

Because everything connects in the end, or only seems to, or seems to only because it does.

U 465

Budge: *You're part of the whole thing.*

Grass: *Whatever the whole thing is.*

Budge: *Exactly.*

DR 54

Cults, Criminal Organizations, Spy Agencies

Today there's just one terrorist network and one police apparatus. Thing is, they sometimes overlap.

P 116

If you've got criminal tendencies, and I'm not saying this is true of you or me, one of the places to make your mark is law enforcement.

L 64

There's a thin line between exterminator and roach.

RS 251

By way of contraband, then, I was not talking about drugs or alcohol or stolen art or weapons, about anything, in short, that they try to confiscate from your person when you enter, say, a prison, "when you bend over to allow them to check your anal cavity for printed matter, narcotics, alcoholic beverages, digging tools, TV sets, implements of self-destruction" (*L* 95). I was also not referring, though they are closer to my theme, to all the counterbands or countergroups, all the counter- or anti-government groups, all the secret organizations and countercultures that traffic in contraband goods in DeLillo's novels: the Happy Valley Farm Commune in *Great Jones Street*, "a rural group that came to the city to find peace and contentment" (*GJ* 36; see 241), or the research entity that created Dylar, a group "supported by a multinational giant" but "operating in the deepest secrecy in an unmarked building just outside Iron City" (*WN* 299), or the Maoist organization in Lebanon in *Mao II*, or the Baader-Meinhof group in the short story of the same name, or "Kommune One" in *Falling Man*, that collective of the late 1960s that claimed Martin Ridnour as a member (*FM* 146).

Nor was I referring to all the religious groups that populate DeLillo's novels, the group *Ta Onómata* in *The Names*, a "doomsday cult" (*N* 116), "zealots of the alphabet" (*N* 75), a group whose name and interest intersect or coincide as band and contraband, or the "post-evangelist" doomsday cult evoked in *Zero K* (*ZK* 41), or the Moonies, that cult or religious group so prominent in 1970s and 1980s in the United States with their belief, laugh if you will but he made a killing, that "the messiah is here on earth and he is a chunky man in a business suit from the Republic of Korea" (*M* 186). Or else the Hare Krishnas in a Bombay airport, not Indians, of course, but "a group of North Americans in saffron robes and running shoes," looking "deeply surprised in their baldness and blotched skin, amazed to be who they were" (*N* 254), and in *Underworld* those same or very similar "Krishna skinheads with handbells, young and pale in ocher robes and high-top sneakers, jumping devoutly up and down" (*U* 470).

There are cult or secret organizations everywhere in DeLillo, on every street corner, one is tempted to say, or in every wallet. As the black street preacher in *Underworld* says, trying to expose the clandestine organization that secretly runs our country: "Unfold this dollar and turn it over to the backside where they keep their secret messages. ... This is Rosicrucian, the beam of light. ... You see the eye that hangs over this pyramid here" (*U* 354). "What's a pyramid doing on a U.S. bill? That's a question you do well to ask" (*U* 364; see 379).

> I've been studying this dollar bill for fifteen year. Take it to the privy when I do my hygiene. And I worked those numbers and those letters all whichway and I hold the bill to the light and I read it underwater and I'm getting closer every day to breaking the code. (*U* 354)

In addition to all these very new or ancient organizations, there is the mafia, always there, ever reliable, whether in *Running Dog* or *Libra* or *Underworld*, anywhere bets are placed and waste managed. The good old mafia, with its fingers in everything when it's at its best, like Carmine Latta's organization in New Orleans (*L* 169), with "prostitutes from here to Bossier City, a place where you could get a social disease leaning on a lamppost," specializing in "casinos, betting parlors, drug traffic," though also "motels, banks, juke boxes, vending machines, shipbuilding, oil leasing, sightseeing buses," not to mention "finance companies, gas stations, truck dealerships, taxi fleets, bars, restaurants, housing subdivisions" (*L* 170, 175). It's a secret organization, the mafia is, but their power is well known, like an open secret, and those in the organization have their own aura. That is especially true of Latta himself in *Libra*, a mob boss who was "like a fairly-tale pope, able to look at you and change your life, say a word and change your life" (*L* 174). The mafia gives meaning to a life through its codes and secrets, operating always "under the surface of ordinary things. And organized so that it makes more sense in a way, if you understand what I mean. It makes more sense than the horseshit life the rest of us live" (*U* 761; see *N* 202). It is this same mafia that plays such a large role in the life of Nick Shay in *Underworld*, or at least in the way he imagines his life, and in this sense there's little difference. For Nick believes his father Jimmy Costanza, a small-time neighborhood bookie, was killed by the mafia, despite the reasoned assurances of a local crime boss to the contrary (*U* 766). He believes it because it is so much better than the alternative, which is that his father simply abandoned his wife and two sons—the worst of all possible crimes for a culture that puts family above all else.

In addition to all these underground or cult organizations, all these contraband groups dealing in contraband outside the government—all these gangsters, thugs, common criminals, and so on—there are all the spy agencies and secret organizations within or on the fringes of government. In *Running Dog* there's the quasi-governmental intelligence operation PAC/ORD, and then, within or outside it, Radial Matrix, an even more covert and secret group, a secret within a secret, "a breakaway unit of the U.S. intelligence apparatus" (*RD* 75; see 45). Such governmental organizations or agencies are often indistinguishable from the organizations they are supposed to combat, as if countering a contraband group required one to imitate or double it and so become contraband oneself—government-funded Contras, for example, enlisted to overthrow foreign governments. As Richard Elster of *Point Omega* aptly puts it in the wake of the US invasion of Iraq in 2003, "A government is a criminal enterprise" (*PO* 33).

There are, then, within the US government, traditional spy agencies like the FBI, especially the one run by J. Edgar Hoover, a massive operation with its "photographs, surveillance reports, detailed allegations, linked names, transcribed tapes—wiretaps, bugs, break-ins," and so on (*U* 559). It's everything one needs to end up "spying on ourselves" (*L* 18).

Then there's the CIA—itself not a single thing but a multifaceted, multilayered organization. Around the Bay of Pigs, for example, there was, as we learn from *Libra*, a group called the Senior Study Effort (SE), but then also SE Augmented, and SE Detailed, and then Leader 4 (*L* 20), each level protected from the others in such a way that those at high levels, and then beyond them the President himself, could claim plausible deniability for anything done at the lower levels. For each, "knowledge was a danger, ignorance a cherished asset," "details a form of contamination," with "each level of the committee designed to protect a higher level" (*L* 21). And, of course, "the White House was to be the summit of unknowing," "as if an unsullied leader redeemed some ancient truth which the others were forced to admire only in the abstract, owing to their mission in the convoluted world" (*L* 22).

But then there was Alpha 66—a secret group within the CIA or maybe just contracted by the CIA: "Alpha was run like a dream clinic. The Agency worked up a vision, then got Alpha to make it come true" (*L* 304). Fearful that JFK wanted to normalize relations with Cuba, this little group of former CIA agents associated with the unsuccessful Bay of Pigs operation plans an assassination attempt (just an attempt, mind you, for the idea was not initially to *kill* the President) that would implicate Cuba and rekindle interest in overthrowing the Castro government (*L* 27–28). But the plot is almost secondary to the secrecy involved in planning and executing it, incidental, really, to the sheer excitement and terror of the CIA operatives involved. Here is how one of the wives of the CIA agents involved described her husband's life in intelligence, his commitment to the Agency's "theology of secrets" (*L* 442):

> The Agency was the one subject in his life that could never be exhausted. Central Intelligence. [She] saw it as the best organized church in the Christian world, a mission to collect and store everything that everyone has ever said and then reduce it to a microdot and call it God. (*L* 260)

God, but with an American face—that is the CIA, or at least was during the good old days of the Cold War. As *The Names* put it: "If America is the world's living myth, then the CIA is America's myth. All the themes are there, in tiers of silence, whole bureaucracies of silence, in conspiracies and doublings and brilliant betrayals" (*N* 317).

The FBI, the CIA, the KGB, the IRS—all these agencies charged with controlling contraband goods also end up trafficking in them themselves (*RD* 40, 64, 133, 137). And, of course, no one knows who is really working for whom. Lyle in *Players* has to ask at one point: "Aren't you required by law to tell me what organization you're with, exactly?" (*P* 156) But not even the people actually working for these agencies always know for whom they are working. James Axton in *The Names*, for example, realizes only near the end of the novel that he may have been working not for a group of insurance companies, as he had believed, but the CIA (*N* 243–244, 271, 315–317). (Axton does get a little hint early on in the novel when he sees his boss's new briefcase, which "looks and feels like a briefcase. Except it has a recording device, a device that detects other recording devices, a burglar alarm, a Mace-spraying device and hidden tracing transmitter, whatever that is" (*N* 11).)

There are secrets within secrets and organizations within organizations, counterintelligence operations, precisely, within intelligence operations. This can get complicated for everyone involved. For example, when Oswald is given advice on how to get hired by a group trying to get information on certain pro-Cuba organizations, he is told to make it clear that he's "a Castro hater" who wants "to pose as a leftist, to infiltrate local organizations" (*L* 310). Hence Oswald would be a real leftist and Castro-lover posing as a Castro-hater who will pose as a Castro-lover in order to infiltrate a Castro-loving group and provide information to the anti-Castro group that, unbeknownst to him, is actually plotting an assassination attempt on Kennedy that will result, it is hoped, in the overthrow of Castro. When Oswald earlier travels to Russia—"the secret that covers one-sixth of the land surface of the earth" (*L* 33)—people wonder whether he might have been clever enough to take advantage of the Naval Intelligence's false defector program as a way of actually defecting, in which case he would be "a real defector posing as a false defector posing as a real defector. Ha ha" (*L* 162). The Russians cannot, of course, be sure one way or another, at least not initially, which is why Oswald sees some rather odd things when he is living in Minsk:

> There's this funny little device on the wall of his flat and it's not a socket, a light switch or a thing to hang a picture from. Not only that. He keeps seeing a car marked "Driving School" going up and down his street. Maybe his street is the site of the final exam, he thinks, except there is never a student in the car. (*L* 205)

There are in DeLillo, then, conspiracies outside government and conspiracies within, conspiracies so complex that it becomes impossible to tell with any certainty one side from the other or whether there really are any clearly defined sides at all. All you can know with any certainty is that everyone is "a spook or dupe or asset, a double, courier, cutout or defector, or was related to one," "all linked in a vast and rhythmic coincidence, a daisy chain of rumor, suspicion and secret wish" (*L* 57). There are the organizations outside government that run contraband and the organizations within that support or finance them or run contraband themselves: band and contraband, intelligence and counterintelligence, spies and contras. The espionage of these groups consists of everything from wiretaps and message intercepts to "spy planes, drone aircraft, satellites with cameras that can see from three hundred miles what you can see from a hundred feet," not to mention the U-2 spy plane of *Libra*, the "dark lady of espionage, the Soviets called it" (*L* 75, 89–90, 190–192), instruments designed to gather "all the secret knowledge of the world" (*L* 77).

It all begins with the simple and obviously not-so-simple attempt to read, influence, or subvert human thinking and intention. And that is done through an initiation into the life of secrets. Take Oswald yet again. He begins reading leftist literature, communist books, in part because of the secret truths they seem to contain:

> The books were private, like something you find and hide, some lucky piece that contains the secret of who you are. The books themselves were secret. Forbidden and hard to read. They altered the room, charged it with meaning. (*L* 41)

Oswald thus begins to believe that he himself is becoming one of the secret men who wrote these secrets books or who were written about in them, men living in "small rooms. Men reading and waiting, struggling with secret and feverish ideas" (*L* 41). These men became his models, right down to their taking of a secret name:

> Trotsky's name was Bronstein. He would need a secret name. He would join a cell located in the old buildings near the docks. They would talk theory into the night. But they would act as well. Organize and agitate. (*L* 41)

We have already spoken of the power of the secret in DeLillo, but "when the name is itself secret, the power and influence are magnified," for "a secret name is a way of escaping the world. It is an opening into the self" (*N* 210). When Oswald thus returns to the United States from Russia, he begins to feel not just that he understands the secrets of others but that he is "in" on their secrets, that he is even central to them, and that he is being spoken to by others. He thus reads the radical newspaper *The Militant* for hidden signs, for a "message buried in the text," believing that one could "read between the lines" and figure out what "they want you to do ... on behalf of the struggle" (*L* 372). He watches TV too and feels "connected to the events on the screen. It was like secret instructions entering the network of signals and broadcast bands, the whole busy air of transmission" (*L* 370). Even the movies on TV seem to be talking to him directly, for example, *Suddenly*, where "Frank Sinatra is a combat veteran who comes to a small town and takes over a house that overlooks the railroad depot. He is here to assassinate the President" (*L* 369), or *We Were Strangers*, where "John Garfield is an American revolutionary in Cuba in the 1930s" (*L* 370). It is as if these late-night films, shown while everyone else was sleeping, "carried his dreams," as if "he was in the middle of his own movie," as if "they were running this thing just for him" (*L* 370).

Oswald is a pretty extreme case, but there are so many spies and spy organizations in DeLillo's novels that it's hard not to be paranoid. Take Jack Gladney's ex-wives, for example, all very different and yet, somehow, all with "ties to the intelligence community" (*WN* 6; see 48, 213, 275). Hence Jack's attraction to Babette, perhaps, who initially seems to have no secrets, no double or counter life, until Jack discovers that she is harboring the secret of all secrets:

> Some of my adoration of Babette must have been sheer relief. She was not a keeper of secrets, at least not until her death fears drove her into a frenzy of clandestine research and erotic deception. (*WN* 213–214)

White Noise will thus come to revolve around the secret of Babette's Dylar and of her affair with the supplier of it, a secret that itself revolves around "an ancient and terrible secret" (*WN* 244), "the secret of our own eventual end" (*WN* 241). To decipher this secret and uncover Babette's secret life, Jack will himself become a sort of spy or double agent, a university professor with a double life. "Was I immersing myself, little by little, in a secret life?" he asks himself. "Perhaps I was beginning to understand my ex-wives and their ties to intelligence" (*WN* 274–275).

Coincidences and Conspiracies

So far everything's operating as per planned.

RS 18

He was too tired to appreciate the irony, or coincidence, or whatever it was. There were too many ironies and coincidences. A shrewd person would one day start a religion based on coincidence, if he hasn't already, and make a million.

L 79

> *Conspiracy's our theme. Shit, you know that. Connections, links, secret associations.*
>
> RD 58

What we are left with, then, is "compulsive information-gathering" (*P* 129), secrecy and espionage, the "haze of conspiracies and multiple interpretations" (*P* 104), "mazes, covert procedures. Strange, strange, strange relationships and links" (*P* 181), "links inside links" (*RD* 111), in short, conspiracy and its "sense of evil design" (*RD* 57), a phrase from *Running Dog* that could apply to DeLillo's writing as a whole. For ours is "the age of conspiracy," "the age of connections, links, secret relationships" (*RD* 111), and DeLillo is perhaps our most prescient voice in this age. As we read in *Great Jones Street*, "There are subtleties. ... There are nuances. There are ambiguities." And "if a person doesn't see that, he's either an asshole or a fascist" (*GJ* 132).

All these secret lives, all this talk of conspiracy, can be very appealing—even to businessmen or tenured professors. As someone says in *Players*, "Imagine how sexy that can be for the true-blue businessman or professor. ... The suggestion of a double life" (*P* 100). Who would not want to get in on the action?

But the truly great thing about truly great conspiracies is that even those who are part of them do not always know they are in them until it's too late. In short, it's unclear who is the informant, who is the government, and who the terrorist (see *P* 134). And that is, of course by design, "You know only what you have to know. First principle of clandestine life" (*P* 186). That is how we get Selvy in *Running Dog*, knowingly leading a secret life without knowing that he himself has been kept in the dark about the true nature of the secret:

> It was becoming clear. He was starting to understand what it meant. All that testing. The polygraphs. The rigorous physicals. The semisecrecy. All those weeks at the Mines. Electronics. Code-breaking. Currencies. Weapons. Survival. ... They'd seen his potential. ... Of course. It was only fitting. All this time they'd been conveying him to the cemetery. (*RD* 183–184)

Hence Selvy is killed not by some foreign government or agency but by Radial Matrix or some rogue element within it, that is, by the very agency he had been trained by and for which he had been working (see *RD* 81).

It's not just the crime organizations, then, or the crimes themselves but, as we like to say, the cover-ups, the conspiracies, like the one covered or covered up by the Warren Commission Report on the JFK assassination, the bedtime reading of Senator Percival's wife in *Running Dog*: "She's been reading the Warren Report for eight or nine years. Nine years, I make it. The full set. Twenty-six volumes" (*RD* 71). The Kennedy assassination of course haunts the novels of DeLillo from the very beginning, from David Bell's trip to Dallas at the end of *Americana*—"I pressed my hand against the horn. I kept it there as I drove past the School Book Depository, through Dealey Plaza and beneath the triple underpass" (*A* 377; see *A* 66, 82)—through *Running Dog* (see *RD* 199), *Players* (*P* 161), and, of course, *Libra*, some seventeen years after *Americana*, as if DeLillo himself were following Bell's itinerary and not the reverse. It is not hard to understand why: the JFK assassination is ground zero when it comes to conspiracies and hidden connections. There are "connections, funny undercurrents, Oswald, for instance. Cuba, for instance. Missing documents. ... running people underground or out of the country" (*P* 154). The Kennedy assassination is the "dark center" of an entire century of secrets and conspiracies, the first and most mysterious in a long litany of events and names that are silently or not so silently repeated, sometimes with an accent: "John F. Kidney, Boddy Kidney, Martin Luther Kang, Jaws Wallace," and so on (*RD* 189). As we read in *Underworld*, "everything connects in the end" (*U* 465), by either conspiracy or coincidence, because within the most highly calculated and plotted conspiracy there is always a good measure of accident and coincidence serving as the counterweight or counterbalance to systems and intentions. The Kennedy assassination is thus the quintessential conspiracy, the holy grail of conspiracies, not because it still promises some grand resolution or revelation, because some mastermind will one day be unmasked behind all the suspicious occurrences and connections before and after November 22, 1963, but because it is the perfect mix of planning and contingency, because anyone who looks into it will become lost in a vast web of secrets with no discernable origin or center. That is the way Nicholas Branch, the retired CIA agent "hired on contract to write the secret history of the assassination," began to see it (*L* 15; see 60):

> If we are on the outside, we assume a conspiracy is the perfect working of a scheme. Silent nameless men with unadorned hearts. ....
> But maybe not. Nicholas Branch thinks he knows better. ... the conspiracy against the President was a rambling affair that succeeded in the short term due mainly to chance. (*L* 441; see 200)

Branch is thus willing to accept the role played by coincidence in many of the strange accidental deaths and ruled suicides of so many people associated with the assassination and the subsequent investigations (*L* 379). But then, of course, as Branch knows the very best conspirators also know, to hide a really good conspiracy one would do well to leave hints of patterns that would ultimately be taken for coincidence, "coincidence so bizarre they have to believe it" (*L* 147; see also 44, 172, 204, 280, 330, 336). So where does that leave us?

There is, therefore, the JFK assassination conspiracy—or whatever it is and whoever was involved—and there are lesser-known conspiracies that have barely made it onto our map. Such would be the case, says Marvin Lundy in *Underground*, of Greenland. First clue: "Did you ever notice that it's never the same size on any two maps? The size of Greenland changes map to map. It also changes year to year" (*U* 315). Greenland seems to have "a secret function and a secret meaning" (*U* 316). It's right there on the map but nobody ever seems to visit it or talk about it:

> I watch the nature channel and I see tribes they wear mud on their body in New Guinea and I see those thingabeests, they're mating in some valley in Africa. … But I never hear a peep from Greenland. (*U* 316)

There are thus large-scale, national or international conspiracies, and little private ones, conspiracies in which everyone is implicated and conspiracies of one, conspiracies to kill Kennedy, to topple Castro, and Jack Gladney's plot to kill his wife's lover and Dylar dealer, a personal plan that begins to feel like a conspiracy in the very nature of things:

> I sensed I was part of a network of structures and channels. I knew the precise nature of events. I was moving closer to things in their actual state as I approached a violence, a smashing intensity. Water fell in drops, surfaces gleamed. (*WN* 305)

This passage from *White Noise* brings us to another aspect of the DeLillo contraband, the way in which things, by doubling themselves, by becoming double, part of a conspiracy with themselves or with the narrative in which they are embedded, begin to shine or to light up from within. Radiance, iridescence—that is the final, phenomenal or phenomenological consequence of contraband.

But before we get to things becoming conscious of themselves, radiating from within, before we can begin to speak of DeLillo's contraband narratives, we have to look at how DeLillo's works double or contraband not only illicit substances and things such as drugs and arms and erotica but language itself.

Secrets and Rumors

Secrets build their own networks.

L 22; see *WN* 275

The men at his level were spawning secrets that quivered like reptile eggs. They were planning to poison Castro's cigars.

L 21

The thing that hovers over every secret is betrayal. Sooner or later someone reaches the point where he wants to tell what he knows.

L 218

Hear the latest secret?

U 405

We read early on in *Libra*: "He was thinking about secrets. Why do we need them and what do they mean?" (*L* 16) Those are two of the central questions not just of *Libra* but of many DeLillo novels, questions to which a few provisional answers can be given. First, secrets create a bond, a community of sorts, not simply because of the information and the power attached to them but because of the *life* they give:

He believed it was a natural law that men with secrets tend to be drawn to each other, not because they want to share what they know but because they need the company of the like-minded, the fellow afflicted—a respite from the other life, from the eerie realness of living with people who do not keep secrets as a profession or duty, or a business fixed to one's existence. (*L* 16; see 30)

Second, secrets tell us who we are. Without secrets, without some measure of a secret life, we cannot separate or distinguish ourselves from others. As one of the principal architects of the JFK assassination plot says about his own six-year-old daughter:

Secrets are an exalted state, almost a dream state. ... there's something vitalizing in a secret. My little girl is generous with secrets. I wish she weren't, frankly. Don't secrets sustain her, keep her separate, make her self-aware? How can she know who she is if she gives away her secrets? (*L* 26)

Whence this definition of the polygraph: a "machine [that] intervenes between a man and his secrets" (*L* 362), in other words, between a man and himself. The fantasy of a life or an afterlife in which every secret is exposed is thus a waking nightmare, a superego turned into its own intelligence operation (see *U* 514). Not everything, it seems, should be said, or exposed, or revealed. As Nick Shay says, "Maybe I have a theory about the damage people do when they bring certain things into the open" (*U* 294), like trying to say the name of God or telling one's spouse about an affair—or about a murder one committed as a seventeen-year-old kid.

Third, there is an aura about the secret and a corresponding aura attached to the one who possesses it or is assumed to possess it. For the secret is a power, and "once you have it, you find yourself protective of it. It confers a culthood of its own" (*N* 247). Take Oswald, for example, the man of secrets: "The secret he'd carried through the Marine Corps for over a year, his plan to defect, was the most powerful knowledge in his life up to this point" (*L* 150). Later in the novel, after his failed attempt on the life of right-wing general and political figure Edwin A. Walker, Oswald attends one of Walker's rallies, getting real close, in handshake range, emboldened and empowered by the secret of his attempt: "The secret he carried with him made him feel untouchable. He was the one, the man who'd fired the shot that barely missed. It was a secret and a power. And he was standing right here, among them ... wearing his .38 under a zipper jacket" (*L* 372). One can almost hear an echo of Jack Gladney here: How stupid this guy was to let me get so close ... (see *WN* 297). Every "conceal and carry" statute will have to reckon with this power and this voice.

But then there's the power that attaches to the one who is thought to have a secret, regardless, it seems, of whether he or she really has it. In *Libra*, again, the name given to that power is *charisma*, and, this time, it's those in power who seem to have it:

> Do you know what charisma means to me? It means he holds the secrets. The dangerous secrets used to be held outside the government. Plots, conspiracies, secrets of revolution, secrets of the end of the social order. Now it's the government that has a lock on the secrets that matter. (*L* 68)

Fourth and finally—and this is the most obvious and thus the easiest to overlook—the secret is a thing of language. It is not some pre-, post-, or a-linguistic fact or meaning stored away in someone's brain tissue but a piece of language, a code of some sort that runs its contraband through the human skull, or through some computer hard drive, but that in every case *means* something to the one who has it and the one who would like to get it.

What links all these groups, all these secret societies and spy organizations, is thus less their common trade in contraband goods than their common circulation within a counterband discourse, their common trafficking in secrets and codes, counterjargons and ideologies, right down to the counterband playing over and over inside their heads. Imagine Mohammad Atta, for example, carrying the secret of what he is planning around within him, trying to act naturally in a supermarket checkout line in Florida, checking out the female cashier while the tape inside his head whispers to remind him, "the idea is to go unseen" (*FM* 172), he who "knew things she could never in ten lifetimes begin to imagine" (*FM* 171). It's a genuine power, this secret, this secret life. Oswald in *Libra* feels something similar: "Nobody knew what he knew. The whirl of time, the true life inside him. This was his leverage, his only control" (*L* 46). That is the power of the secret. It seems to intimate that, to use a phrase from *Libra* that first appears when a woman on a street corner gives Lee Harvey Oswald a leaflet titled *Save the Rosenbergs*, "there is a world inside the world" (*L* 13, 47, 153, 277), a world—a whole world of language—that is darker, more interesting, more compelling, and maybe even bigger than the world in which it is found.

The secret is, in short, a kind of shadow language, a double language, at once visible on the surface and yet suggestive of something deeper, something more ominous and more electrifying. As someone says in *Great Jones Street*:

> The true underground is the place where power flows. That's the best-kept secret of our time. You're not the underground. Your people aren't underground people. The presidents and prime ministers are the ones who make the underground deals and speak the true underground idiom. The corporations. The military. The banks. This is the underground network. This is where it happens. Power flows under the surface, far beneath the level you and I live on. (*GJ* 231–232)

What all underground organizations and spy organizations, all contraband or counterband groups, have in common, what they all share, is thus the secret, not some particular secret, of course, but the idea of the secret, a fascination with the secret life, "a life in which every breath is governed by specific rules, by patterns, codes, controls" ("HM" 36). What links all these organizations, legal or illegal, is their belief in a counterculture or counterworld, another world order that runs parallel to or beneath the surface of the "real" world, a counterband world that is, in certain ways, more real than the world it doubles, a dark web beneath the web or right on the surface of the web, a counter-language or a conspiracy language that is more compelling than the language it shadows.

Secret organizations and the organizations charged with countering them in secret are everywhere in DeLillo's work not because, or not simply because, they are inherently intriguing or compelling, because of their plot value, as it were, but because they are things of language, because their thingness, to recall *Great Jones Street* again, is their wordness. For what all these contraband organizations traffic in first and foremost is language, in secrets and codes, in covert communication systems that initially seem to be controllable but that are very soon themselves in control, systems in which one gets inevitably enmeshed, caught up, absorbed by underground patterns and webs, by all the whispers and rumors that are always bubbling up from just below the surface. It is thus never simply band against contraband in DeLillo, some wholly visible, legitimate, superstructure or authority opposed to some underground organization, but always one underground or secret organization against another, one underworld vying for power with another, one underworld beneath, beyond, or opposed to another.

We saw a moment ago how the CIA is an agency designed for producing and then keeping secrets; it is also an agency for producing the most widely circulated rumors. Take, for example, the CIA overthrow of the government in Guatemala, which was brought about less through force than through "broadcast techniques" and "cryptic messages from spy movies of the forties. 'Attention, Eduardo, the moon is red'" (*L* 127), through the production of "rumors, false battle reports, meaningless codes, inflammatory speeches, orders to non-existent rebels. It was a like a class project in the structure of reality" (*L* 125). Sound familiar to anyone? DeLillo was on to fake news before fake news even became a real thing.

Stories of the contraband Hitler film in *Running Dog* would be exemplary of this culture of rumor and the secret. "I hear things all the time," says Lightborne, the art dealer trying to obtain the film, "I get word. The air is full of vibrations. Sometimes there's an element of truth. Often it's just a breeze in the night" (*RD* 17). Lightborne is speaking here not simply about a contraband or underground film but about a film that actually takes place underground, in Hitler's bunker, a film of Hitler's last days, April 1945, in Berlin (*RD* 18–19). It's just one of the many things in DeLillo's work that happened or are rumored to have happened or are remembered as having happened in some underground. And Hitler, of course, is or used to be the primary subject of such rumors, all the "Hitler gossip" and "sensational rumors" surrounding, for example, "the last days in the *führerbunker*" (*WN* 274).

In *Cosmopolis* it's just the rumor, the word, of a "credible threat" that sets everything in motion, the kind of threat or risk that James Axton in *The Names* is paid to assess (*C* 166). Even something so simple, so seemingly banal, as Terry Chang's description to Keith Neudecker in *Falling Man* of "an underground [poker] game, private game, high stakes, select cities," takes on the aura of a mystical gathering with its shibboleths and its rituals: "It's like a forbidden religion springing up again. Five-card stud and draw" (*FM* 202), "like early Christians in hiding" (*FM* 203).

DeLillo's writing is an attempt to put a glass to our collective ear so that we might make out the secret plans being hatched in the motel room next door. It's an attempt to let us hear the faint rumbling of underground language, contraband language, running just below the surface, like the NYC subway and everything else that's screeching and rattling down there in the tunnels of the City That Never Sleeps, "the ghost engines [that] droned everywhere—down sewers, under basement stairways, in air conditioners and cracks in the pavement. All these complicated textures" (*P* 206). As Globke's assistant Hanes says in *Great Jones Street*: "It's all under the surface, of course. Surface events are practically nil" (*GJ* 131). It's a claim about things, to be sure, but also and perhaps especially about language.

What ultimately drives people, what inspires belief, moves economies and currencies, is thus not what is known on the surface but the secrets and secret patterns below, at once controlled and uncontrollable—the "traded voices, traded news and rumors—buzzes, rumbles, scuttlebutt" ("HM" 30–31; see "IA" 64, "AE" 90). In *White Noise* it's rumor that brings people together, that creates the bond, and especially in times of crisis. It always starts small, with "small crowds collected around certain men," "the sources of information and rumor" (*WN* 129). But then it begins to take on a life of its own, the rumor does, having its source in no one and everyone: "There was a growing respect for the vivid rumor, the most chilling tale" (*WN* 153). "At noon a rumor swept the city" (*WN* 160).

Even science can get caught up in rumor. In *Ratner's Star* someone named J. Graham Hummer hears rumors that "something big is about to be announced. Seriously, the air is rife" (*RS* 31). When a conference is later called by astrophysicists to announce the discovery of an "invisible mass" in the universe, news "spread rapidly, causing rumor to flourish, much of it humorous in nature, centering on the notion that ninety percent of the universe is missing" (*RS* 168). (The concerned reader of *Ratner's Star* will find comfort in what is reported in *Underworld*, namely, that due to climate change the ten percent of the universe that's left can be expected to "expand in warm weather" (*U* 129).)

There are many other great rumors in DeLillo, real whoppers, like the one in *Underworld* about a huge cargo ship filled with heroin—unless it's toxic waste, or excrement—circling the globe for years now, unable to pull into port. Like most other rumors, "this ship thing is a dumb rumor that builds on itself" (*U* 302; see 278). No one is the source of it and so no one is responsible: "You know how rumors work. Nobody tells you. You just hear" (*U* 329). You just hear and then you just want to spread it, even if you don't believe it. You spread the rumor not because you think it's true but, yes, "for the edge. The bite. The existential burn" (*U* 406; see 410, 413).

Elsewhere in *Underworld* there is the mid-1950s rumor that "Pope Pius was having mystical visions," perhaps due to "drinking dago red until three in the morning" (*U* 536), and then the rumor of all rumors, the story of the appearance of Esmeralda on a billboard out by the airport in New York, with

> word passing block to block, moving through churches and superettes, maybe garbled slightly, mistranslated here and there, but not deeply distorted—it is clear enough that people are talking about the same uncanny occurrence. And some of them go and look and tell others, stirring the hope that grows when things surpass their limits. (*U* 818; see "AE" 94)

Secret or underground organizations and the secrets, rumors, and conspiracies they engender, the "textures, entanglements, riddles, [and] words" in which they traffic (*RD* 107)—these are the things, the textures, of DeLillo's writing. Near the end of *Americana*, we already see the close connection between finding links or textures and the act of writing itself: "What I was engaged in was merely a literary venture, an attempt to find pattern and motive, to make of something wild a squeamish thesis on the essence of the nation's soul. To formulate. To seek links" (*A* 349).

Language—literature—is thus itself at once code and secret, the medium in which to hide links and the means to finding links. What is a secret but a counter-word or counter-language, a hidden though always, in principle, revealable language—unless, of course, there are secrets that go beyond anything that can simply be revealed, unless some kind of ritual or initiation, some rigor or discipline, some practice of reading and writing, is required to have any chance of gaining access to the secret. For there is also, as we will see, in works such as *The Names* and *Ratner's Star*, something like a secret of writing—not a secret contained or ciphered in writing but a secret of writing itself. As Ratner himself explains from his "ultrasterile biomedical membrane environment" (*RS* 211), at pretty much the dead center of the novel, there are underground writings, "mystical writings," writings with an underground meaning, a secret or latent meaning beneath their manifest content: "The writings have a substructure, a secret element of the divine" (*RS* 222). There are the explicit things, the writing on the surface, and then there is "the secrecy of things, the hiddenness, the buried nature" (*RS* 220), a truth below what appears to be the truth:

A hidden essence. A truth beneath the truth. What is the true name of G-dash-d? How many levels of unspeakability must we penetrate before we arrive at the true name, the name of names? Once we arrive at the true name, how many pronunciations must we utter before we come to the secret, the hidden, the true pronunciation? (*RS* 221)

And then there is the secret of ourselves, of our lives and our deaths, the secret of our utterly contingent birth and "the secret of our own eventual end" (*WN* 241). As a son says to his dying father in *Love-Lies-Bleeding*:

> I don't think I know what to say. I never did. … You would say, Not everything we feel has to be expressed, or can be expressed. We withhold some things. Some things are too powerful, or too breakable. We withhold, we suppress, we whisper. … We whisper to our lovers. Why? Because some things are too precious to enter the world. (*LL* 76)

There are secret fears, secret desires, and then the ultimate secret of death—about which we have no knowledge but only intimations—a taboo or contraband subject that is the dark center of just about every one of DeLillo's works. And then, finally, there is the secret of God, not the secret that God keeps from us but the secret that God is, a secret that cannot be revealed but that must somehow be expressed in a word or a language to be invented (see *U* 295–296).

Undergrounds

Noise from the streets rose uncertainly tonight, muffled, an underwater density. Air conditioners, buses, taxicabs. Beyond that, something obscure: the nonconnotative tone that appeared to seep out of the streets themselves, that was present even when no traffic moved, the quietest sunups. It was some innate disturbance of low frequency in the grain of the physical city, a ghostly roar.

P 148

The whole history of mathematics is subterranean, taking place beneath history itself, misunderstood, ignored, ridiculed, unread, a shadow-world scarcely perceived even by the learned.

RS 195

In speaking of contraband, then, I was speaking not of any kind of illegal product or of the organizations that traffic in them but of the fact that, in DeLillo's works, there is always a substructure, a second level, always an underworld or alterworld beneath the world, an underground below the ground. In short, there is always a superstructure and a substructure, what is happening above ground and what is happening below in some subworld or subconscious. Always two levels—two at the very least—two bands or layers, a surface and an underside, or a surface and another surface, and then the tension that results from the disconnections or the secret connections between them, the things one feels only in the night or only when, as in an eclipse, night comes upon the earth in the middle of day, in contraband fashion.

Though a novel actually titled *Underworld* would not come for a couple of decades after DeLillo's first works, the theme of an underworld or a counterworld is present from the very start. Already in *Americana*, the place of the father—as well as of film (and this is no coincidence)—is in the underworld, below ground, in the basement, a place that David Bell remembers as if the past, or his memory of the past, were itself an underworld: "In the flickering basement ... I thought of him standing by the projector" (*A* 85). We come to realize that Bell, who will spend most of his time in the novel making a movie, has never completely come out of that basement. That's because no one ever completely emerges from such a basement, the place where all the big things happen in a life.

In *Mao II* the novelist Bill Gray, obsessed by the plight of a UN worker held captive in a basement in Beirut, finds himself compelled to write about that basement room, as if there were some special connection between that room and writing itself, between the hostage and the novelist, that basement and the written page: "the words lead him into that basement room" (*M* 160; see 107–112). "There was something at stake in these sentences he wrote about the basement room. They held a pause, an anxious space he began to recognize" (*M* 167).

It is also in a basement that Win Everett will plan the assassination attempt on JFK, the basement becoming for him a refuge, "a place to refine and purify, to hone his sense of the past" (*L* 178). As for Oswald, the central figure in Everett's plot, he too lives for the most part below ground, "a fatherless boy" living with his mother in a "basement room in the Bronx" (*L* 4), or later, "underground" (*L* 271), trying to keep out of sight. And two days after being captured in the flickering light of a movie theater, just hours after the assassination, he will himself be killed as the police are moving him out of the jail "via the basement" (*L* 433). Oswald's life thus ends below ground, in a basement, in perfect symmetry with the place where, on DeLillo's telling, it began—the NYC subway, which runs beneath so many of DeLillo's works. Here is how *Libra* begins: "This was the year he rode the subway to the ends of the city, two hundred miles of track" (*L* 3). It is there that Oswald first gets the idea, it seems, of an underground life, a life of secrets and, as we have seen, of power:

> It did not seem odd to him that the subway held more compelling things than the famous city above. There was nothing important out there, in the broad afternoon, that he could not find in a purer form in these tunnels beneath the streets. ... The view down the tracks was a form of power. It was a secret and a power. ... Never again in his short life, never in the world, would he feel this inner power, rising to a shriek, this secret force of the soul in the tunnels under New York. (*L* 4, 13)

As for Billy Twillig, math prodigy tapped to decode the message supposedly received from a faraway star, his father Babe worked in the same NYC subway, just like Eddie Robles in *Underworld*, who spent his whole working life in a little booth selling tokens (yes, there were tokens back in the day) and practicing chess moves (*U* 224; see 233). From the lowest comes the highest, from the most vile the most ethereal, and vice versa. As soon as Billy is born, Babe wants to bring his son "down into the tunnels" (*RS* 69), to introduce him, in "a sort of Theban initiation," "to the idea that existence tends to be nourished from below, from the fear level, the place of obsession, the starkest tract of awareness" (*RS* 4). As for the initiation, father and son—just like Oswald and his father minus the father—"rode the local for a while, standing at the very front on the first car to get the motorman's viewpoint" (*RS* 4).

Billy's life as a math prodigy would take him far away from NYC, but not necessarily from the underground. At age fourteen, he would be brought out to an Asian desert to work at Field Experiment Number One, an "armillary sphere" (*RS* 23), "a vast geometric structure ... about sixteen hundred feet wide, six hundred feet high. Welded steel. Reinforced concrete" (*RS* 15–16). It's an impressive structure above ground, but in the second part of the novel we learn that there is a mirror image of the superstructure below. All the advances in decoding the message thought to come from a planet near faraway Ratner's Star will thus end up coming not from Field Experiment Number One, the structure above ground, but from the Logicon project below. In short, in a single title, *Ratner's Star*: the lowly rat and the lofty star, the lowest and the highest, the one inside the other, *rats* in *Star* and *stars* in *Ratner's*.

That is why there are so many rats in DeLillo, why DeLillo would make of the local fauna of NYC a metaphysical theme. Billy Twillig, for example, thinks he sees a rat in the subway when his father takes him down for that Thebans initiation (*RS* 5), while Oswald keeps "a watch for sewer rats" (*L* 3), the kind from which legends are born in NYC, "an endless source of stories, the size of the rats, the attitude of unfearing, how they ate the bodies of those who died in the tunnels" (*U* 439–440, see 194, 233; *M* 172). Here is one of those stories: "Did I ever tell you about the rat downtown?" (*U* 205) Nick Shay has taken his date—"a German woman, a philosophy student, yes, and a sort of future, now that I think of it, terrorist type" (*U* 205)—back to her apartment after going to a jazz club, and when they walk in they see a rat, "a phenomenal rat, big and fast," and what happens, Nick recounts, "my date goes right after it … What is happening to my jazz date? It's disintegrating into a rat hunt" (*U* 206). We are not told, but she was probably a Hegelian.

The theme of the underground or of the underworld is, obviously, absolutely central to *Underworld*, where the word itself refers, just for starters, to the NYC subway, to the Eisenstein film "Underworld" or "Unterwelt" (*U* 424), to the gangster film of the same name (*U* 431), and then to the mob, which may or may not have taken Nick's father Jimmy Costanza and "dropped him into the lower world" (*U* 119; see 106). As Nick likes to think, "The earth opened up and he stepped inside. … I think he went under. … I think he just went under" (*U* 808–809). And just as Field Experiment Number One above ground is mirror-doubled in the ground below, so Martin Lundy will keep all his baseball memorabilia, including his model recreation of the Polo Grounds, in his basement (*U* 187), itself a kind of unconscious or subconscious, whether individual or collective, because, as Marvin knows full well, "there's an ESP of baseball, an underground … a consciousness, and I'm hearing it in my sleep" (*U* 179). Lundy is an adept at hearing this underworld, but on October 3, 1951, others seemed to be on the same wavelength, countless others, in fact, a whole crowd, hearing something about baseball and something that went far beyond it, a foreboding caused by the contrabanding of events—by an underground nuclear test thousands of miles away that was somehow felt in the Polo Grounds that day:

> There was a hidden mentality of let's stay home. Because a threat was hanging in the air. … They sensed there was a connection between this game and some staggering event that might take place on the other side of the world. … People had a premonition that this game was related to something much bigger. (*U* 172)

It can all sound a little mystical or mysterious, this unconscious of America's national pastime, but it somehow communicates with all the other undergrounds and underworlds in the novel, including the fallout and bomb shelters built in response to similar intimations of a catastrophic future right below the surface—or right *on* the surface—of the present: "People hide in their basement rooms. They take to the bunkers and tunnels as weapons roll identically off the line and begin to light up the sky" (*U* 465).

The underground, the basement, the NYC subway, the underground of Field Experiment Number One, even the Convergence of *Zero K*—itself described as a sort of "sub-planet" (*ZK* 258)—all show, through a series of descents and ascents, that the superstructure always bears traces of its substructure, which is, as it were, the hidden law of the superstructure. Above as below, then, the pyramid as well as the tomb: "We built pyramids of waste above and below the earth. The more hazardous the waste, the deeper we tried to sink it. The word plutonium comes from Pluto, god of the dead and ruler of the underworld" (*U* 106).

3

Counterpoints and Counternarratives

Fiction is all about reliving things. It is our second chance.

"PH"

This is the most secret part of the narrative. It must be free of naming.

RS 106

Bandwidths

There was the laughing man at the far end of the room. There was the fact that they would all be dead one day.

FM 228

Something about the way I think and feel. He caught the back-and-forthness.

M 51

This, finally, is where we can begin to carve out a space for another sense of contraband, a contraband notion of contraband, if that's not too tautological or too academic, a contraband in and of language, one that is not unrelated to the etymology of the word, which comes from the Italian, appropriately enough for DeLillo, *contrabbando*, made up of *contra-*, meaning "against," of course, and *bando*, "proclamation," from the Latin *bannus*, *bannum*, meaning edict, ban, penalty, in the plural, *banns*, as in marriage *banns*, marriage proclamations—which permits me to say here that marriage too will have its own contraband in DeLillo, in the form of betrayal or infidelity, sometimes accompanied by confession, and often in a motel room, a contraband space par excellence. The word *contraband* is thus a word for a category of things and a word about words, a word about language and the limits, legal or otherwise, of language. It names at once illicit things or substances and the proclamation or ban against those things. In speaking of DeLillo's contraband, then, I am referring here not so much to drugs or drink or weapons or works of art sold on the black market or of the secret organizations through which all these things circulate but to language as contraband, language as the substance and the very medium of contraband. For if contraband, in the guise of illegal goods and substances, carried along by secrecy or conspiracy, is a privileged subject in DeLillo's writing, it is also the very form, mode, or style of that writing. It is a name for DeLillo's various attempts to forge a counter-language, a language of the surface for what is just below the surface, just beneath what is visible, explicit, and expected, a contraband language that might initially sound like a kind of white noise but whose layers and textures can ultimately be distinguished, its rules deciphered or decoded. That is the kind of contraband I want to try to sneak in here, a thing of language, a language-thing, even when, and this is probably not a coincidence either, that which occasions this literary contraband is contraband in the more literal or traditional sense. There would thus be literature that is barred or banned, that becomes contraband or contrabanned, and Don DeLillo has had his share of barred works over his career, from *Americana* to *White Noise*, but then there is *contraband literature*, literature that works through the techniques of contraband.

Recall, for instance, the famous opening lines of DeLillo's best-known novel, *White Noise*, where Jack Gladney begins listing all the things coming out of the station wagons on moving-in day at the College-on-the-Hill. DeLillo fans can almost recite the list by heart:

> Carefully secured suitcases full of light and heavy clothing; with boxes of blankets, boots and shoes, stationary and books, sheets, pillows, quilts; with rolled-up rugs and sleeping bags; with bicycles, skis, rucksacks, English and Western saddles, inflated rafts [a first slightly off-kilter note, but we tend to let it slide ...], stereo sets, radios, personal computers; small refrigerators and table ranges; the cartons of phonograph records and cassettes; the hairdryers and styling irons; the tennis rackets, soccer balls, hockey and lacrosse sticks, bows and arrows [another somewhat odd note, to be sure, but then, even more unexpectedly, though in retrospect it seems as if we have been waiting for it all along ...], the controlled substances, the birth control pills and devices; the junk food still in shopping bags—onion-and-garlic chips, nacho thins, peanut creme patties, Waffelos and Kabooms, fruit chews and toffee popcorn; the Dum-Dum pops, the Mystic mints. (*WN* 3)

That is how a counterband narrative begins, with an incongruous element slipped in between the sporting gear and the junk food, smuggled in, as it were, along with the other items, smuggled in but also meant to be sniffed out, or rather, meant to be detected as trying to pass undetected—and that's the difference between literal contraband, if we can call it that, and literary contraband. While the college freshman might hope to sneak something past his or her parents or campus security by packing it inside other things, DeLillo wants us to detect the incongruous or contraband element, which is usually highly coded and often rather funny, producing a bit of friction within the fiction, a blip in the narrative, a dissonance between two narrative registers, the band (the wholesomeness of another college move-in day) and the contraband (the drugs and the sexual devices that will get broken out as soon as the station wagons pull away).

The contraband thus runs here from the most serious and ordinary items to the most surprising and incongruous and from the generic (blankets, pillows, phonograph records) to the ultra-specific (Waffelos and Kabooms, Dum-Dum pops, and Mystic mints—all items that probably need a trademark sign beside them), though it can also, on occasion, run in the other direction, from the less to the more serious, as in this list of priorities after the evacuation of a town, again in *White Noise*: "When the siren sounds two melancholy wails, street captains will make house-to-house searches for those who may have been inadvertently left behind. Birds, goldfish, elderly people, handicapped people, invalids, shut-ins, whatever" (*WN* 206). "Controlled substances," then, though maybe already those "saddles" and "rafts" and "bows and arrows," slightly odd notes that seem to foreshadow even odder ones. Here is Grass in *The Day Room* explaining why his wife never visits him in the hospital: "She has her bridge club. She has tennis in a bubble. There's antiquing on the weekend in the country. Her bow and arrow. Her insect larvae. There's her foot fetish. Her bicycling through the wine country. She has her massive coronaries" (*DR* 12).

The contraband effect is thus produced—particularly in DeLillo's earlier novels—by means of an unexpected, incongruous element, often near the end of a sentence or passage, a jolting, attention-grabbing, and thereby often comical leap in thought or language. Here's one more, already in the first hundred pages of *Americana*, where the incongruous element again involves the other kind of contraband I just spent so much time saying I did not mean to talk about. David Bell says:

> I called up the head priest one night, the pastor, and we had an interesting talk. Hell of a nice guy. ... He told me all about the human soul. The soul has a transcendental connection to the body. It informs the body. The soul becomes aware of its own essence after it separates from the body. Once you're dead, your soul can be directly illuminated by God. I sent him a case of Johnnie Walker Red. (*A* 86; see *AZ* 9)

Here the contraband element gets smuggled in—and again we can hear it coming, at least in retrospect, which is another thing about contraband, its temporality—under the cloak of God, amid what sounds to be some pretty serious talk about religion. A profane element gets inserted, as it were, into the midst of a very sober if not sacred subject. And let me say here just in passing that if DeLillo is a great writer of religion it is because the contraband works always in two directions, turning what is sacred into the profane through parody or pastiche, whatever that might mean, and sacralizing the everyday, making a miracle out of, say, the appearance of a young girl's face on a billboard advertisement for Minute Maid orange juice. So, Johnnie Walker, that's the unexpected, incongruous, and yet, in retrospect, perfectly appropriate contraband element, Johnnie Walker Red, to be precise, which is good but not as good as the Black (not to mention the Blue—I've never even seen the Blue), which suggests that all those assurances about the immortality of the human soul were helpful, appreciated, but maybe not quite good enough to merit the Black.

Two discourses, then, one serious and the other playful, one, let's say, high and the other low, one surface and one just below the surface, festering, full of implications, ready to "express itself" (*C* 186). And since Johnnie Walker is on the table, consider the following from *Libra* where a juxtaposition between two incongruous elements—the ingredients for DeLillo contraband, as I am understanding it here—are laid out in an explicit contrast, here occasioned by the narrator's thoughts about a certain KGB center in Moscow:

> The nice thing about the Center was the inexpensive caviar and salmon available in Building 12 across the square, and the J&B and Johnnie Walker at a dollar a bottle. The not-so-nice thing was the heavy sense of Stalinist terror. (*L* 164)

Once again, the counterband effect is created in part through one of those contraband elements we looked at earlier. Sex—if not necessarily erotica—can work in a similar way. Here is David Bell from *Americana*, talking about the film he is making to his old friend Ken Wild, keeping it clear and simple before jump-cutting, as it were, to a quite different topic:

> What I'm doing is kind of hard to talk about. It's a sort of first-person thing but without me in it in any physical sense, except fleetingly. ... The anti-movie. The single camera position. The expressionless actor. The shot extended to its ultimate limit in time. I just got laid incidentally. (*A* 263)

From *Americana*, then, to *Zero K*, some four and a half decades later, the narrator's one-track mind continues to divide in two (like an image and its counterimage in a mirror):

> At home he stood before a full-length mirror reciting from memory speeches he was working on about risk appetites and offshore jurisdictions, refining his gestures and facial expressions. He had an affair with an office temp. He ran in the Boston Marathon. (*ZK* 14)

Contraband here names at once the counterband, the counter-meaning or counter-narrative, and the tension or contact between two narrative lines, two story lines, two voices, two meanings, the one smuggled inside the other or simply juxtaposed with the other. It's a single thing, this contraband, but it immediately divides and manifests itself in different ways by moving, for example, from a narrative in the present to one in the past or from one more or less contemporaneous scene or thought to the next in contrapuntal fashion, not unlike what we see in, say, the Proteus chapter of Joyce's *Ulysses*, the novel most frequently invoked in *Americana* (see *A* 143, 145).

The contrabanded back-and-forth of DeLillo's narratives can thus take place through the juxtaposition—whether in first- or third-person narration or simply in dialogue—of different places or scenes or thoughts, different trains or bands of thought, between perceptions and memories or perceptions and associations. Here's a touch of contraband between something Oswald sees happening at a party—his wife being offered a cigarette—and his thoughts about a book he had ordered.

> A man offered Marina a cigarette from a black-and-white case. Lee had his collection. He'd written to an obscure press in New York for a twenty-five-cent booklet called *The Teachings of Leon Trotsky*. Back comes a letter saying it's out of print. At least they sent a letter. He saved their letters. The point is they are out there and willing to reply. He was starting a collection of documents.
> She would never refuse a cigarette. (*L* 235)

We thus watch Lee watching Marina and hear Lee thinking about a booklet about Leon that he had hoped to receive in the mail. And Leon, like Lee, had once lived in the Bronx—which is another thing we are supposed to think about.

Here's another example, from the same novel, a back-and-forth between encyclopedia entries Oswald had once gone through—he's up to the *k*'s, it seems—and Oswald's dreams and aspirations, the two finally getting telescoped together in the name of a bird:

> He had his one-volume encyclopedia of the world, which his aunt Lillian said he read like a boy's novel of the sea. Kinetic energy. Grand Coulee Dam. He would join a communist cell. They would talk theory into the night. They would give him tasks to perform, night missions that required intelligence and stealth. He would wear dark clothes, cross rooftops in the rain.
> How many people know a killdeer is a bird? (*L* 37)

Contraband narrative can thus name the back-and-forth between two different trains of thought of the same person in the same place or the thoughts or actions of two different people in different places (like NYC and the American desert in *Running Dog* or NYC and Hamburg in *Falling Man*, to name just two), a back-and-forth between different, simultaneous conversations or between different topics within the same conversation. Here's George Haddad in *Mao II* making small talk with Bill Gray about coffee and then shifting suddenly to try to convince Bill to chuck his typewriter and get himself a word processor: "Drink your coffee. There's a new model that Panasonic makes and I absolutely swear by it. ... You transform freely, fling words back and forth" (*M* 164). Word processing—that's what contraband is all about, though one has to wonder whether the typewriter's "return" (sometimes accompanied by a little bell) is not more appropriate for the contrabanded narrative than that more seamless, soundless word processor.

The transition between different bands is thus sometimes on the macro-level, between two distinct narratives, sometimes on a micro-level, occasioned by a simple shift in perception on the part of one of the characters. For example, to pick just one among a thousand possible examples, in this sex scene between Lomax and Grace Delaney in a New York hotel in *Running Dog*, it is a sound outside the room that triggers the shift in narrative: "Lomax leaned over to lick her navel. Someone pushed a room-service tray along the corridor" (*RD* 216). There we are in bed with Lomax and Grace Delaney (it's quite a party) and then, all of a sudden, we are out in the corridor as we, following them, hear the room-service tray outside. It is compelling narration, but it is also true to experience, which is never simply singular or linear but always discontinuous, always coming to us in waves or in fragments, with realizations that happen not, as we say, in "real time" (whatever that means) but almost always in retrospect.

Sometimes, then, the counterpoint, or what I am calling here the contraband, can be occasioned by a perception or by memory, by a shift between two temporal bands or tracks, a transition between what is happening in the present and a memory of the narrator or character of something from the past. This then allows the present to be thought *either* in terms of what will have been recorded for the future and repeated in the future *or* in terms of a repetition or playback of the past. There is, for example, in *Underworld* a contraband narrative between the story of Marvin Lundy and his wife Eleanor looking for the famous Bobby Thomson baseball in San Francisco and a hilarious narrative of Marvin and Eleanor, early in their relationship, traveling through Eastern Europe, Marvin's bowel movements becoming more rank and embarrassing the further they travel East. The two narrative bands then more or less converge as Marvin recalls that it was on that very trip, just as their train was passing through a tunnel and the transistor radio someone was listening to cut out, that Bobby Thompson hit his shot heard 'round the world (*U* 313; see *L* 85 for a forerunner—a sort of exhibition game—of this scene).

Memories return in contraband, extraordinary moments, historical moments, or else ordinary things—simple phrases that one's parents used to say. When Bill Gray in *Mao II* goes to sleep on the ferry from Cyprus to Lebanon, a sleep from which he will never awaken, he recalls, he replays, those simply everyday phrases: "His father. I keep telling you and telling you and telling you. / His mother. I like it better with the sleeves rolled down" (*M* 216). Those are the kinds of things that come back in contraband: simple, everyday things, absolutely unremarkable and yet oddly unforgettable.

Sometimes the contraband happens through the interweaving of two strands of conversation, close enough to be part of the same conversation and yet somehow disjointed. Here's a fairly simple contraband scenario, two speakers not quite talking over one another but not responding in sequence either:

> Toinette: San Francisco. To stay with friends. Four or five days. Then back to New York.
>
> Lia: I've never been to New York. So many places.
>
> Toinette: They're not really friends. They're people I met somewhere, married forever. We keep in touch. I don't know why I'm going really. (*LL* 89)

Or instead of two lines of thought in two different people that barely intersect, there can be a single line of thought that divides so that one might follow both the truth of the matter and the false assumptions or implications triggered by it:

"They met at Disney World. It'll be all right."
"When were you in Los Angeles?"
"You mean Anaheim."
"When were you in Anaheim?"
"You mean Orlando. It's almost three years now." (*WN* 15–16)

At other times, the contraband can happen between a conversation or a narrative line and the individual thoughts of one of the characters. Here is Jack Gladney in a restaurant, about to pay the bill and then suddenly recalling his wife's affair with Mr. Gray:

> I called for the check. Extraneous flashes of Mr. Gray. A drizzling image in gray shorts and socks. I lifted several bills from my wallet, rubbing hard with my fingers to make sure there weren't others stuck to them. In the motel mirror was my full-length wife, white-bodied, full-bosomed, pink-kneed, stub-toed, wearing only peppermint legwarmers, like a sophomore leading cheers at an orgy. (*WN* 268)

Contraband is able to combine distraction and obsession, getting lost in other thoughts or else perpetually returning to the same thought, being caught off guard by something just encountered or picking at some past thought like a sore or a scab.

The contraband can run from the serious to the less serious, for example, from thoughts about sex and union with another immortal soul to choices at the gas pump:

> How subtly we shifted emotions, found shadings, using the scantest movement of our arms, our loins, the slightest intake of breath, to reach agreement on our fear, to advance our competition, to assert our root desires against the chaos in our souls.
> Leaded, unleaded, super unleaded. (*WN* 199)

Or from the least significant, a piece of lint, to the most profound.

> A staticky piece of lint clung to the TV screen.
> In bed we lay quietly, my head between her breasts, cushioned as if against some remorseless blow. I was determined not to tell her about the computer verdict. I knew she would be devastated to learn that my death would almost surely precede hers. (*WN* 172)

Contraband is the name for all these juxtapositions, all these times, places, or narrative lines in counterpoint. Here, in just three sentences, and without any real transition, we go from (Jack) thinking about death to (Jack) hearing clothes in the dryer to (Jack) meeting Murray in the supermarket:

> Shouldn't death, I thought, be a swan dive, graceful, white-winged and smooth, leaving the surface undisturbed?
> Blue jeans tumbled in the dryer.
> We ran into Murray Jay Siskind at the supermarket. His basket held generic food and drink, nonbrand items in plain white packages with simple labeling. (*WN* 18)

One could cite almost any page of *White Noise* for similar examples. Here's just one more, some two hundred pages later, a similar three-step ending yet again with Murray:

> I bounded upstairs to find my glasses.
> "*The National Cancer Quiz*" was on TV.
> In the lunchroom in Centenary Hall, I watched Murray sniff his utensils. (*WN* 214)

Sometimes it is not narrative or perception or memory but just a little shift in linguistic tone that does the trick, a juxtaposition of two or more different registers of conversation, light-hearted banter and the story of a family tragedy in *Americana* (*A* 228–230), or, in *Ratner's Star*, serious scientific discourse and adolescent sexual and scatological humor (see *RS* 34, 48, 374–375). Or this, a simple shift from a spiritual register to a physical, everyday one through the introduction of a made-up, slightly off-key adjective: "Death is a religious experience. It is also nuts-and-boltsy. Something fails to work, you die" (*P* 63).

In each case, there is a transition, sometimes just quick or abrupt, sometimes downright jarring, between one paragraph and the next, one sentence or even one phrase or word and the next. There is also, just as frequently, and perhaps even more uniquely DeLillo, more signature DeLillo—and this is, of course, well known—a repeated back-and-forth between one scene, narrative, or narrative track and another. *Libra*, DeLillo's fast-paced, rapid-fire narrative about the Kennedy assassination, is perhaps the best example of this. The novel alternates between chapters that follow Oswald from the time he was a boy growing up in the Bronx to the time of the assassination, about a decade in Oswald's life (with separate chapters devoted to his time in Atsugi, Japan, Fort Worth, Texas, Moscow, Minsk, back to Fort Worth, Dallas, New Orleans, Mexico City, and then Dallas again), and chapters that follow a small group of ex-CIA operatives and Bay of Pigs veterans from the first sketches of the assassination plot in April 1963

(April 17, to be exact, "the second anniversary of the Bay of Pigs" (*L* 31)) to the assassination some seven months later. These two narrative strands or bands, these two narrative frames, ultimately converge in Dallas on November 22, 1963, and they both end three days later with the funeral of Lee Harvey Oswald in Fort Worth. The chapters thus go back and forth, with many back-and-forths within each chapter, allowing some events or details to be recounted twice or even three times, that is, from Oswald's perspective, from the perspective of those plotting the attempt, and, finally—we will talk about this level of narrative later when we look at all the figures of writers in DeLillo's work—from the perspective of Nicholas Branch, the retired CIA officer who had been contracted many years later to write the secret history of the assassination. The novel will thus culminate in a scene that moves back and forth at breakneck speed between descriptions of the crowd, Oswald in the Book Depository, the men behind the grassy knoll, and then, as the first shots ring out, the reactions of the spectators, those in the motorcade, the Kennedys and Connallys, people taking pictures in the crowd, the Secret Service agents, and so on (*L* 391–406). Back and forth it goes, from one paragraph or sometimes even one sentence to the next. About three-quarters of the way through the novel, just as the two narrative threads or bands are about to converge, the enigmatic David Ferrie gives us not only an explanation for Oswald's role in the assassination but also the very principle of the contrapuntal narrative:

> Think of two parallel lines. One is the life of Lee H. Oswald. One is the conspiracy to kill the President. What bridges the space between them? What makes a connection inevitable? There is a third line. It comes out of dreams, visions, intuitions, prayers, out of the deepest levels of the self. It's not generated by cause and effect like the other two lines. It's a line that cuts across causality, cuts across time. It has no history that we can recognize or understand. But it forces a connection. It puts a man on the path of his destiny. (*L* 339)

Falling Man does something similar. Divided into three parts, each titled with a proper name that masks or double-bands another name—"Bill Lawton," a name that sounds to children like "Bin Laden" (*FM* 73), "Ernst Hechinger," the "real name" of Martin Ridnour, and "David Janiak" (the real name of the performance artist known as "Falling Man")—the narrative runs both forward and backward (in memory, through the narrator) in order to put two narratives into a collision course and record their moment of impact. It goes back and forth between the narrative featuring Keith Neudecker in the hours, days, and weeks just after the plane attacks on 9/11, Keith's memory of those attacks and his experience of being in the towers, and a narrative with Mohammed Atta in the weeks, days, and hours just before the attack, the two narratives with two temporalities running side by side, one backward and the other forward, until they collide on the morning of 9/11 in the space of a single, devastating sentence:

> A bottle fell off the counter in the galley, on the other side of the aisle, and he [Mohammed Atta] watched it roll this way and that, a water bottle, empty, making an arc one way and rolling back the other, and he watched it spin more quickly and then skitter across the floor an instant before the aircraft struck the tower, heat, then fuel, then fire, and a blast wave passed through the structure that sent Keith Neudecker out of his chair and into a wall. (*FM* 239)

It is a narrative structure that could be heard, though only in retrospect, in this simple sentence right at the beginning of the novel describing Keith as he walks in the smoke and rubble right after the collapse of the towers: "He walked away from it and into it at the same time" (*FM* 4). That's DeLillo's narrative contraband in a single declarative sentence.

There is a similar notion of contrabanded time in most DeLillo novels, like *The Body Artist*, or *Point Omega* (constructed as a kind of ellipsis revolving around two points), or *Zero K*, or the play *Love-Lies-Bleeding*, narratives where we move forward and then backward in time, or at once forward and backward, sometimes revolving around a film or a performance or the review of a performance. In each case what we get is a double-banded temporality, one in the present, at room temperature, as it were, and one on the back burner, or else—pick your metaphor—in the freezer, waiting to be resurrected in a subsequent paragraph, sequence, or section of the narrative. DeLillo's writing has enough energy and enough intelligence, enough bandwidth, as we might say today, for both the story and the counter-story, the narrative and the counter-narrative.

Battle of the Bands

It's all double, Gary. Double consciousness. Old form superimposed on new. It's a breaking down of reality. Primitive mirror awareness. Divine electricity. The football feels. The football knows. This is not just one thing we're watching. This is many things.

EZ 129

> *Sometimes I think everything I've done since those years, everything around me in fact, I don't know if you feel this way but everything is vaguely—what—fictitious.*
>
> U 73

Sometimes, then, the transition is, as it were, on a macro-level, between two narratives or two narrative threads that eventually cross or intersect, and sometimes it takes place within a single scene—for example, in the infamous opening pages of *Underworld*, where the back-and-forth between several narrative bands or strands shifts our focus or attention between what's happening on the field in the Polo Grounds, what's happening in the crowd with Bill Waterson and Cotter Martin out in the bleachers, what Frank Sinatra, Jackie Gleason, Toots Shor, and J. Edgar Hoover are doing in the more expensive seats, and what's happening in the announcer's booth, which is also to say, on the radio. And that is just the beginning of a narrative contraband that takes us at once slowly forward from that single shot in the prologue, the home run by Bobby Thomson of October 3, 1951, itself doubled or contrabanded by a Soviet nuclear test in the Kazakhstan desert, and then, beginning in Part I of the novel, set in 1992, backward, until the two bands converge in 1951 and 1952, before then returning us to 1992 and beyond. Rapid expansion and then contraction—*Underworld* is the big bang of DeLillo's contraband narratives.

As we will see, the techniques of film provide us with a privileged way to think this movement of DeLillo's narrative. In *Mao II*, for instance, there is a series of back-and-forths, a series of jump cuts, as it were, between what's happening on the field in Yankee Stadium, the Moonie couples getting married, and what's happening in the stands between the parents and family members—a scene that repeats in advance, in effect, that opening scene of *Underworld*, where the Polo Grounds replaces Yankee Stadium and a baseball game stands in for the mass-marriage, a masterpiece of counterpointed, contrapuntal, or, as I am choosing to call it here, *contraband* writing.

It is this doubling, this repetition and displacement, this replaying or rescreening, this retrospective recognition, this playing of one narrative or band off the other, this trafficking in contraband, that produces so much of what is original and unique in DeLillo's work. Whether the back-and-forth is chapter by chapter, scene by scene, paragraph by paragraph, or sentence by sentence, the contrapuntal or counterbanded narrative confuses temporalities and, ultimately, turns language upon itself. Take, for example, in *End Zone*, the hilarious back-and-forth dormitory room conversation about the football season ending, a dress being sewn, and a plane crash in which the president of the college is fatally injured (*EZ* 180). The humor comes from the fact that, when woven together like this, these very different narrative strands all ask to be treated with the same degree of seriousness. But things become even more madcap, more delirious, more DeLillo, when these narrative bands begin to turn on and around language itself, a language that is both referring and referenced, self-referring, therefore, used to describe objects but then itself made into the central object of discussion, two different bands, then, two different tracks, one related to *things* and the other to the *words* used to describe those things:

> "I've had conversations with the guy. He's pretty interesting, albeit a little bit stereo."
> "What do you mean—stereo?"
> "I mean psycho. Did I say stereo? What a funny word to use."
> "You said albeit a little bit stereo."
> "Did I say albeit? That's incredible, Gary. I'd never use a word like that. A word like that is out of my province."
> "But you used it, Jimmy. I'm certain."
> "I must have been speaking in tongues," Fife said. (*EZ* 203)

It's a funny little passage, an attempt to capture what college students of the time might have simply called "shooting the shit," and yet the conversation about some guy ultimately turns into a conversation about their conversation, culminating in a reference to "speaking in tongues," a central theme in DeLillo's work. Albeit ironic or tongue-in-cheek, the reference turns us back to language: we go from talking about the guy who is a little bit psycho—and, notice, Fife says *psycho*, which is a funny word to use, because it's also the name of a famous movie, the one at the center of *Point Omega*—to talking about the *words* used to talk about the guy, to talking about the process by which the talking is done, the possibility of a glossolalia that is at the origin of Fife's speaking and, why not (because what kind of coincidence is *psycho* anyway?), DeLillo's writing. That too is part of the contraband effect, and it makes DeLillo's writing at once a whole lot funnier and less serious than we might tend to think and a whole lot more serious and profound than we might have thought. For the contrabanding of narratives does not just layer one band onto another but weaves or interweaves them with one another, cutting up or interrupting the narrative, turning them upon one another, each individual band becoming more like a Möbius strip in the end than a ticker tape.

Someday, someone, some professor of Latent English—taking his or her cues from the Professor of Latent History in *Great Jones Street* (*GJS* 74–76)—will have to do a rigorous taxonomy of the various kinds of contraband techniques in DeLillo's works. As we have seen, the transition can be occasioned by a contrapuntal back-and-forth in the narrative sequence or chronology of events, itself occasioned by a perception, or an association, or a memory, or by a shift in linguistic register, as language begins to take itself as its own object and surface and subsurface, word and thing, become confused.

In *White Noise* there is a passage in which we get not just an *example* of contraband but something like one of the principles for pulling it off. Babette's father has just run through a long litany of his physical ailments, any combination of which should cause a daughter to be concerned; he concludes by telling his daughter not to worry about any of these but something else. Don't worry, he basically says, about his limp, the cough, the insomnia, the smoking, his bad teeth, his shakes, his sudden and unexplainable weight loss, his bad eyes, and so on: "Worry about the car," he says, "The steering's all awry. The brakes were recalled three times. The hood shoots up on pothole terrain." And then the giveaway: "Deadpan. Babette thought this last part was funny. The part about the car" (*WN* 256). So there it is; the contraband has to be deadpan. As we read in *The Names*, "Deadpan. Absolutely deadpan to the end" (*N* 32; see *U* 286). It has to be deadpan because that's what creates the tension, the contrast, the contraband, precisely, between thing and words, between *what* is being said and the *manner* in which it is being said.

Deadpan, that's the key to DeLillo's literary contraband, and it is at work in all those riffs, gags, sketches, and shticks for which *White Noise*, most notably, is rightly famous. But they are everywhere, already abundantly represented in *Amazons*, for example, with its long riffs on stupidity and stupid things (*AZ* 87–88), on the legendary father-daughter talk (*AZ* 215), on the catastrophes that are always threatening us: "It's self-evident, isn't it? There's just every kind of catastrophe looming around the bend," for example, in case one needs convincing, "What about fossil fuels? ... What about nuclear weapons falling into the hands of terrorists? ... What about continental drift? ... What about monosodium glutamate? ... What about red dye number two? ... What about grade-A beef that's really horse meat and chicken necks?" (*AZ* 247) Or the whole schtick about peeing in sinks—a competition of sorts—that gets replayed in *White Noise* ("I've peed in sinks. I peed in a sink in Oklahoma City once." ... "I peed in a sink in Yellowknife. That's the northernmost point I've ever peed in a sink in" (*AZ* 123–124)), or the one that picks up on the old "where were you when x?" died game, a shtick that's so fun it too gets reprised in *White Noise*. What's funny here is precisely the juxtaposition between the supposed seriousness of the historic event and the precise recall of the most trivial circumstances surrounding its announcement:

> Where were you when Jimi Hendrix died?. ... I was in Sarasota, Florida, playing tennis with my uncle J.R. when we heard it on somebody's transistor. It was the first set and J.R. was ahead three games to two. I was wearing cut-off jeans. Where were you when Janis Joplin died?. ... I was in Williamstown, Massachusetts, with my mother and father and my cousin J. R. Junior. We drove up to watch the leaves change color. We heard it on the car radio. We were doing forty-five in a thirty-mile-an-hour zone. There was a green Toyota in front of us. My mother was cleaning her sunglasses. (*AZ* 255–256)

Now none of this literary contraband depends, of course, on any explicitly "counter" or "contra" words in DeLillo's writing, even though DeLillo, as a writer of counterintelligence and counterterrorism, of counteraggressions, counterinsurgencies, and counter-investigations of various kinds, packs his novels with all sorts of counter-words, from "counterpoint" ("MD" 121), "countermotion" (*WN* 299), "counterforce" (*C* 52; *L* 100), "counterpoise" (*C* 5), "countermand" (*ZK* 200), and "counter-argument" (*N* 327) to "counteract" (*WN* 140, 287), "countermeasure" (*FM* 40; see *L* 219), "counter-surroundings" (*BA* 48)—as in the way Mr. Tuttle in *The Body Artist* is able to place Lauren "in a set of counter-surroundings, of simultaneous insides and outsides" (*BA* 48)—and so on. In his essay "The Power of History," DeLillo even speaks of a "counter-history." But these words are, strictly speaking, not necessary for the contraband effect, which is a thing of language that goes far beyond a special set of words.

The contraband effect is achieved through various kinds of artifice and technology, various forms of reproduction and repetition that modern technologies make even more available to us. Through this contraband, two or more tracks or bands intersect or collide but never completely merge with one another or become conflated with one another, never become, as a German idealist might say, sublated, the one by the other. For the one is never in DeLillo's hands the dialectical counterpart to the other but that which resists and irritates the other or else enlivens and *underscores* it from within. To cite Jacques Derrida (though just this once) on the notion of contraband itself in *Glas*, a text from 1974, just three years after *Americana*, a text itself written in contraband, that is, not simply on two figures but in two bands or two tracks, in two columns, one on Hegel and the other Jean Genet, "The contraband is *not yet* dialectical contradiction. ... The contra-band *remains* something other than what, necessarily, it is to become" (*Glas* 244a). In the passages I have cited—and these are, as I have insisted, just examples, because such passages are everywhere—one linguistic register, voice, or narrative comes to interrupt or haunt the other, playing over it or beneath it like a second sound track. For there are always in DeLillo's fiction at least two tracks or two bands at work, two *bandes*, as one would say in Derrida's French, playing side by side, a narrative and a counter-narrative, a voice, a sound track, a *bande sonore*, and a *contrebande*—always at least two and often several at the same time.

Cleo Birdwell in *Amazons* organizes and paces her narrative, her memoir—sometimes even in spite of herself—through a kind of contrabanded narrative that jumps between the time she is writing her memoir, perfectly wholesome childhood memories of Badger, Ohio, and less wholesome memories of a long road trip with the New York Rangers: "I've been trying not to do this in short, quick bursts because it doesn't seem very reflective or thematic that way. But this is how my memories of those events are arranged, in bursts and flashes, in little jumps from city to city" (*AZ* 43). Cleo's narrative thus follows her time with the New York Rangers through all the big NHL cities (Boston, Chicago, Toronto, Buffalo, Philadelphia, Minneapolis-St. Paul), each city being marked by a new sexual partner (a former NHL player, the team coach, the general manager, a tennis star, a sports writer, etc.) and a new sexual act or a new twist on an old one (genital, manual, manual-genital, with foreplay, without foreplay, strip Monopoly, you name it). When combined with those childhood memories of Badger, Ohio (see *AZ* 80, 210), what you get is a contrabanding of songs of innocence, if you will, and moans of experience. Nowhere is this more powerful, or more hilarious, than when Cleo recounts for more than a dozen pages "Christmas in Badger" to sportswriter Murray Jay Siskind, who is naked in bed with her. It is an elaborate form of foreplay, an account of the food preparations, the choosing of the Christmas tree, the selection of gifts, the wrapping of those gifts, the writing of Christmas cards, the caroling through town, the setting up of the family's nativity scene, each of these heart-warming accounts punctuated by a new stage in Murray's sexual arousal (*AZ* 286–297). Cleo goes into such poetic detail because, you see, in Badger, "'we cared about Christmas, and standards, and neatness, and precision, and doing things right, and customs, and traditions, and never settling for second best,' I said. / Murray took my hand off his penis" (*AZ* 294).

So it's touching and then it's not touching, just hilarious, and then it's both touching and hilarious. It's *bander*—which in French, and in Derrida's French in *Glas*, means not only to band or to bandage but to get it up—and *débander*, or *contra-bander*, which means the opposite, as if contrabanding were a sexual as well as a narrative technique. Even after a dozen pages of this, we, like Murray, want to hear more, though we know that every Christmas, like every childhood, like every banding experience, must ultimately come to an end.

He wanted to hear about the opening of the presents on Christmas morning, and the crisp, browned surface and juicy meat of the turkey. ... But he seemed too, too excited by it all, and I thought it would be best if we called it a night then and there.
   Too much innocence can burst the heart. (*AZ* 297)

Under the rubric of *contraband*, then, I am trying to take account of a whole range of phenomena, literal contraband, to be sure, but also, and especially, contraband narrative, double narratives, various kinds of word-running, the smuggling in of other discourses, historical events, and narratives into fiction, for example, as well as the power of the double, the doppelgänger, the duplicate, the technical or industrial knockoff, and so on. Counterband narrative is what takes place when two or more narratives run alongside one another, intersecting, interrupting, supplementing, and augmenting one another; one can think of it as a narrative and a sub- or counter-narrative, a text and its subtext, but also as a conscious text or narrative and a subconscious one, an open narrative and a secret one, a serious narrative and a playful one, one narrative above ground and the other just below, in the underworld, one narrative, as it were, in the day room and the other in the motel, one narrative of the bare leg and the other of stockings, one narrative quintessentially American and the other not quite or not only, or the one narrative "live" and the other already a replay, a replay that, in retrospect, seems to have made that "live" narrative possible in the first place.

4

Media and Mediatization

"Where's the media?" she said.
"There is no media in Iron City."
"They went through all that for nothing?"

WN 92

His fear was going undocumented in city after city. He was disturbed by the prospect that the riot or terrorist act which caused his death would not be covered by the media. The death itself seemed not so much to matter.

N 194

Newspapers, Magazines, Tabloids

She had this stopped feeling you get when there's something awesome in the news, this stoppage in the body, the cold stilled excitement that prepares you for something vast.

M 185

It would have been awful to be out of the country when Elvis died. I don't think I could have survived that. ... Imagine not being able to enjoy the media coverage. What's the point of being American if you're going to be out of the country for a thing of that magnitude?

AZ 256

UNIVERSE SAID TO CEASE EXPANDING; BEGINS TO FALL BACK ON ITSELF; MILLIONS FLEE CITIES.

RS 50

Contraband narratives, then, two or more narrative strands side by side, juxtaposed: there are any number of ways to pull this off, but it often happens most spectacularly in DeLillo through media of various kinds—newspapers and magazines, to be sure, but also, and especially, radio and television (even the telephone), and, beginning in the 1990s, the internet. It will be worth our while to look briefly at each of these in order to see just how such technologies of repetition and retransmission impose their unique brand of contraband on narrative, just how they threaten not just to double or repeat but to replace that which we might think they simply imitate or report. Contraband or counterband is another way of saying that whatever is real or whatever seems to be real has a counterband, not a representation, exactly, but a repetition, an underside or shadow that is actually essential to the original—a second iteration that makes the original thing what it is.

There are, especially in earlier DeLillo novels, magazines like *Look* and *Life* (*L* 424) and *Time* (*U* 250, 252), but then also the fictional *Running Dog*, a radical magazine that takes its name from a slogan from the Vietnam era—"capitalist lackeys and running dogs" (*RD* 30; see 112 and *GJ* 20, where *Running Dog* is already the name of a news service)—the magazine for which Moll Robbins is writing a series of articles on the sex industry. How radical the magazine is is a matter of debate. "We say 'fuck' all the time," says Moll when asked. "My point exactly" is the skeptic's response (*RD* 21).

There are magazines, then, some real, some fictional, and then there are tabloids, all very real, the kind sold in supermarket checkout lines featuring stories of the rich and famous or life after death or UFOs, or Elvis alive, or Bigfoot, the lost city of Atlantis, or Mark David Chapman changing his name to John Lennon, and so on (*WN* 145–146, 234). Nick Shay moves his mother out of NYC to Phoenix in part to get her "out of the daily drama of violence and lament and tabloid atrocity and matching redemption" (*U* 86). When, later in *Underworld*, the stories begin spreading about the appearance of Esmeralda on a NYC billboard and Sister Edgar begins expressing an interest in this story, her younger colleague, Sister Gracie, tries to dampen her enthusiasm: "This is tabloid. This is the worst kind of tabloid superstition. ... Be sensible. Don't abdicate your good sense" (*U* 819; see "AE" 95).

Newspaper stories and headlines are thus another way to introduce contraband elements into the narrative, for example, in *Players*, "Mystery of Stock Exchange Murder Unraveling Slowly" (*P* 65), or, in *Ratner's Star*, an imagined eight-column headline announcing the recent scientific discovery of a collapsing universe (*RS* 50), or, in *Mao II*, the ticker tape announcement on June 3, 1989, in Times Square of the Ayatollah Khomeini's funeral (*M* 185; see 197, 233, and "HS" 177).

But there is one other, one last newspaper headline worthy of mention here, this one neither tabloid nor fiction but a real headline perfectly adapted for contraband fiction and so imported by DeLillo more or less as it was first printed. In his essay "The Power of History" (published September 7, 1997, not long after the appearance of *Underworld*), DeLillo speaks of his developing interest in the famous baseball game at the Polo Grounds in 1951—a game he remembers being in a dentist's chair for when the famous home run occurred—and his desire to learn more about the game. He thus recounts going to the library, "to the basement," as chance would have it, "of a local library to find a news account of the game," and finding "an unexpected connection," a "juxtaposition" of two headlines on the front page of *The New York Times* of October 4, 1951: "*Giants capture pennant*—this was the dramatic substance of the first headline," and "*Soviets explode atomic bomb*—this was the ominous threat of the second." A juxtaposition, a counterpoint—both of these are DeLillo's words—that seemed to have come right out of a DeLillo novel: "The home run that won the game—soon to be known, vaingloriously, as 'The Shot Heard 'Round the World'—had found its vast and awful counterpoint. A Russian mushroom cloud" ("PH"). Here's how the novel would recall or reproduce it:

> The front page astonished [Bronzini], a pair of three-column headlines dominating. To his left the Giants capture the pennant, beating the Dodgers on a dramatic home run in the ninth inning. And to the right, symmetrically mated, same typeface, same-size type, same number of lines, the USSR explodes an atomic bomb—*kaboom*—details kept secret. / He didn't understand why the Times would take a ball game off the sports page and juxtapose it with news of such ominous consequence. (*U* 668)

Juxtaposition and counterpoint—the very contraband effect that DeLillo had been using in narratives since the 1970s was right there in black and white in *The New York Times*, all the news that's fit to print side by side, just waiting to be put into narrative. The short story "Pafko at the Wall" would be the first version of the opening pages of that narrative and "The Triumph of Death," the Prologue to *Underworld*, the final take—this title, "The Triumph of Death," taken from a painting rather than a newspaper, itself the perfect conjunction or contrabanding of those two stories from the *Times*.

Radio

The radio came on. I hurried out of the room, fearing that some call-in voice, some stranger's soul-lament, would be the last thing I heard in this world.

WN 244

> They listened to Life Line on the radio. It was a commentary on heroism and how it had fallen into disuse.
>
> L 251

> He listened to the radio, to an evangelist talking about retail prayer and wholesome prayer. Pray for yourself, pray for the world.
>
> L 30; see 78

> Who is for real and who is sent to take notes? ... Weird Beard says, Eat your cereal with a fork. Do your homework in the dark. And trust your radio before you trust your mother.
>
> L 266

In addition to newspapers and tabloids there is the even more promising contraband medium of radio, which is especially prominent in DeLillo's early work or in works such as *Underworld* that are set in a time when radio was king in America. With its sometimes absurd, sometimes disturbing juxtaposition of news or talk and advertising, radio was already performing, in some sense, the very contraband effect that DeLillo's narratives would seek to perfect. Such juxtaposition is already on display in *Americana*: "The radio was announcing a sale on ground round steak and then some old-time rock came on, lush and mystical, cockney voices wailing through a prayer wheel of electric sitars" (*A* 111). Later in the novel, there is a back-and-forth between a live family conversation around the dinner table, a seemingly serious conversation about theories of the soul in ancient religions, and a recorded radio announcement by President Eisenhower (*A* 183). By the time of *White Noise*, this contrabanding effect of radio will be fully integrated into the narrative, the interventions of radio not just described but fully reproduced in the narrative itself. Here are just three examples—all of them from the car radio playing in the background during the airborne toxic event:

> A helicopter flew over, headed in the direction of the accident. The voice on the radio said: "Available for a limited time only with optional megabyte hard disk." (*WN* 112)

> There was an epic quality about them that made me wonder for the first time at the scope of our predicament. / The radio said: "It's the rainbow hologram that gives this credit card a marketing intrigue." (*WN* 122)

> It's an event all right. It marks the end of uneventful things. This is just the beginning. Wait and see.

> A talk-show host said: "You are on the air." The fires burned in the oil drums. (*WN* 151)

In *White Noise* the contraband does not even stop when the action is nearing a climax and the protagonist, not to mention the reader, should be concentrating on what is about to happen rather than listening to the radio. "I reached into my pocket, rubbed my knuckles across the grainy stainless steel of the Zumwalt barrel. The man on the radio said: 'Void where prohibited'" (*WN* 303).

Once again, there are two narratives playing side by side, one in the room, or coming out of the head of someone in the room, and one coming from the radio. We see the same contraband effect in *Libra*, published two years after *White Noise*: "She was afraid he would turn into one of those men who make a saintliness of their resentment, shining through the years with a pure and tortured light. The radio said high seventies. God is alive and well in Texas" (*L* 18).

Contraband radio, then, CB radio as it were. Anyone who wants to know or to remember what radio was in America, radio before TV or the internet, could do worse than to start with DeLillo. We read in *Great Jones Street*: "This was America's mechanical voice, its doll voice, coughing out slogans into the dawn, testing itself in the event of emergency, station after station fading away in the suffering breath of the national anthem" (*GJ* 25).

Radio is thus always playing in the background, radio as a place of language, of talk, of talk radio (see *WN* 247, 263), of news (see *BA* 23, 70), of ball games on a hot summer day. It is a quasi-miraculous language machine, a place where we can come into contact with different languages, different English languages—eastern, southern, western—but then also foreign languages. Indeed radio used to be the place a certain America or a certain American might first encounter another language: "The radio was tuned to the Italian station ... *baci a tutti*" (*U* 709; see *GJ* 164). Radio is "the place where words are recycled," says Gary Harkness in *End Zone*, as well as an opening to the rest of the world, in times of both war and peace, "the place where villages are burned. That's my Indochina. I listen only at certain times of day for certain periods of time. When time's up, I bring it into silence. It's almost a ceremony. ... It becomes almost a spiritual exercise. Silence, words, silence, silence, silence" (*EZ* 239–240).

The radio is the place—was the place—where one first heard certain kinds of music and oftentimes in a car, the car radio having the advantage of adding speed to sound: "The car was filled with the sounds of big beat, gospel, ghetto soul, jug bands and dirt bands ... with luck I'd catch a scrap of catatonic Monk or Sun Ra colliding with anti-matter" (*A* 350). It was on the radio, the car radio, that one might first hear, like a revelation or a secret from the underworld, Bob Dylan singing "Subterranean Homesick Blues" (*A* 375), or else "the week's top songs" (*U* 771), or the oddly compelling voice of a

Wolfman Jack, "a howling disc jockey vectored into the desert from some bandit station below the border" (*U* 453).

The radio is or was also the instrument of evangelism, not the place where the apocalypse was announced but the place of the apocalypse itself, the place of "revivalist preachers, men of a certain creepy eloquence" (*L* 360), the place, in *Americana*, of Warren Beasley, "considered a prophet by some, a menace by others" (*A* 94), whose radio program, "Death Is Just Around the Corner" (*A* 93), consisted of Joyce-inspired radio monologues, an alternative form of writing, writing as David Bell might have imagined it and as DeLillo will at once execute and incorporate it:

> Time to pluck the lint from your omphalos. ... Mollycuddling and bloomless bride. ... I've got the Stephen Dedalus Blues and it's a long way to Leopoldville. ... We have awakened from the nightmare of history. ... And lead us not into annihilation but deliver us from rubble, for thine is the power and the power and the power, forever and never, oh man. (*A* 231–232, 234)

What we have here is already the announcer or preacher as performance artist, doing live shows or putting them on tape for rebroadcast and posterity (*A* 371; see also 365–366). Here's a description, some quarter of a century later, of Lenny Bruce that sounds like something that could have come out of one of Warren Beasley's monologues in *Americana*:

> Lenny switched abruptly to ad lib bits. Whatever zoomed across his brainpan. ... he finally closed the show with a monologue that had a kind of abridged syntax, a thing without connectives, he was cooking free-form, closer to music than speech. (*U* 586)

In *Underworld* the radio is not just one of the most obvious technological signs of the times but also the instrument that carries the narrative, as the voice of Russ Hodges, the Giants announcer, carries onto the rooftop where Nick Shay has taken his radio to listen to the game on October 3, 1951 (*U* 93, 133), or onto a train in Europe where American GIs and Marvin Lundy are listening intently, Hodge's "account of the game interrupted whenever the train entered a tunnel, and that's where Marvin was when Thomson hit the homer, racing through a mountain in the Alps" (*U* 313). (No word at this point on whether Greenland was in any way involved.) Those listening are, as we hear in *Underworld*, "the game's remoter soul. Connected by the pulsing voice on the radio" (*U* 32), and the one game that seems not only not harmed but maybe even enhanced by this remoteness is baseball. Even Lee Harvey Oswald would have recognized that: "He walked home, hearing a lazy radio voice doing a ballgame. Plenty of room, folks. Come on out for the rest of this game and all of the second" (*L* 12–13). This is the same Oswald who got himself invited a couple of times onto public-affairs shows to "talk about Cuba and the world ... the United Fruit Company, the CIA, collectivization, the feudal dictatorship of Nicaragua, movements of national liberation" (*L* 328–329), the same Oswald who, wouldn't you know it, ends up after his defection working in a factory in Minsk "making radios for the masses" (*L* 197).

So there's news, sports, and weather (often on the one's), music, serial dramas (*U* 698), talk radio—with its "long queue of underground souls waiting to enter the broadcast band" (*U* 167)—and the occasional university radio station, like the one in Madison, Wisconsin, that gets taken over by student protesters during a Vietnam War protest (*U* 603), the riot out on the campus, "if that's what it was," "being augmented and improved by a simulated riot on the radio" (*U* 599). That's the contraband effect, the amplification and transformation of what's going on "out there" by its technological mediation. It is during that same radio station takeover, in fact, that a "sexy voice on the radio repeated the DuPont slogan ... Better Things for Better Living ... Through Chemistry" (*U* 602)—a slogan that had previously found its way into *Americana* (*A* 130), as if radio were able to tune in from time to time to the same DeLillo station, WDDL, let's call it, in order to channel a word or phrase from some past work.

There is something about the radio that calls us or calls us back. It is the radio that brings Albert Bronzini to that small room where George the Waiter has just shot up, not long before he is shot dead by Nick Shay: "He heard a radio playing round the next bend and decided to follow the sound" (*U* 769). Same goes for Win Everett, the prime mover behind the assassination attempt on Kennedy: "He heard an old familiar voice on the kitchen radio, some voice from the old days of radio," and he was "struck by the complex emotion carried on a voice from another era, tender and shattering" (*L* 222). It's the power, it seems, of disembodied voices coming from afar. For "an old voice, a radio voice from another era can bring back everything" (*L* 362).

There are radio voices from the past, but then also radio voices in the present that seem to be tapping into something that surpasses the present. Such is the voice of Russ Knight, Weird Beard—another version of the radio prophet Warren Beasely, it seems—talking in Dallas on KLIF, right before the assassination of JFK:

In the dark they picked up the first pulse of Dallas on the radio, a scratch and rustle at the edge of the band, and they listened to an eerie voice ride across the long night. ... "Don't you know the rumors he travels with a dozen look-alikes when he goes into no man's land? ... Oh the air is swollen. ... All the ancient terrors of the night. We're looking right at it. We know it's here. We feel it's here. It has to happen. Something strange and dark and dreamsome. Weird Beard says. Night is rushing down over Big D." (*L* 381–382; see 223, 265, 417)

Television

For most people there are only two places in the world. Where they live and their TV set.

WN 66

I tried to tell myself it was only television—whatever that was, however it worked—and not some journey out of life or death, not some mysterious separation.

WN 105

If a thing happens on television, we have every right to find it fascinating, whatever it is.

WN 66

The boy is growing up without television, which may make him worth talking to, as a sort of wild child, a savage plucked from the bush, intelligent and literate but deprived of the deeper codes and messages that mark his species as unique.

WN 50

In the second half of the twentieth century—and it's already different today—TV, even more than radio, provided not just, to cite a phrase, "the soundtrack of our lives" but the contraband to them. For some people, like Lyle in *Players*, "watching television was ... a discipline like mathematics or Zen" (*P* 16; see 40). But for most of us it was just there, blaring or droning on in the background, the sound more significant than the image (see *A* 66, *DR* 69), providing a second narrative, another voice, whether totally understandable or barely audible. DeLillo made a name for himself, as it were, with these contrapuntal interventions—particularly in *White Noise*, though not just there. Here are two, the second supplemented by the sounds of clothes in the dryer:

We went back to Denise's room. The voice at the end of the bed said: "Meanwhile here is a quick and attractive lemon garnish suitable for any sea food." (*WN* 178; see 96, 239)

We listened to the tap and scratch of buttons and zipper tabs. It was time for me to leave for school. The voice upstairs remarked: "A California think-tank says the next world war may be fought over salt." (*WN* 226)

Many similar examples of televisual and telephonic contraband could be pulled from *White Noise*, but it would be a mistake to think that DeLillo's interest in TV emerged only in the mid-1980s. David Bell in *Americana* already works for a TV network and is himself the producer of the "Soliloquy" TV series.

There are also frequent references to TV shows in DeLillo's work, and they are never just any shows. In *Libra*, for example, Oswald and his mother watch *Racket Squad* and *Dragnet* (*L* 5)—telling names, to be sure, as is the thing Oswald watches on the static screen after the programming is over, because in those days, imagine, a channel would actually "sign off" around midnight: "the DuMont test pattern" (*L* 6), which—check it out, Google it— looks like a target. There's also *I Led Three Lives*, "the story of an ex-Marine who has infiltrated the Soviet intelligence apparatus as part of the U.S. Navy's false defector program" (*L* 164). In *Underworld* there is Jackie Gleason, aka Ralph Kramden from "The Honeymooners" (*U* 103, see 413), who plays such a prominent role in the novel's Prologue. As Nick later says, "We felt better with Jackie in the room, transparent in his pain, alive and dead in Arizona" (*U* 106). Alive and dead because, for the Shay family from the Bronx, Gleason in those "Honeymooner" reruns brought the past back into the present, east to west, New York to Phoenix, the moon to the sun if one wants to wax poetic. Because everyone remembers not just "Harty har-har" (*U* 30) but "To the moon, Alice! To the moon!" Everyone remembers it, a gesture, a voice, something more than just another piece of TV trivia, like "bet you don't know the name of Tonto's horse" (*U* 288–289).

Throughout DeLillo's work there are also, in addition to all these references to TV, reflections about it. For example, "Were people this dumb before television?" (*WN* 249) Babette in *White Noise* has a far more positive outlook on what used to be called "the boob tube" (yet another of those phrases that is totally hardly recognizable in a world where TVs no longer have tubes). Her view is that TV could be domesticated, turned into a family bonding experience: "She seemed to think that if kids watched television one night a week with parents or stepparents, the effect would be to de-glamorize the medium in their eyes, make it wholesome domestic sport" (*WN* 16).

And so the Gladneys had their family hour, at the end of the week, when they would huddle around the TV, the new American hearth, to watch some family oriented program, like disaster TV: "That night, a Friday, we gathered in front of the set, as was the custom and the rule, with take-out Chinese. There were floods, earthquakes, mud slides, erupting volcanoes" (*WN* 64). Jack's colleague Alfonse (Fast Food) Stompanato (see *WN* 9) could have done a theoretical analysis or the color commentary on it:

> Japan is pretty good for disaster footage. India remains largely untapped. They have tremendous potential with their famines, monsoons, religious strife, train wrecks, boat sinkings, et cetera. But their disasters tend to go unrecorded. Three lines in the newspaper. No film footage, no satellite hookup. This is why California is so important. (*WN* 66; see 90–92, 162)

TV can be a site of isolation, an instrument that returns nothing but one's own image or the reflected image of others in the room (see *FM* 118), "a study in the art of mummification" (*GJ* 136). But it can also be the site of the outside coming inside, the place where the outside enters our home, our heads, our voices, our narratives, and our dreams in, yes, a contraband fashion. Though television is everywhere in DeLillo, *White Noise* is the user's manual to thinking television in DeLillo and, thus, television in America, and, thus, America itself, from, say, the 1960s through the 1990s. Every negative thing ever said about television is no doubt true, and yet "TV offers incredible amounts of psychic data. It opens ancient memories of world birth, it welcomes us into the grid" (*WN* 51). As Murray Siskind, the prophet of pop culture, puts it in that novel, it all comes down to "waves and radiation":

> I've come to understand that the medium is a primal force in the American home. Sealed-off, timeless, self-contained, self-referring. It's like a myth being born right there in our living room, like something we know in a dreamlike and preconscious way. (*WN* 51)

That's one way to take TV, not as a medium cool that deadens and disconnects but as a "force" that moves, motivates, and manipulates, sometimes connecting people to the grid in a comforting way, sometimes getting them all hot and bothered. Here is a description of James Axton's father—a description, note, from 1982, well before FOX News or the 24-hour news cycle:

> Most of his anger came from TV. All that violence, crime, political cowardice, government deception, all that appeasement, that official

faintheartedness. It rankled, it curled him into a furious ball, a fetus of pure rage. The six o'clock news, the seven o'clock news, the eleven o'clock news. ... The TV set was a rage-making machine, working at him all the time, giving him direction and scope, enlarging him in a sense, filling him with a world rage, a great stalking soreness and rancor. (*N* 178–179)

The guy would clearly not make it a week in today's news environment.

News, weather (*WN* 22, *A* 43), traffic, political commentary, business reports, dramas, commercials, it's all there, and if one doesn't like one band or program or channel, all one has to do, like Gary in *The Day Room*, is "Click" (*DR* 68, 78–79, 96–97). Channel surfing—that is perhaps another way to think the contraband effect of Don DeLillo.

The fascination of TV consists in its sound, DeLillo suggests, but also in the repetition of its images: "There is something about troops entering a square, jogging row after row in lazy cadence. She keeps changing channels to see the troops" (*M* 178). And then there's nothing quite like live TV—especially when what is "live" gets replayed in a loop. In *Cosmopolis*, for example, there's the assassination, live on the Money Channel, of the managing director of the International Monetary Fund: "Happened only a minute ago. Eric watched it happen again, in obsessive replays" (*C* 33).

Since TV is everywhere in "real life," it becomes the primary referent for that life: "We stood there watching a surge of florid light, like a heart pumping in a documentary on color TV" (*WN* 227). "I looked for a blanket to adjust, a toy to remove from a child's warm grasp, feeling I'd wandered into a TV moment" (*WN* 244).

But then there's what is called "reality" or "hyperreality" TV (*V* 68). The first act of *Valparaiso* is a series of TV interviews between various media people and Michael Majeski, who had become famous for a misadventure that took him not to Valparaiso, Indiana, where he was supposed to go on business, but Valparaiso, Chile (*V* 21, 31). The second act, set in a TV studio, is a talk show, filmed before a live studio audience and hosted by Delfina Treadwell (no relation, it seems, to the Treadwells of *White Noise* who get stranded in the Mid-Village Mall). As Teddy, her sidekick, puts it, Delfina is "our life-spirit, the shining soul of daytime America" (*V* 64) who summons us "to a hyperlife of laughter and tears and tenderness and rocking socking sensation" (*V* 63). Because "off-camera lives are unverifiable" (*V* 83), Delfina encourages Michael not just to say what he thinks but to confess right there on national TV his "unspoken thoughts" (*V* 69), everything he is "hiding in [his] heart" (*V* 75). She wants, in a word, his "soul in a silver thimble" (*V* 90), his "naked shitmost self," and she will get something of that self when Michael finally does confess, on camera, live, to trying to flee his past by attempting suicide during his flight to Chile (*V* 91). It is this kind of spectacle that Richard Elster accuses Jim Finley of wanting to capture in his movie, some kind of "public confession," the film of "a man breaking down" (*PO* 53–54).

Valparaiso is a play, a "live" play, about the "hyperlife," the disembodied life, to which the media invites us, the fascination of having our bodies in one place and our images and voices elsewhere, in a doubled, projected, contraband world where one is both already a little bit dead and more than a tad immortal:

> The cameras will swing toward the audience in the course of the show. ... Point to yourselves on the giant monitors. I understand the need for this. I encourage this. Wave to yourselves. See yourselves cross that critical divide into some plane of transcendence. (*V* 64)

TV seems to suck the life right out of its subjects and replace it by an unreal, imaginary life—a life of light and particles. Livia, Michael's wife, says of Delfina: "She's a trick of light. That's all she is. Poke a finger right through her" (*V* 92). And yet the life of TV seems to be other, even more real than the real, a transcendence that lends one a sort of radiance or glow that is unavailable in real life. Livia says of her husband, "I see him complete when he's on TV. It's the realized potential of the man. ... He becomes an exceptional being." In short, "He glows ... He shines" (*V* 85), his life itself takes on a "luminous quality" (*V* 51). Jack Gladney sees something similar when he suddenly and unexpectedly catches a glimpse of his wife's televised image: "The face on the screen was Babette's. ... Was this her spirit, her secret self, some two-dimensional facsimile released by the power of technology ... I tried to tell myself it was only television ... and not some journey out of life or death, not some mysterious separation" (*WN* 104–105).

It is, it seems, this contrabanding of life, this doubling or self-doubling of life, that leads to a certain transcendence and causes things to glow from within. Delfina says to the camera in the studio or in the studio in the theater for those who saw DeLillo's play "live":

> Someone dies, remotely known to you, but how real and deep the loss. Who is he? An image aloft in the flashing air. Not even that. A set of image-forming units, sand-grain size, that shape a face on-screen. How can it be? A life so unfleshed takes up intimate space. Someone spun of lightwaves and repetitious sounds. How is it possible? ... There is something in these grids of information that strikes the common heart as magic. (*V* 106)

Underworld is, among many other things, a study in the way TV took over our lives in the second half of the twentieth century. Having or not having one's own TV, watching TV alone or with others, seeing others on TV and sometimes even oneself—these are central themes in *Underworld* (see *U* 104, 116, 754). At a certain point, everyone has a TV—even Ismael Muñoz, who had been living in the Wall, an abandoned building "unlinked to the usual services" and so without TV, a predicament or a "stern mercy" that changes when Ismael hooks up a bicycle to an old generator and then the generator to a TV: "Now here it is, suddenly. You touch a button and all the things concealed from you for centuries come flying into the remotest room. It's an epidemic of seeing" (*U* 812). And TV comes to the Wall just in time, that is, in time for a nationwide story about the Wall itself—the story of Esmeralda Lopez's rape and murder: "There is a news report of the murder, their murder, and it is freaking network coverage, CNN—tragic life and death of homeless child" (*U* 816). Ismael and his crew are thus caught in the coverage of a crime that has taken place in their very neighborhood and, thanks to their makeshift TV, they become fascinated by it, mesmerized by themselves in contraband: "They gawk and buzz, charged with a kind of second sight, the things they know so well seen inside out, made new and nationwide. They stand there smeared in other people's seeing" (*U* 817). The whole world is watching, including them, but the magic here is that they can *see* themselves being *seen* by that world.

We witness something similar in *Underworld* in the videotape, captured by a little girl in the back of her family car, of a shooting by the Texas Highway Killer that runs endlessly on TV news (*U* 232). So taken is the killer himself by the image of his own killing that he actually calls in to a local news station to talk live with the news anchor: "He talked to her on the phone and made eye contact with the TV" (*U* 270; see 215–217).

We are implicated by TV, "smeared" by other people's seeing, even when we are those other people. DeLillo obviously did not invent the "selfie," but his brand of counterband writing has been an attempt to think it in advance. Though David Bell is making a film and not filming himself for TV, the point of the DeLillo contraband could not be clearer. Near the end of his film Bell interviews himself and, in effect, says hello to his future self, watching himself both in the present and at some distant remove:

> "Is there anything else you'd like to tell the camera?" "Simply hello. Hello to myself in the remote future, watching this in fear and darkness. Hello to that America, whatever it may be doing or undoing. I hope you've finally become part of your time, David. You were always a bit behind, held back by obsolete sensibilities." (*A* 286)

There is much more to be said about this smear and this second sight, about the way in which we see ourselves with the eyes of others, and the way in which, sometimes, we only become ourselves through this second sight. In anticipation of that, here's a little trailer, featuring Lee Harvey and Marina Oswald on a sidewalk in Fort Worth, Texas, well before either of them had ever come to a TV near us:

> One evening they walked past a department store, just out strolling, and Marina looked at a television set in the window and saw the most remarkable thing, something so strange she had to stop and stare, grab hard at Lee. It was the world gone inside out. There they were gaping back at themselves from the TV screen. She was on television. ... She turned and looked at the people, checking to see if they were the same as the ones in the window. They had to be the same but she was compelled to look. She didn't know anything like this could ever happen. She walked out of the picture and then came back. ... She was amazed every time she saw herself return. (*L* 227; see *U* 354)

(By the way, "Scout was the name," the name of Tonto's horse.)

Telephone

Maybe I shouldn't have called. I just wanted to say hello. Nothing special. I'm naked and I've been calling people all over the country.

A 249

Nothing is beyond the telephone, you're saying. There's nothing out there. Some vastness I can't see or name.

DR 45

I picked up the telephone and listened to the dial tone, music of a dead universe. The sound fascinated me.

GJ 166

Radio and television are no doubt DeLillo's most commonly used technologies of narrative contraband, technologies not just referenced in the narrative but used to create the contraband effect. But there are other medias and technologies that are well worth giving a listen to. For example, the telephone. Someday, someone, decades or centuries from now, will be able to follow the transformations in American teletechnology, beginning with the telephone, by rereading DeLillo from *Americana*, where David Bell's name already recalls the "Bell System—communications for home, industry, and four-fifths of the universe" (*A* 41), through *Point Omega*. It just might be *Americana*, for example, that will one day inform future generations that "there were thirty-six small holes in the mouthpiece of my telephone" and "only six holes in the earpiece," and that, for someone like Bell, "this disparity seemed significant" (*A* 96). It may well be that one will read *Great Jones Street* in order to be reminded of what a disconnected phone was or meant, not just a broken phone but a working phone with no connection: "A telephone that's disconnected, deprived of its sources, becomes in time an intriguing piece of sculpture," "an object rather than an instrument, an object possessing a kind of historical mystery" (*GJ* 31; see 70). Or what it meant for a phone—what we used to call a landline—to be in a fixed place, ready to start ringing at any moment, a visitation or an intrusion of the outside world within one's own four walls:

> Telephone. It seemed incredible and I merely stared at the sucking black shape. Each note seemed louder and more shrill, the protest cry of a thing that preferred its latent state. Telephone. I walked across the floor and picked up the receiver. (*GJ* 143)

Or what it meant for a phone to ring in an empty house or apartment, a theme that connects *Americana*, DeLillo's first novel, to the pseudonymous *Amazons*, "I called my apartment again. No answer. Nothing. The sound of a phone ringing in an empty room. / New York, New York" (*AZ* 50), to *Point Omega*, not to mention the play *The Day Room*: "No one's there. I'm dialing my number at home, just to see if it rings" (*DR* 50; see *A* 353, *PO* 100). Or what it meant to have a "dial tone" or to plan an entire evening around making a long-distance call, "waiting for the hour of the rate change and then placing a chair by the telephone and working the numbers carefully, face down in the rotary dial" (*U* 231). Or that being called to a public or shared phone in a high school or college dormitory inevitably meant that someone in your family had died (*EZ* 94). One may even come to know what phone sex was before the 1–900 number (*A* 249).

The telephone brings those who are far away close, even when one is just talking for the sake of talking: "He called Janet and talked. He talked and listened. The smaller the talk, the better he felt" (*U* 414). Stripped down to pure sound, the telephone is a kind of communication between souls: "I hung up and went for a walk. The women were in their lighted homes, talking on the phone. ... I listened to the women talk. All sound, all souls" (*WN* 273). And then there are the intimations, even between these souls that seem so close and familiar, of distance, separation, and, ultimately, death. When Marian, up in Wisconsin, tells Nick over the phone, in Arizona, that "she wanted to get married," she doesn't know how Nick is reacting because "a telephone silence can be hard to read, grim and deep and sometimes unsettling" (*U* 604). The connection is thus sometimes close, sometimes uncertain, and sometimes deeply disconcerting. James Axton in *The Names* senses all of that at once in a conversation with his estranged wife, Kathryn, as the somewhat unexpected—contrabanded—coda to this passage helps drive home:

> Her voice was dense, chambered, the telephone a sign and instrument of familiar distance. ... There were many silences. We said goodnight, dark, sorry, making plans to meet in Piraeus for the trip to the airport. After that we would talk again, talk often, keep each other informed, stay in the closest possible touch.
> Ashes. (*N* 134)

Tape Recorders and Answering Machines

"Come early," she said. "You can help me toss the salad. We'll talk over old time." "There are no old times, Wendy. The tapes have been accidentally destroyed."

A 25

Please / leave / a mess/age/ af/ter / the / tone.

BA 67

The contraband effect can be achieved, as we have seen, by introducing incongruous elements, by shifting between different narratives or linguistic registers, by incorporating teletechnologies such as radio and television into the narrative, or by running side by side two or more *bandes sonores*, that is, two or more tracks or voices. From *Americana* onward there is thus always a band and a counter-band, one track with or against another, sometimes in coordination and sometimes running interference, one track always in counterpoint with the other. Sometimes there are contraband tapes in the literal sense of the word, secret or underground tapes, basement tapes, as it were, for example, in *Underworld*, the bootleg tapes of Lenny Bruce's routines, his blue material, which circulated among "Lenny's teenage fanatics," "kids from Brooklyn and Queens who did his bits word for word, memorizing off his albums but more religiously from the rare tapes slyly recorded by traffickers in contraband goods" (*U* 625). In an age of mechanical reproduction, the contraband tape, the knockoff or reproduction, the glorious rip-off, becomes just as valuable, sometimes even more so, than the original itself, assuming we still know what an original is.

Tape recorders, then, bring one narrative band into juxtaposition with another in a rather explicit and powerful way. When Keith Neudecker in *Falling Man* explains how he used to carry a little recorder around with him, Florence, who used to listen to music on the portable tape player she left behind in her briefcase the day she had to evacuate one of the towers (*FM* 93), asks Keith, "What did you say when you talked into it?" Keith responds, predictably, unpredictably, original in its repetition, "I don't know. My fellow Americans" (*FM* 54)—yet another reference that will someday have to be explained (the presidential address … Nixon … Watergate … which all revolved, come to think of it, around tape recordings).

In *The Body Artist* everything also revolves around a tape recorder, that is, around Lauren Hartke's relationship with Mr. Tuttle, who shows up one day in Lauren's house in Maine, imitating both her and her husband Rey, who has just committed suicide. Lauren ultimately realizes that Mr. Tuttle is able to imitate her and her late husband's voices not because he had once heard them live but because he had heard tape recordings of them. He is thus imitating or reproducing not the live voices of Lauren and Rey but the reproductions of them (*BA* 56–57), reproductions that thus repeat the past but with some crucial differences and odd variations (*BA* 55). That then raises to a whole new level the question of just what Mr. Tuttle is doing or, indeed, what he *is*: he seems to be neither speaking spontaneously nor merely repeating or reproducing. He is like a living tape recorder or audiobook with a certain capacity for innovation or invention. He repeats Rey but also seems to embody him, which is why Lauren asks him not just to speak like her husband but to "do" him: "Talk like him. Do like him. Speak in his voice. Do Rey" (*BA* 71).

> It did not seem an act of memory. It was Rey's voice all right, it was her husband's tonal soul, but she didn't think the man was remembering. It is happening now. This is what she thought. She watched him struggle in his utterance and thought it was happening, somehow, now, in his frame, in his fracted time, and he is only reporting, helplessly, what they say. (*BA* 87)

But, again, what does it mean to "Do Rey"? Is it Rey, she wonders, live Rey, or just memoray, live Rey or, as one used to ask, Memorex˚? What is clear to Lauren is that "this was not some communication with the dead. It was Rey alive in the course of a talk he'd had with her, in this room, not long after they'd come here" (*BA* 61).

There is a tenuous difference between the thing and the repetition of the thing—the voice and its recording, the original and the man who embodies the original, the voice and its contraband in spoken conversation, in recordings, or indeed in art. Mr. Tuttle challenges all the categories: neither man nor child, at once ghostly voice and living tape recorder, he is "outside the easy sway of either/or" (*BA* 69). And that is why Lauren ends up herself recording Mr. Tuttle and then incorporating this uncanny voice into her own performance art piece, doing this voice herself "live," first on the telephone (*BA* 101) and then at the end of an interview being recorded on a "message-storing digital voice recorder" (*BA* 108) as she suddenly switches to Mr. Tuttle's voice, "spooky as a woodwind in your closet. Not taped but live. Not lip-sync'd but real" (*BA* 109), Mr. Tuttle as the contraband of Rey, the Rey-band, and Lauren as the contraband of Mr. Tuttle—the one "doing" the other.

The Body Artist explores this questionable difference between the voice and its playback or its repetition, the voice and its electronic, robotic, or synthesized version on a tape recorder or what used to be called an "answering machine." I don't know if Siri will ever appear in a DeLillo novel—in fact, that's a good question for Siri—but she certainly could.

> She called Mariella and got the machine. A synthesized voice said, *Please / leave / a mess/age/ af/ter / the / tone*. The words were not spoken but generated and they were separated by brief but deep dimensions. She hung up and called back, just to hear the voice again. How strange the discontinuity. It seemed a quantum hop, one word to the next. She hung up and called back. One voice for each word. Seven different voices. Not seven different voices but one male voice in seven time cycles. But not male exactly either. And not words so much as syllables but not that either. She hung up and called back. (*BA* 67)

Contraband sounds and voices interrupt our lives just as constantly as they interrupt DeLillo's narratives—whether live and direct or transmitted and recorded, everything from the gramophone, with its mass-produced voices designed to be passed on from one generation to the next (*U* 36), to the answering machine with its messages left for very specific individuals. It's an odd thing, still today, leaving a voice message on a phone—consigning one's voice to the memory banks of our telephone provider. It used to be an odder thing, however, when one called and left a message on a "home phone" with an answering machine. You would talk, knowing that your voice could be heard in the living room, say, of the person you were calling, but not knowing for certain whether he or she was actually there listening—or whether he or she was alone—and just not picking up. Such is Bill Gray's experience calling Brita in *Mao II*:

> Do you know how strange it is for me to sit here talking to a machine? I feel like a TV set left on in an empty room. I'm playing to an empty room. This is a new kind of loneliness you're getting me into, Brita. How nice to say your name. (*M* 91)

Bill Gray "hears" himself speaking aloud in Brita's empty apartment and then imagines what will happen to his voice between the time Brita's recorded voice says "Nobody's home. Please leave a message" and the time his recorded message gets played back:

> The loneliness of voices stored on tape. By the time you listen to this, I'll no longer remember what I said. I'll be an old message by then, buried under many new messages. The machine makes everything a message, which narrows the range of discourse and destroys the poetry of nobody home. (*M* 92)

It will not be long before this entire technology requires an even more elaborate explanation than the one just given, beginning with just what a home phone or an answering machine was.

But then there's one final tape recording to be mentioned, a recording of that famous home run in October 1951, the so-called "shot heard 'round the world." While thousands originally heard Russ Hodges call that shot on the radio that day, many millions more would have been deprived of that moment were it not for someone's bright idea to tape the game while listening to it—a contrabanding for which we have not only an audio account of the game but, now, DeLillo's *Underworld* to thank:

> There's a man on 12th Street in Brooklyn who has attached a tape machine to his radio so he can record the voice of Russ Hodges broadcasting the game. The man doesn't know why he's doing this. It is just an impulse, a fancy, it is like hearing the game twice, it is like being young and being old, and this will turn out to be the only known recording of Russ' famous account of the final moments of the game. (*U* 32)

To hear a game twice at the same time, to be at once young and old—that too is the contraband effect, a contraband that can be relatively low tech, more or less internal, no more than a voice in the head, or else very high tech, a memory facilitated by external tapes or drives, externalizations of oneself and one's perceptions—radio, television, telephone, recording devices of various kinds—externalizations that, as we will see, actually allow one to recognize oneself in the first place. These contraband technologies do not just imitate or reproduce our experience but actually structure it and tell us who we are. This, then, is the writing of recoil rather than reflection, the writing of repetition and displacement—as well as the writing of ghosts. For if every voice can be recorded, every body filmed, then each of us is a ghost in advance, already dead before our time and already immortalized through these contraband technologies.

Internet

> *The internet is a counternarrative, shaped in part by rumor, fantasy and mystical reverberation.*
>
> "RF"

> *Bud's wife worked on the line at Texas Instruments, mounting microchips on circuit boards, Bud said, for the information highway.*
>
> U 265

> *http://blk.www/dd.com/miraculum*
>
> U 810

It should come as no surprise that an author who had integrated the technologies of radio, television, telephone, film, and so on, so deeply into his work should take an interest in the internet. Beginning in the 1990s, particularly in *Underworld*, references begin creeping in, and, by the final pages, the entire novel will have been drawn in to this new digital reality, sucked into cyberspace. That is because the final—or at least the penultimate—scenes of the narrative are "lived" not through direct narration or any kind of audible or filmed account but through the internet. It happens, appropriately, through the mediation of a younger generation. Nick is living in Phoenix with Marian and, still, his Going-Nowhere-Fast son Jeffrey, a bit of a deadbeat in his father's eyes and yet a kid who sometimes hits the nail right on the head:

> Everybody is everywhere at once. Jeff likes to say this, our son, who still lives at home and still says things with the smirky sort of shyness he has brought with him out of adolescence. (*U* 805)

Jeffrey could be talking here about modern life, contemporary travel, with everybody always on the go, but he could also be talking about the internet, that vast contraband network that allows everyone to be everywhere all at once, a mass fantasy for oneself and others right there at one's finger tips.

Near the end of the novel, then, Nick discovers that his son has been visiting a website devoted to miracles (*U* 806): "He enters seventeen characters and then *dot com miraculum*. And the miracles come scrolling down" (*U* 807). It's an interesting site, not only to Jeffrey but also to his parents: "There are reports that crippled dogs have risen and walked. Jeff tells us this and smirks shyly, either because he thinks it's funny or because he thinks it's funny and believes it" (*U* 806). It's like cyber-tabloid only better because the images move and are connected. It's good, wholesome, entertainment; Murray Siskind would have surely approved. But then there's something that hits home: "At dinner one night he tells us about a miracle in the Bronx" (*U* 807). It's the story we have been following throughout the novel:

> A young girl was the victim of a terrible crime. Body found in a vacant lot amid dense debris. Identified and buried. The girl memorialized on a graffiti wall nearby. And then the miracle of the images and the subsequent crush of people and the belief and disbelief. Mostly belief, it seems (*U* 808). Her name is Esmeralda. (*U* 810)

A "lurker" to such things, Jeffrey "feels he doesn't have the credentials to relate a tale of such intensity, all that suffering and faith and openness of emotion, transpiring in the Bronx" (*U* 808). But his father says "what better place for the study of wonders" (*U* 808). That's what brings him, our narrator, into the story of Esmeralda's miraculous appearance and Sister Edgar's reaction to it. An exceptional event even when it's manufactured, as this one will prove to be, the miracle is the contraband to everyday experience, the underside, beyond all evidence and proof, which is no doubt why just about every DeLillo novel ends with one. But the point here in *Underworld* is that everything is mediated through the internet. The tale is told in two keystrokes, a binary pair, like 0 and 1, two short sections labeled *Keystroke 1* and *Keystroke 2*. The first keystroke tells the story of Esmeralda's violent end and her miraculous apparition, as well as Sister Edgar's even more miraculous reaction to it. *Keystroke 2*—the contraband keystroke—gives us a number of reflections on the internet itself. First, there is Sister Edgar's place in the web:

> In her veil and habit she was basically a face, or a face and scrubbed hands. Here in cyberspace she has shed all that steam-ironed fabric. She is not naked exactly but she is open—exposed to every connection you can make on the world wide web. (*U* 824)

And then the web itself:

> There is no space or time out here, or in here, or wherever she is. There are only connections. Everything is connected. All human knowledge gathered and linked, hyperlinked, this site leading to that, this fact referenced to that, a keystroke, a mouse-click, a password—world without end, amen. (*U* 825)

Two keystrokes, different and yet joined by a screen that reads "*Searching*" (*U* 817, *U* 818). It's not as if DeLillo had been waiting all his life for the internet, but the internet must have surely appeared to him as something his writing had always been anticipating—all the connections, rumors, and fantasies brought together in one vast network, driven by science and yet animated by a kind of faith. We read of Sister Edgar, "She is in cyberspace, not heaven, and she feels the grip of systems" (*U* 825).

The ultimate miracle of *Underworld* is thus perhaps not the appearance of Esmeralda, since it is probably just an illusion anyway, the billboard's old advertisement appearing through the new one when hit by the subway headlights, but the internet itself. That's what the narrator ultimately suggests: "The real miracle is the web, the net, where everybody is everywhere at once, and he is there among them, unseen" (*U* 808).

The miracle is thus perhaps not some great or momentous happening within the world but the mediatization and opening of the world—something within the world that appears bigger or more encompassing than the world in which it is found, a counterworld that can contain and replace what we used to call the world itself. That's what the internet promises or at least asks us to consider: "Is cyberspace a thing within the world or is it the other way around? Which contains the other, and how can you tell for sure?" (*U* 826).

There is a world inside the world, "a life inside this life" (*RS* 370), a contraband world and a contraband life inside what we call this world and this life—a mohole, as it were, woven throughout our universe, a dark web inside or beneath the web we think we know so well. "He enters seventeen characters and then *dot com miraculum*. And the miracles come scrolling down" (*U* 807): Maybe that's because, as we hear in *End Zone*, "the number seventeen is a numeral of immortal life" (*EZ* 93–94).

5

Arts of Duplicity

Before pop art, there was such a thing as bad taste. Now there's kitsch, schlock, camp and porn.

RD 148

Marvin walked in his sliding step, his sort of explanatory shuffle, it was a comment on the literature of shuffles.

U 188

Painting and Sculpture

On all the walls, everywhere, were dozens of paintings. Mostly abstract. The real thing. Just lines. Just squares. Just circles. All black. Practically all black. Huge, powerful, looming canvases.

AZ 100

You're looking at a picture on a wall. That's all. But it makes you feel alive in the world. It tells you yes, you're here. And yes, you have a range of being that's deeper and sweeter than you knew.

C 30

It was by a famous painter whose name she could never remember but he was famous, he was dead, he had a white mask of a face and glowing white hair. Or maybe he was just supposed to be dead. Scott said he didn't seem dead because he never seemed real. Andy. That was it.

M 62

When an artwork includes or cites another artwork, whether from literature or some other art, the gesture is never innocent, never naïve, never without effects of contraband. That is doubly true in DeLillo, where artworks are everywhere, everything from paintings and sculptures to earthworks, graffiti, and performance pieces, not to mention photography and film, which are so ubiquitous they will need a section of their own. In addition to more or less passing references to Rousseau (*N* 287), Hopper (*P* 47), Rothko (*C* 30), and Dürer (in the form of "Otto Durer Obenwahr," a name that came from David Bell's colleague "Theodore Warburton," in his final memo before retirement, "three names from two, anagrammatized, a last jest from corporate exile" (*A* 375)), there is, for example, Whistler, a small print of "the famous Mother" (*U* 748), hanging over the extra-marital mattress of Klara Sax and Nick Shay's brief but torrid affair as an admonition or an Oedipal reminder for both mother and son. It was already a strange affair, he being seventeen and she in her thirties, "something you didn't want to tell your friends about," but then there was "Whistler's fucking Mother hanging on the wall" (*U* 751).

Paintings thus often function in DeLillo as reminders or remonstrations, as counter-discourses or visual provocations that run counter to everyday discourse. In each case it's another form of contraband and, more often than not, a reminder of death in life. In *Falling Man* Lianne's mother, Nina Bartos, a retired art history professor, "the So-and-So Professor of Such-and-Such" (*FM* 9), is given two still lives, *natura morta*, by the Italian painter Giorgio Morandi (*FM* 12). They are a gift from her longtime lover, Martin Ridnour, an art dealer with another name and a secret past (see *FM* 42–45, 145). Still lives of bottles and other shapes, these paintings remind Nina of the World Trade Towers, now collapsed. They are paintings that Nina imagined she would look at as she was dying, pictures that somehow tell us about "being human, being mortal": "I think these pictures are what I'll look at when I've stopped looking at everything else. I'll look at bottles and jars. I'll sit here looking" (*FM* 111). But that's not what happens in the end, since Nina will have given them back to Martin before she dies. "All the paintings and drawings carried the same title. *Natura Morta*. Even this, the term for still life, yielded her mother's last days" (*FM* 211).

There's the short story "Baader-Meinhof," which is not really about the 1970s and 1980s terrorist group but about a 2001 art exhibit in NYC on the deaths of the group's members in prison, "a cycle of fifteen canvases" ("BM" 105), "Ulrike dead in each, lying on the floor of her cell, head in profile" ("BM" 105). The last of the fifteen paintings, "the largest by far and maybe most breathtaking," "the one with the coffins and cross," is called *Funeral* ("BM" 118). The main character goes to the exhibit of these paintings for "three straight days" ("BM" 107), obsessively, like the narrator of *Point Omega* going to see *24 Hour Psycho*, because it takes that long to begin to see a thing like that.

Then there's the painting *The Triumph of Death*, "a sixteenth-century work done by a Flemish master, Pieter Bruegel" (*U* 49–50). It is a reproduction of this painting printed in the *Life* magazine of October 1, 1951, that floats down in the confetti storm of the Polo Grounds into the hands of J. Edgar Hoover, who thinks: "The dead have come to take the living. The dead in winding-sheets, the regimented dead on horseback, the skeleton that plays a hurdy-gurdy" (*U* 49). He is at once repulsed and fascinated, "morbidly fond" (*U* 574), which is why he folds the picture and puts it "neatly in his pocket ... to study further" (*U* 54). The painting becomes central to *Underworld*, but perhaps already to *Mao II*, where TV footage of a crowd at a soccer match is compared to just such a painting:

> It is like a religious painting, the scene could be a fresco in a tourist church, it is composed and balanced and filled with people suffering. ... They show the fence from a distance, bodies piling up behind it, smothered, sometimes only fingers moving, and it is like a fresco in an old dark church, a crowded twisted vision of a rush to death as only a master of the age could paint it. (*M* 33–34)

Finally, there's Andy, the inimitable Andy Warhol, whose art is not necessarily about death but whose life is, Andy at a black-and-white mask ball at the Plaza in 1966 "wearing a mask that was a photograph of his own face" (*U* 571), inimitable and yet perpetually imitated, everything from the silk screen called *Crowd* and the Mao series of 1973—"Photocopy Mao, silk-screen Mao, wallpaper Mao, synthetic polymer Mao" (*M* 21), "a reproduction of a pencil drawing called *Mao II*" (*M* 62)—to Andy's Coca-Cola series, the real thing, as it were, which Brita Nillson encounters a version of on the sweatshirts of Maoist boys in training in Beirut, "a sweatshirt with Coke bottles pictured across the front, row after row" (*M* 150). There's Andy's Mao, Andy's Coke, but then also Gorby I, Alexander Kosolapov's repetition of Warhol's repetition—because it's all about the work of art in the age of mechanical reproduction, the film, the photograph, the lithograph, the T-shirt. There is still today, to be sure, the aura of the unique, of the original, the unreproducible, the one-off, but there is also—and today especially—the aura that comes from reproduction itself (see *M* 15). As Acey Greene, a black female artist from Chicago (*U* 389–394), the second city, says in the can-do contrabanding spirit of Andy, "It's not Marilyn I want, it's fake Marilyn" (*U* 474).

In addition to painting, there is sculpture, often large, muscular sculpture, and often produced by women, like Sullivan in *Americana*, known for her "power-art, meaning art produced by electric tools" (*A* 107), or Klara Sax with her massive art project to paint decommissioned B-52s, 230 of them, out in the desert (*U* 83). Using "automotive spray guns ... to prime the metal" (*U* 68), the planes are then hand-painted, an homage to the "nose artists" who once "painted pinups on the fuselage"—*Long Tall Sally*, for example, the "sexy woman" painted on the nose of the plane as "a charm against death" (*U* 77). When Nick drives out into the desert to see this work, he is overwhelmed by the beauty and power of it all and knows enough not to "linger": "See it and leave. If you stay too long, you wear out the wordless shock. Love it and trust it and leave" (*U* 83).

But there is more than that in the end. There are the contrabanding opposites we saw earlier between past and future, the most primitive and the most contemporary:

> And truly I thought they were great things, painted to remark the end of an age and the beginning of something so different only a vision such as this might suffice to augur it. ... And I wondered if the piece was visible from space like the land art of some lost Andean people. (*U* 126)

There's *Long Tall Sally*, therefore, and then there's her ancient counterpart, at the center of the short story "The Ivory Acrobat," a delicate piece this time, an unearthed sculpture (or a mass-produced replica thereof) dating back to 1600 B.C., the "reproduction of an ivory figurine from Crete, a bull leaper, female, her body deftly extended with tapered feet nearing the topmost point of a somersaulting curve" ("IA" 65). It's an image or a story that seems to have been with DeLillo since at least *The Names*, where we read of "Minoans ... Grand ladies. Slim-waisted and graceful" (*N* 84; see also 37).

There is thus painting, sculpture, and then all kinds of mixed media in between, from collages (*A* 108) to lithographs (*A* 336) to, in *Zero K*, *gesso on linen*, Ross Lockhart's final words, as it turns out, a term that the narrator, Ross's son, says he tried "to absolve ... of its meaning and to think of it as a fragment of some beautiful lost language, unspoken for a thousand years" (*ZK* 268; see 251). *Gesso on linen*—ancient words, he imagines, for plaster of Paris.

In *Zero K* there is also an art exhibit in a NYC gallery featuring a single rock, just one big rock—really big, but just a rock: "The rock simply sat there" (*ZK* 215). It's the kind of thing that inspires contemplation: "I allowed myself a minute or two with the rock" (*ZK* 215). It is as if DeLillo is recalling something from *Ratner's Star*—"I find peace in the contemplation of rock art" (*RS* 102)—or from *End Zone*, which ends with a reference to "the black stone of Abraham" (*EZ* 241), an echo of the round stone that Anatole Bloomberg found out in the desert and painted black as a "burial marker" for his recently deceased mother:

> I was sure I would never recover from the unspeakable heartbreak and Jewishness of her funeral. So I didn't go home. Instead I went into the

desert with a paintbrush and can of black paint. Among all those flat stones I found a single round one. I painted it black. It's my mother's burial marker. (*EZ* 188)

In DeLillo's work, rock is a serious thing, whether simply found out there in nature, like this one in southern Greece, "a massive anvil rock, maybe five hundred feet tall, a dark presence, a power like a voice in the sky" (*N* 183), or "the rock mass" of the Acropolis, which looms, as it were, over much of the novel (*N* 230), or marked by human hands, like the one, again in *The Names*, that is graffitied with the Greek name for "names." James Axton is talking here to his son—the one who writes, as we will see, and so has his own interest in names:

> It was a fallen rock, a ten-foot boulder standing by the roadcut to our left, a flat-faced reddish block with two white words painted across its width, the pigment running down off the letters in rough trickles, the accent mark clearly in place.
> *Ta Onómata.* ...
> "Do you know what it means?"
> "The Names," I said. (*N* 188; see 299)

Finally, in *Love-Lies-Bleeding* there is Alex Macklin, former painter turned earth artist. Alex's final project, never completed, was a sort of dream work, at once contemporary artwork and ancient ruin, exhibit hall and underworld:

> A room, a cube. I don't have a name for it. First we cut a passage in. A rough narrow entranceway, cramped, with jutting rock. ... A chamber, a cubical room. Fashioned out of solid rock. ... Art that's hidden in a mountain. An incredible. ... sort of stone enclosure that you would drench with paintings of your dreams. ... [Or maybe] a bare room without a signature. Just there. Except it won't be there. (*LL* 59–61)

A room, a tomb, a work of art, a place of uncertain survival, it resembles a small-scale version of what art is or will become in the Convergence of *Zero K*. As Jeffrey Lockhart says of his step-mother: "And Artis now in this barely believable place, this desert apparition, soon to be preserved, a glacial body in a massive burial chamber" (*ZK* 14–15). It could have been signed Alex Macklin: "Untitled, unfinished. But not nothing" (*LL* 83).

Of course, what would art be without an "art world," that is, a place to buy, sell, and consume art? What would it be without a place like New York? There are thus artists but then also art dealers and collectors, always just a little bit suspect: Lightborne in *Running Dog*, Norman, behind bars, in "Hammer and Sickle" ("HS" 151), Martin Ridnour in *Falling Man*, and, in *Underworld* (*U* 376), "Carlo Strasser, the amateur art collector and whatever else he was, in his splendid Italian shoes, with a farmhouse, she recalled, near Arles" (*U* 478; see 386). And then there are all the galleries (*U* 376) and exhibits, like the Morandi exhibit in Chelsea that Lianne goes to (*FM* 209) or the exhibit in *Mao II* where Karen inadvertently or absentmindedly pulls a spoon off a painting, leaving "the premises with part of an artwork in her possession" (*M* 173). But she did the right thing: "She took the greatest possible care of the food-encrusted spoon from the art gallery" (*M* 178–179). Though "a spoon is not a painting of a spoon" (*DR* 75), a lesson we have all learned from Magritte, when it comes off a painting it seems to become something else altogether—a contrabanded spoon, as it were, no longer art exactly but still not something with which to eat soup.

But that then raises the whole question of what a spoon—or any other ready-made object—is doing in a painting anyway. In *Amazons* the point is made with a frustration bordering on fury by an ex-hockey player looking at a modern painting in a snazzy Manhattan apartment: "Explain the spoon. … The painter didn't just put it there because he had too many soup spoons around the house. It's not something he stuck there, meaning to come back and get it later when the soup was hot" (*AZ* 102). The answer he gets from the painter's owner is as clear as a tautology: "You simply accept it for what it is. … Once upon a time these pictures may have been difficult. But … we now know they are simple. The canvas is canvas. The paint is paint. We respond to it as paint. And we respond to the spoon as a spoon. It is a spoon" (*AZ* 102–103). It's a good explanation, but the ex-hockey player is hardly convinced, because "the other paintings don't have spoons … Explain that. If you can't explain the spoon, explain no spoon" (*AZ* 103). The moral of the story seems to be that "some people just have to stay away from modern art. They owe it to themselves. It makes them insane with rage … 'Explain the spoon.' It could kill you faster than a California mudslide" (*AZ* 107).

Finally, there are the millionaires and billionaires who begin spending some of their fortunes on art, a serious pastime that requires not just serious money but, if you are going to do it right, serious study. Such is the case of Ross Lockhart in *Zero K*:

> I used to think I was a serious man. The work I did, the effort and dedication. Then, later, the time I was able to devote to other matters, to art, educating myself to the ideas and traditions and innovations. Came to love it. … The work itself, a picture on a wall. Then I got started on rare books. (*ZK* 31)

One can of course always read this compulsive collecting with a more suspicious eye, as Jeffrey, his son, will not fail to do: "Figurative, abstract, conceptual, post-minimal ... I tried to convince myself that Ross was using them to smother my response to his bloated portfolio" (*ZK* 54). And yet the art will remain after the death of Ross Lockhart, art after the heart has stopped beating for a time in the Convergence: "It was my father's former office and two of the paintings he owned were still on the wall, dark with strips of dusty sunlight, both of them. ... The two paintings were the spectral remains of my father's presence here" (*ZK* 165–166). Art as a reminder of the dead and, in the Convergence, as we will see, the dead as art—*Art*is and Lockh*art*, both in a state of suspended animation.

Theater, Performance Art, Graffiti

> *He found himself bored, often, at the theater. ... This kind of torpor was generated by three-dimensional bodies, real space as opposed to the manipulated depth of film.*
>
> *P* 100

> *The true play could not be found in theaters. The true play was ourselves and we needed shadows on which to chalk our light, speed to conquer sequence, infinitesimal holes in which to plant our consciousness.*
>
> *A* 346–347

> *Maid: Do we have names in this?*
>
> *DR* 61

And then there is theater, often at the center—and we shouldn't be surprised—of DeLillo's own plays. *The Day Room*, for example, revolves around the search for the Arno Klein theater company, a secret theater group with no theater or announced performances. "They turn up in some remote part of the city. They simply appear. In Amsterdam they used squatters' buildings. A different building every night" (*DR* 74; see *U* 601). Devoted fans spend their entire lives following rumors, traveling the world trying to catch a performance. As Lynette says: "I've been trying to see this group for half my life, it seems" (*DR* 67). So secret is the group it is unclear whether it really even exists, or whether there really is an Arno Klein, or whether there is any difference between everyday life and the performances of a theater company that would supposedly double and contraband it. "Maybe they're just a never-ending rumor" (*DR* 73; see 83). And if they do exist, perhaps their performances can be determined to have taken place only after the fact, surmised in retrospect: "Did you ever think that might be *them*? The taxi man and sweeper. That was possibly the spot" (*DR* 72). *The Day Room* is thus a play in two acts where the second act may or may not be the counter-act of the first, where the characters in the hospital in the First Act may be patients who have slipped out of the "Arno Klein Psychiatric Wing" or else actors playing characters in the play, actors playing with, and perhaps under the direction of, the elusive Arno Klein. One cannot tell the patients from the doctors or the characters playing patients and doctors from the characters playing actors playing patients and doctors. Entirely white, the Day Room would seem to be the counter-room of the real world, countering it, encountering it, and becoming confounded with it (see *DR* 26–27).

It's a play, then, full of reflections about the form of the play itself, about the set, stage directions, audience, the difference or the distance between the play and what's outside the play, the difference between theater and imagination. As Gary says about the Arno Klein theater group: "I'm satisfied just imagining they exist" (*DR* 70). The play's the thing, then, but it is more than the conscience of the king that is at stake. It is the very relationship between band and contraband, the thing and the play on the thing.

Like the play, though often without the possibility of a repeat performance, is performance art, works that cannot or cannot easily be reproduced or repeated. There is, for example, the artist in *Great Jones Street* who is trying to produce an earthquake, a seismic event, a "kinetic shiver" (*GJ* 77), and in *Mao II*, the 1988 performance piece "The Lovers: The Great Wall Walk," in which "a man and a woman"—Marina Abramovic and the German artist Ulay, for the record—who walked "the length of the Great Wall of China, approaching each other from opposite directions" (*M* 70; see *RS* 287).

That then brings us to Lauren Hartke (yet another name, like Lockhart, with both *art* and a *k* in it—a DeLillo twofer), Lauren the body artist, with her "slow-motion repetitions of everyday gestures" (*BA* 58), "always in the process of becoming another or exploring some root identity" (*BA* 105), some identity, it goes without saying, that is not simply "her own" or that is her own only by way of others: Mr. Tuttle, for example (*BA* 101), or an old Japanese woman she sees in town (*BA* 35)—both of whom she will try to imitate in her new show, right down to simple gestures like the way the Japanese woman holds her hands:

> Her hands were fisted up inside the sleeves of her jacket, for warmth, and she watched the woman, sleeves seemingly empty, and cursed herself for not having thought of this for the piece, because it was fantastic,

no hands, it was everything she needed to know about the woman and would have been perfect for the piece. (*BA* 115–116)

Lauren's gestures are extraordinary for the way they imitate or contraband the ordinary, everyday things like breathing or standing up slowly against a doorpost or making an exaggerated facial expression. It is not so much imitation or repetition but, precisely, contrabanding that Lauren is attempting:

> It wasn't outright impersonation but she heard elements of her voice, the clipped delivery, the slight buzz deep in the throat, her pitch, her sound, and how difficult at first, unearthly almost, to detect her own voice coming from someone else, from him, and then how deeply disturbing. (*BA* 50)

Lauren is contrabanding, all right, but it's not clear whom or what. As we saw earlier, she starts using, repeating, Mr. Tuttle's voice, which is itself a repetition, a replay or playback, it seems, of Rey's, Rey's voice as it is heard on a tape recorder. Lauren's piece is thus called Body Time (*BA* 104), suggesting, it seems, the time of the body, or time in the body, time inscribed in the body. What is it about?

> Something about past and future. ... What we can know and what we can't. ... Maybe the idea is to think time differently. ... Stop time, or stretch it out, or open it up. Make a still life that's living, not painted. (*BA* 107)

It's a piece that takes us to the limits of language. It begins with Lauren as the old Japanese woman and ends with her as "a naked man, emaciated and aphasic, trying desperately to tell us something" (*BA* 105):

> The last of the bodies, the naked man, is stripped of recognizable language and culture. He moves in a curious manner, as if in a dark room, only more slowly and gesturally. He wants to tell us something. His voice is audible, intermittently, on tape, and Hartke lip-syncs the words. (*BA* 107)

Of course, the performance piece is also double-banded, taped, synced, two-tracked at the very least: in addition to the voices Lauren herself produces, voices within voices, the piece is accompanied by the "anonymous robotic voice of a telephone answering machine delivering a standard announcement" (*BA* 106), and projected onto the back wall of the performance site is the video feed of an empty road in Finland (*BA* 107). If one were to produce an image or a performance piece of DeLillo's own writing—or at least certain aspects of it, simple gestures and thoughts against the background of another technologically produced or reproduced narrative—this might well be it.

But Lauren is not the only body artist or body teacher in DeLillo. Babette in *White Noise* gives classes in "Eating and Drinking: Basic Parameters," a title that, she admits, "is a little more stupid than it absolutely has to be" (*WN* 171). But if the name of the course is a little stupid, the thing is not, and Babette defends it: "I'm not a very ingenious person but I know how to break things down, how to separate and classify. We can analyze posture, we can analyze eating, drinking and even breathing" (*WN* 192). In short, "she teaches them how to stand, sit and walk" (*WN* 27; see 75, 105). What performance could be more basic and what defines more fully the parameters of our lives?

But then there are the performances of Falling Man, an imitation or contrabanding of the man who leapt from one of the burning towers on 9/11, an imitation of the simple, natural gesture of falling, though the key, here, is to freeze or to stick the fall, to embody somehow "the jolt, the sort of midair impact and bounce, the recoil, and now the stillness, arms at his sides, one leg bent at the knee" (*FM* 168), to end up "dangling there, above the street, upside down," wearing "a business suit" (*FM* 33). We later find out through an obituary that the performance artist is thirty-nine-year-old David Janiak (also spelled with a *k*) (*FM* 219), whose performance recalls a photograph by American photographer Garry Winogrand (1928–1984), though Janiak's gesture is even more ominous. For if a bystander in the Winogrand photograph can smile at the trick of the falling or dangling man, those who see Janiak find no amusement in the stunt: "Headlong, free fall, she thought, and this picture burned a hole in her mind and heart, dear God, he was a falling angel and his beauty was horrific" (*FM* 222). Lianne thus sees the contrabanded performance of what her husband Keith (with a capital *K*) saw in person, falling man, the real one, the first one, the original, absolutely incomparable in this life. The performance piece thus seems to repeat the incomparable—like the two Morandi paintings that somehow embody for Lianne both Keith and the falling towers. Here are the final lines of *Falling Man*: "Then he saw a shirt come down out of the sky. He walked and saw it fall, arms waving like nothing in this life" (*FM* 246).

DeLillo is obviously interested in having characters who perform with their bodies, who gesture for a living, if you will, or as a pastime. But he is also interested, and this is true of *every* novel, in himself describing gestures. He is interested in people doing ordinary things, like sitting or walking or buttering toast ("We became meticulous and terse, diminished the scope of our movements, buttered our bread in the manner of technicians restoring a fresco" (*WN* 118; see *L* 16 for more toast-buttering)), or sleeping on a train ("My son slept sitting in a chair like some boozed commuter, head rolling on his chest" (*WN* 154)), or shagging fly balls ("He moved across the dirt and weeds, kicking up dust, purposely delaying his break for the ball so that he could make an over-the-shoulder or backhand catch" (*A* 359)) or working on a garbage truck (*U* 704), or doing yoga (*N* 250), stylized gestures all—as if the writer felt the challenge of describing certain movements or gestures, Tai-Chi, for example, with its "moves and countermoves" (*RD* 5, 27; see *LL* 89), hand exercises in therapy (*FM* 40), kickboxing in pajamas ("S" 190), or else dancing (*ZK* 186, see 207), tap-dancing (*P* 78–79), belly dancing (*N* 220), or striptease (*L* 261–262). Or everyday gestures like checking for one's keys and wallet before leaving home (*ZK* 183), or walking up a flight of stairs and touching the "newel" at the top (and the point here, as we will see, is as much the word "newel" as the newel thing), or sitting down in a deck or lounge chair, shaking an orange juice carton, or putting on a sweater. So interested is DeLillo in gestures that he will have Bill Waterson give Cotter Martin a little clinic in them as they sit in the stands in the Polo Grounds on that fateful afternoon in October 1951. Bill says, "I take my seventh-inning stretch seriously. I not only stand. I damn well make it a point to stretch" (*U* 30), at which point he "has some fun doing various stylized stretches, the bodybuilder, the pet cat, and he tries to get Cotter"—the fourteen-year-old black kid who has cut school to be at the game—"to do a drowsy kid in a classroom" (*U* 31). And you can almost see him obliging.

There is often something either self-conscious or self-referring about many of these gestures, as if the gesturer saw himself or herself from afar, already part of a certain narrative or codified form, as if the narrative voice were already layered onto the gesture itself. Here is a sampling of just a dozen such gestures, all by girls or women—just to counter the image of DeLillo as a "male" or "masculine" writer—gestures that are all recognizable and could probably be given titles if one wanted, like "little girl feeding ducks" or "little girl angry with her mother," all the way down to "woman pretending to sleep":

1. "The girl took bread in fragments from her father and pitched them over the rail, holding her hand open like someone signaling five" ("R" 47).
2. "She sat next to her mother, arms at her sides, slim white legs pointed straight out, a show of mock obedience. They were not talking to each other" (*L* 135).
3. "She tilted her head in the hopeful way of a tourist who wishes to ask directions" ("R" 49).

4. "She sat up and turned the pages, trying to disguise herself as someone who routinely reads for fifteen minutes before dropping into easy sleep" ("IA" 61).
5. "[She] managed to get our attention by the sheer pleading force of the look on her face. Her hand was over the mouthpiece of the phone. She did not speak but only formed the words. *The Stovers want to come over*" (*WN* 42).
6. "She took a deep drag on her cigarette and exhaled smoke in rapid expert streams from nose and mouth, a routine she used when she wanted to express impatience with her immediate surroundings" (*WN* 86).
7. "[She was] using her thumbnail to gouge price stickers off the items she'd purchased, a determined act of vengeance against whatever was out there doing these things to us" (*ZK* 248).
8. "She went slackjawed and held her hands out, palms up, like where did this come from, like what did I do to deserve this, eyes wide, a dumbfounded cartoon child" (*PO* 67).
9. "She was crying, making the motion or taking the shape, but without tears, her mouth stretched flat, the animated light missing from her eyes" (*M* 220).
10. "She shook hands all around. She was an enthusiastic handshaker. She pumped way up and down, like someone just learning how to do it" (*AZ* 314).
11. "She stood with her right arm fully extended as though taking aim with a pearl-handled Colt. All she wanted to do was shake hands, I luckily saw" (*AZ* 323).
12. "She slipped under the quilt, turning on her side and facing the wall to prove she was serious. Slowly now, into that helpless half life of self-commentary, the voice film that runs between light and dark" (*M* 91).

Arguably the ultimate performance piece, art installation, or earthwork in all of DeLillo is the Convergence itself of *Zero K*, not a *natura morta*, like the Morandi paintings, but a genuine "still life," a term that is almost as paradoxical as the living or not-quite-dead people frozen beneath the earth: "Tableau vivant, I thought, except that the actors were dead and their costumes were super-insulated plastic tubes" (*ZK* 140). The narrator seems to be following the insight of his stepmother Artis, who says that they ought to regard the Convergence "as a work-in-progress, an earthwork, a form of earth art, land art" (*ZK* 10). It is not unlike Alex Macklin's last work where "the earth is the guiding principle. ... Return to the earth, emerge from the earth" (*ZK* 10), perfectly appropriate for Artis, an archaeologist who once was on a dig—"burial mounds," of course—not far from the Convergence

(*ZK* 30–31). The place is itself like an artwork, a room, a tomb, a gallery, where the work coincides with or contrabands the space itself:

> An art gallery, I thought, with nothing in it. The gallery is the art, the space itself, the walls and floor. Or an enormous marble tomb, a mass gravesite emptied of bodies or waiting for bodies. (*ZK* 148)

This is not postmodern but postmortem art (*ZK* 232), "art that belongs to the afterlife. It was art that accompanies last things, simply, dreamlike and delirious. You're dead, it said" (*ZK* 119).

But then there are the "people" themselves in the Convergence, like "a new generation of earth art, with human bodies in states of suspended animation" (*ZK* 16), bodies shaved and frozen,

> Rows of human bodies in gleaming pods. ... Here, there were no lives to think about or imagine. This was pure spectacle, a single entity, the bodies regal in their cryonic bearing. It was a form of visionary art, it was body art with broad implications. ... And was there something nearly prehistoric about the artifacts ranged before me now? Archaeology for a future age. (*ZK* 256)

It's pure spectacle, though it is not intended for any spectator or audience: "It's made simply to be here. It's here, it's fixed, it's part of the foundation, set in stone" (*ZK* 51). It's an archaeology for a future that, as always in DeLillo, can only be compared to things from the past: "I thought finally of lavishly choreographed dance routines from Hollywood musicals of many decades past, dancers synchronized in the manner of a marching army" (*ZK* 257)—the Rockettes, maybe, as in *Underworld*, or a chorus line of two hundred and sixty Long Tall Sallys.

These bodies are seen both as a group, as part of a crowd, as it were, and as individuals, each one an artwork unto itself, simply there "in empty method, a living breathing artform" (*ZK* 149). Artis, then, as artwork, at once herself and her own double, herself and her own contraband, buried beneath the ground, waiting to be unearthed, and yet already open to memory, to being remembered, as when Jeffrey returns to NYC and sees a woman in the New York subway that reminds him of her:

> There was a woman on the subway platform, across the tracks. She stood at the wall, in wide trousers and a light sweater, eyes closed, and who does this, on a subway platform, people milling, trains coming and going. (*ZK* 225)

This is, he thinks, the woman he had seen earlier on the street, eyes closed, just standing there, like a statue, like a mannequin, like Artis: "She stood in open space, an unexplained presence" (*ZK* 210)—unexplained but nonetheless reminiscent of Artis in the Convergence.

That's precisely how contraband works on the reader in DeLillo. One scene, through memory, begins to impose itself upon another. A woman with her eyes closed in the rain recalls, for Jeffrey, for the reader, Artis, who says earlier in the novel, "I think about drops of water. How I used to stand in the shower and watch a drop of water edge down the inside of the sheer curtain" (*ZK* 17; see 211). But then it is hard not to think of Janet Leigh in *Psycho*, or, rather, in *Point Omega*, pulling the shower curtain down, with six—or was it four?—curtain rings spinning (*PO* 9, 109), or maybe even the drops of water in *White Noise*, or Eric Packer contemplating his own reflection on the surface of the glass tower in which he lives: "A surface separates inside from out and belongs no less to one than the other. He'd thought about surfaces in the shower once" (*C* 9), or Tap, the nine-year-old aspiring novelist in *The Names*: "I told them about a letter I'd received from Tap. He liked the sound the water made in the shower when it hit the plastic lining of the shower curtain" (*N* 257). It is easy to write all this off as the repetition of a motif or a theme, a pattern or an obsession; it is instead the multiplication of a contraband, the constant redrawing and then drawing aside of a shower curtain separating inside from out, one novel from another.

Finally, in the Convergence, the phenomenon of contraband makes art of everyday objects in a room, as well as of the room itself, things phenomenalized in order to resemble themselves:

> I was led to a room in which all four walls were covered with a continuous painted image of the room itself. There were only three pieces of furniture, two chairs and a low table, all depicted from several angles. I remained standing, turning my head and then my body to scan the mural. The fact of four plane surfaces being a likeness of themselves as well as background for three objects of spatial extent struck me as a subject worthy of some deep method of inquiry, phenomenology maybe, but I wasn't equal to the challenge. (*ZK* 252)

Later, still in the Convergence, the doubling continues "along a corridor that had murals of ravaged landscapes, on and on, scenes meant to be prophetic, a doubled landscape, each wall repeating the facing wall" (*ZK* 257). This is not gallery art but the art of an underground gallery, underworld or contraband art, an art where thing and image *converge* for just a moment before dividing into band and contraband.

And then there is graffiti art, in *Underworld* but also already in *Americana* (*A* 4; see 18). If DeLillo seems to have a penchant for these more popular forms of art, in addition to cinema, it is perhaps because he is a writer of movement and gesture. There is thus political graffiti, war graffiti, on the walls of a war-ravaged neighborhood of Beirut (*M* 229, 239), and then, of course, the graffiti artists of *Underworld*, who "spray-painted a memorial angel every time a child died in the neighborhood," angels in blue and pink on what was called "the Wall" (*U* 239; "AE" 76), and artists who, like Ismael Muñoz, tag subway cars—underground art that is made to be appreciated both below ground and above (see *U* 343). It is Klara Sax's art dealer who first draws Klara's attention to Ismael: "A kid who does graffiti. He does trains, subways, whole trains ... I don't know his name. I only know his tag. Moonman 157. ... The kid's a goddamn master" (*U* 377). A "legend of spray paint" (*U* 245) at the age of sixteen, that is, "not too old and not too young" for this kind of art, Ismael was "determined to kill the shit of every subway artist in town" (*U* 433). DeLillo's description mirrors well the movement and power of Ismael's painting:

> Every car spray-painted top to bottom with his name and street number. ... The letters and numbers fairly exploded in your face and they had a relationship, they were plaited and knotted, pop-eyed cartoon humanoids, winding in and out of each other and sweaty hot and passion dancing—metallic silver and blue and cherry-bomb red and a number of neon greens. (*U* 394–395; see 433)

Letters and numbers, like DeLillo's writing. "The whole point of Moonman's tag was how the letters and numbers told a story of backstreet life" (*U* 434). It's an artwork that is made fast and that moves fast. And, like Klara Sax, Moonman has assistants, kids with "dozens of cans out and ready, all by prearrangement, and he called a color and they shook the can and the ball went click" (*U* 440). If you don't have access to cameras and film and all the other technologies of the moving image, you make do with paint plastered across a moving surface, like a subway train: it's "art that can't stand still," that "climbs across your eyeballs night and day, the flickery jumping art of the slums and dumpsters, flashing those colors in your face—like I'm your movie, motherfucker" (*U* 441).

These art forms move and even begin to move into one another, graffiti into film or video, and everyday programs, like the market report on the business channel, into performance art, which then loops back to graffiti. Here is Ismael watching one such business report, the letters moving across the ticker tape, the underband, as it were, like a series of subway cars tagged with numbers and letters:

He loves the language of buying and selling and the sight of those clustered sets of letters that represent enormous corporate entities with their jets and stretches and tanker fleets. ... Electronics slightly up, transports down, industrials more or less unchanged. (*U* 814)

Photography

I looked at a million photographs because this is the dot theory of reality, that all knowledge is available if you analyze the dots. ... Reality doesn't happen until you analyze the dots.

U 175, 182

Why do these photographs have a power to disturb him, make him sad? Flat, pale, washed in time, suspended outside the particularized gist of this or that era, arguing nothing, clarifying nothing, lonely.

L 183

In a mosque, no images. In our world we sleep and eat the image and pray to it and wear it too.

M 37

Given everything that has already been said about doubling and duplicity, about seeing oneself at a distance or seeing oneself as another, a special place has to be reserved for photography. Already in *Americana* photographs are central, plastered everywhere (*A* 14, 63, 79). We are not even a hundred pages into this first novel when we see a young man kneeling down as if to worship a photograph, though he is really just taking a photograph of it, while everyone else—including David Bell—watches on with reverence. It happens in the lobby of the building in which Bell works:

> In a far corner there was an exhibit of prize-winning war photographs. One of them was an immense color blow-up, about ten feet high and twenty feet wide. In the center of the picture was a woman holding a dead child in her arms, and behind her and on either side were eight other children; some of them looked at the woman while others were smiling and waving, apparently at the camera. A young man was down on one knee in the middle of the lobby, photographing the photograph. I stood behind him for a moment and the effect was unforgettable. Time and distance were annihilated and it seemed that the children were smiling

and waving at him. Such is the prestige of the camera, its almost religious authority, its hypnotic power to command reverence from subject and bystander alike, that I stood absolutely motionless until the young man snapped the picture. (*A* 86)

And already in *Americana* photographs are juxtaposed not only with what is outside them but with one another, put in contraband, photographs of war, for example, set in counterpoint to advertisements:

I sat on the rim of the tub and flipped through a magazine article about the war. Each page of the article was adorned with color photographs. Opposite a picture of several decapitated villagers was a full-page advertisement for a kind of new panty-girdle. (*A* 104)

Just a list of the different *kinds* of photographs in DeLillo would be long, everything from "blow-ups of still photographs" (*A* 14) and "group photos" (*A* 63; see 79) to the family photo albums (*WN* 30, *LL* 94, "*S*" 189), travel photographs (*FM* 148, 157, 194; or slides, see *U* 473, 493), spy and FBI photos, for example, "an 8 × 10 police photo" of Lenny Bruce's "bloated body"—a little treasure in the "personal files" of J. Edgar Hoover (*U* 574)—"autopsy photos," then, of the rich and famous, sold as memorabilia (*U* 319), photographs of hostages, alive or dead—the vehicles for terrorists to express their demands or to command attention (*M* 164)—even photos in magazines used as "inspiration" for adolescent boys, "a photo of Jayne Mansfield," for example, (we're talking the 1950s) "with her knockers coming out of a sequined gown" (*U* 515), or "photographs of great and near great scientists" (*RS* 20; see 303), Enrico Fermi, for example, in the local library named after him, a photograph "showing the scientist with an early model of the first atomic bomb" (*U* 232), or entertainers, musicians, like a picture of "Charlie Parker in a white suit in some club somewhere. Great, great, great picture" (*U* 326), or photographs of famous ballplayers, such as those that capture the two ends of the Shot Heard 'Round the World, "a photograph of President Carter and his daughter what's-her-name standing in the Rose Garden with Bobby Thomson and Ralph Branca, a strained smile on every face" (*U* 323) and a similar photograph with President Reagan (*U* 190; see 466, 528), or photographs of the legendary game itself, that Giants-Dodgers game of October 1951 in the Polo Grounds (*U* 53), or a picture of Klara Sax, though she cannot recognize herself in it, at the famous Black & White Ball—"What is it about this picture that makes it so hard for me to remember myself?" (*U* 79) Finally—in order to bring this list to a more or less arbitrarily conclusion—there are passport photos, different from most of these others because they are "snapped anonymously, images rendered by machine" (*FM* 142). For Martin Ridnour (who himself no doubt has another passport under the name "Ernst Hechinger"), these "old passport photos," enlarged, are themselves works of art, "faces looking out of a sepia distance, lost in time" (*FM* 141), another form of reproduced or reproducible art, somewhere between governmental information gathering and the art of photography (*FM* 209).

> This is where she [Lianne] found innocence and vulnerability, in the nature of old passports, in the deep texture of the past itself, people on long journeys, people now dead. Such beauty in faded lives, she thought, in images, words, languages, signatures, stamped advisories. (*FM* 142)

Of course, the most famous, most talked and written about photo in all of DeLillo is the photograph of the sign touting "THE MOST PHOTOGRAPHED BARN IN AMERICA" (*WN* 12), a tourist attraction whose status comes not from the barn being photographed but from the photographs of the sign, the sign of "The most photographed barn in America" becoming the most photographed sign of "The most photographed barn in America," the most photographed sign thereby lending its authority to the most photographed barn and, one would like to think, to the barn itself, though in the end no one really even looks at the barn. As Murray Siskind says, "We're not here to capture an image, we're here to maintain one. Every photograph reinforces the aura" (*WN* 12). "What was the barn like before it was photographed?" … "We can't get outside the aura. We're part of the aura" (*WN* 13; see *WN* 89). It is the photo, therefore, not the thing, that now has the aura, which is why "they are taking pictures of taking pictures" (*WN* 13). It is close to a religious experience, not unlike the miraculous appearance of the face of a young girl, recently murdered, on a billboard in New York:

> Being here is a kind of spiritual surrender. We see only what the others see. The thousands who were here in the past, those who will come in the future. We've agreed to be part of a collective perception. This literally colors our vision. A religious experience in a way, like all tourism. (*WN* 12)

And then there is Oswald, using a box camera to take a picture of himself so that his daughter has something to "remember him by"—"his thin smile carried forward by light and time into the frame of official memory" (*L* 278-279).

> He posed in a corner of the yard, the rifle in his right hand, muzzle up, but end pressing on his waist, just inches from the holstered .38. The

magazines, the Militant and the Worker, were in his left hand, fanned like playing cards. (*L* 278)

When it comes to Oswald and the assassination of JFK, this is, of course, just exhibit number one in the entire photo library that had to be reviewed by Nicholas Branch, everything from photographs of skulls sent to illustrate "exit velocities" (*L* 299) to pictures of Kennedy himself taken by people yelling out as the motorcade passed by, "Hey we want to take your picture" (*L* 398)—to say nothing of home movies, like the one made by a Dallas dressmaker standing on the abutment over Elm Street.

Pictures—that's where the truth is now, the reality of the thing. You just need to learn how to blow up the dots and read the reality behind or within them, like Matt Shay in *Underworld*, spending his time in the service analyzing the dots in military surveillance photographs, or Marvin Lundy looking for "amateur film footage" of the famous Giants-Dodgers game in order to identify the person who may have gotten hold of the legendary ball: "It was work of Talmudic refinement, zooming in and fading out, trying to bring a man's face into definition, read a woman's ankle bracelet engraved with a name" (*U* 177).

Photographs are like little contrabands of narrative in their own right, which is why they often begin or end or else frame a DeLillo work. Take *Amazons*, for example, where family photos are mentioned in passing near the beginning of the novel, somewhat as a throwaway, it seems (*AZ* 37), only to return at the very end. Our narrator, Cleo Birdwell, the first woman to play in the National Hockey League, has just seen a film crew in Central Park and wants "to stop and watch," for that is "how they make magic." But she thinks instead, "there's no time to dawdle. The Kramer is now" (*AZ* 385). She thus returns—as if heeding Barnett Newman's "The Sublime Is Now"—to her New York apartment to tend to her lover, former NHL player Shaver Stevens, who has been put to sleep for five solid months in a Kramer cube housed in her apartment. It is not quite the Convergence of *Zero K* but it's close. Shaver is not quite "on ice," but the effect is the same, and the sight of him in his Kramer cube inspires her to get her Kamera and a few rolls of film from the fridge (because that's where they needed to be kept in those days):

> That night, in bed, I thought of the pictures I have of myself. I have pictures of myself, a small girl, skating on the pond in Snowy Owl Glen. My skates are *white*. ... Maybe it was these pictures, and what they recalled, that gave me the idea of getting out my old Instamatic the next day. I blew the dust off it and found some rolls of color film

in the butter tray in the refrigerator. Then I took dozens of photos of Shaver in the Kramer cube. (*AZ* 389)

It was, Cleo says, "a serious idea, even profound, even pseudo profound," and the whole thing ends, the scene as well as the novel, with this: "Click" (*AZ* 390).

There are thus photographs everywhere in DeLillo, in pretty much every novel, but no novel has more reflections upon the nature of photography than *Mao II*. The two central characters are Bill Gray, a mildly accomplished and yet world famous novelist, and Brita Nilsson, whose project, in the beginning of the novel, is photographing famous—and preferably reclusive—authors, but who, by the end, has switched her photographic attention to hard-to-find terrorists (*M* 25; see 15). As Brita notes, "The writer's face is the surface of the work. It's a clue to the mystery inside" (*M* 26). When photographing someone, therefore, it is important for her to "obliterate the sure thing and come upon a moment of stealthy blessing" (*M* 41), a "stealthy blessing" that is always a reminder of death, the contraband to every photograph of a living subject. As Bill Gray himself knows, the photographs that Brita is taking of him do not simply precede his death but declare it in advance: "These pictures are the announcement of my dying" (*M* 43). Taken in the present, they are already destined for the future or are already in the future, already their own archival replacement: "They're here but also there, already in the albums and slide projectors, filling picture frames with their microcosmic bodies, the minikin selves they are trying to become" (*M* 10). As Bill the novelist says, himself doubling as a pretty good theorist of photography:

> Sitting for a picture is morbid business. A portrait doesn't begin to mean anything until the subject is dead. ... The deeper I pass into death, the more powerful my picture becomes. Isn't this why picture-taking is so ceremonial? It's like a wake. And I'm the actor made up for the laying-out. (*M* 42)

In *Mao II* there are yet other examples of this essential technology in the age of mechanical reproduction, photographs in old magazines like *Life* and *Look*, "the generosity of those old covers, the way they seem a pity and a consolation" (*M* 146), but especially photographs of crowds, as if the individual had become something else in the age of photographic reproduction, crowds of refugees (*M* 147), crowds in agony (*M* 174), crowds after the death of the Ayatollah Khomeini, throngs following the body, aerial shots and shots from the ground (*M* 188–189), and then photographs, as we saw earlier, on walls and T-shirts used to consolidate the power of terrorist groups (see *M* 231).

While the novel begins with people taking photographs of the Moonie wedding in Yankee Stadium in NYC, it ends with someone photographing a wedding in Beirut:

> Someone is out there with a camera and a flash unit. Brita stays on the balcony for another minute, watching the magnesium pulse that brings an image to a strip of film. She crosses her arms over her body against the chill and counts off the bursts of relentless light. The dead city photographed one more time. (*M* 241)

We are talking about Beirut here as "the dead city photographed," but since this was the time when it was popular to say that New York was "just like Beirut," the light seems to flash—as it does so often in DeLillo—in two places at once or in the same place at two different times. So it is that Scott, Bill Gray's assistant, tries to capture something about Bill's writing through a reference, once again, to the Bronx-born photographer Garry Winogrand—yet another Garry (for there are many in DeLillo, though this one has more r's than usual) and yet another connection to the Bronx. After Brita speaks of "sentences with built-in memories," Scott says:

> When I read Bill I think of photographs of tract houses at the edge of a desert. There's an incidental menace. That great Winogrand photo of a small child at the head of a driveway and the fallen tricycle and the storm shadow on the bare hills. (*M* 51)

It's probably a pretty good insight about Bill Gray, and if Scott had read DeLillo he would have had even more reason to think of Winogrand, not just because of falling man, as we saw, but because of that same tricycle, featured at the end of both *White Noise* and *Ratner's Star*, tricycles that, after all the oppositions and all the binaries, are always near the end of a DeLillo novel, never far from the miracle, right there as the wheels are about to come off or the sun is about to set.

Film

We don't need Bibles. We have movies. Anytime we want, we can see Charlton Heston in chains.

RS 21

> "Who was the greatest influence on your life?" he said in a hostile tone. "Richard Widmark in Kiss of Death. When Richard Widmark pushed that old lady in that wheelchair down that flight of stairs, it was like a personal breakthrough for me."
>
> WN 214

> The modern sensibility had been instructed by a different kind of code. Movement. The image had to move.
>
> RD 80

From *Americana* to *Zero K* to the short story "The Starveling" there are movies, videos, newsreels, in short, moving images of all shapes and kinds, the quintessential twentieth-century contraband medium. David Bell remarks just three pages into *Americana*, setting the stage for everything to follow: "The war was on television every night but we all went to the movies" (*A* 5; see *DR* 62). Not even ten pages later, there is a reference to "American pyramids" like Kirk Douglas and Burt Lancaster (*A* 12), "Kirk as Van Gogh. Burt as the Birdman of Alcatraz" (*A* 59), but especially Burt as Sergeant Warden in *From Here to Eternity*, a movie that takes place on the eve of the Second World War and begins—nice coincidence—on a military base in Hawaii outside "The Day Room." It was seeing Burt on the Hawaiian beach with Deborah Kerr that caused David Bell to feel, as he says, "for the first time in my life … the true power of the image. … I carry that image to this day. … Burt in the moonlight. It was a concept; it was the icon of a new religion" (*A* 12–13). That no doubt explains why this film returns so regularly, almost like a ritual, throughout *Americana* (*A* 144, 192, 309) and then again in *Running Dog* (*RD* 42). And it no doubt also explains the relationship between pyramids and light, pyramids as stars and stars as pyramids. David Bell says he once saw that light and that pyramid in person:

> There was a movie I had to see. I sat through it twice. … In my mind he would be forever caught in that peculiar gray silveriness of the movie screen, his body radiating a slight visual static. I saw him in person once at Yankee Stadium. … I was glad I had not asked anyone to come to the movies with me. This was religion and it needed privacy. (*A* 135)

"American pyramids," says David Bell, an image that returns in *Great Jones Street*: "The whole concept of movies is so fundamentally Egyptian. Movies are dreams. Pyramids. Great rivers of sleep. The great and the glamorous with their legendary sphinxlike profiles" (*GJ* 73). Pyramids, monuments, and, perhaps, dreams of immortality: we should probably not be surprised to see a reference to pyramids and to dreams of immortality—yet again in the desert, and yet again with movies in the background—in *Zero K* (see *ZK* 76).

As David Bell says in *Americana*: "Once again, as on so many occasions in my life, I was stirred by the power of the image" (*A* 31). A "child of Godard and Coca-Cola" (*A* 269)—that is a description not only of David Bell in *Americana* but, it seems, of DeLillo himself, who packs his novels with cinematic references, beginning with Godard, his *Breathless* (*A* 277), for example, but then also Fellini (*A* 287), Antonioni (*A* 220), and Kurosawa, *Seven Samurai* (*L* 178; see 145, 295) and the famous closing scene of *Ikiru*, Watanabe on a swing in the snow (*A* 287; see 248, 290), along with actors like Belmondo (*A* 287), Bogart (*A* 287), Lauren Bacall (*A* 161), Gregory Peck (*L* 229), John Wayne (*L* 93), and Richard Conte—careful here, "the early Richard Conte" (*RD* 177; see *A* 161).

Movies are—or at least were—the closest thing Americans (though not just Americans) have to a common culture, from certain iconic images to the most obscure trivia, like "famous movie cowboys and the names of their horses" (see *N* 55). Movies are thus referred to and described throughout DeLillo, passing references to people with a "*film noir* face" (*WN* 214), to cheapo 50s movies (*P* 205), "B-movies, TV movies, rural drive-in movies," and movies featuring car crashes, "part of a long tradition of American optimism. ... full of the old 'can-do' spirit" (*WN* 218).

At Leighton Gage, David Bell was himself, we must not forget, in a film studies program and he made films that sound a lot like the novels that DeLillo would eventually write. Bell's junior thesis, for example, was "a thirty-minute film ... about a man who goes into the desert and buries himself in the sand up to his neck" (*A* 32; see 146), a scenario reminiscent of the ending of *Running Dog*. Bell even talks of the way film is able to isolate and free things from history and death in a way that sounds, decades in advance, a bit like *Point Omega*:

> Merry and I explored the desert and I did a lot of filming. ... Through the camera lens passed the light of a woman's body. I felt I could do things never done before. A hawk glanced off the sun and I plucked it out of space and placed it in the new era, free of history and death. (*A* 33)

In the early pages of *Americana* we see David Bell at once making short films for a TV network and describing his life in cinematic terms: "I became involved in the actual production of shows. Meanwhile, life with Merry went on the same way, a blend of jump-cuts and soft-focus tenderness" (*A* 37); "it was all there but the soundtrack and I could imagine a series of cuts and slow dissolves working in Merry's mind" (*A* 36; see 101). Much of *Americana* will thus revolve around Bell making a movie—"Dave Bell's my name; cinematography's my game" (*A* 222)—part documentary, part home movie, a genre difficult to describe, though it perhaps resembles what is described in *Valparaiso*, a sort of 16 mm 8 ½:

> A feature-length documentary film. A self-commenting super-vérité—okay—in which everything that goes into the making of the film *is* the film. Everything that leads up to the film and flows out of the film *is* the film. Including the film. A film that what? That consumes itself as the audience watches. (*V* 36)

In the end, this is probably a better description of the novel *Americana* than it is of the film inside it.

But Bell is just the first in a long series of moviemakers in DeLillo. In *The Body Artist* there is Rey Robles, whose obituary following his suicide details his relatively successful cinematic career: Rey Robles, 64, born Alejandro Alquezar, cinema's Poet of Lonely Places, who "directed two world-renowned movies of the late 1970s," *My Life for Yours* and *Polaris*. Once, "at the Cannes Film Festival, Mr. Robles told an appreciative audience, 'The answer to life is the movies'" (*BA* 27–29). And then there is Jim Finley in *Point Omega*, who had made just one prior film, on Jerry Lewis (*PO* 25–26), but who now wants to make a film with Richard Elster about the Iraq War, about "his time in government, in the blat and stammer of Iraq" (*PO* 21). His plan is to make a simple movie, "no plush armchair with warm lighting and books on a shelf in the background. Just a man and a wall … A simple head shot" (*PO* 21; see 45). Again, it's not unlike David Bell's own film in *Americana*: "The camera's on a tripod. I sit alongside. You look at me, not at the camera. I use available light. Is there noise from the street? We don't care. This is primate film-making. The dawn of man" (*PO* 71).

In *The Names* we are treated to long discourses about film from Frank Volterra, a filmmaker and an old friend of James Axton and, James suspects, an even better old friend of his estranged wife (*N* 106). A bit reminiscent of Brand or Bell from *Americana*, he went to film school at NYU and had written plenty of "unfinished scripts" when he suddenly showed up in Greece to film the cult *Ta Onómata*. For him, everything was about "film": "This is what there was, to shoot film, cut film, screen it, and talk about it" (*N* 109–110).

If the desert is always important in DeLillo, a space in contraband to the city, it is in part because of its cinematic quality. In *The Names*, Volterra, in Jordan and hot on the trail of the language cult, sees a natural connection between film and the desert:

> The desert fits the screen. It is the screen. Low horizontal, high verticals. People talk about classic westerns. The classic thing has always been the space, the emptiness. The lines are drawn for us. All we have to do is insert the figures, men in dusty boots, certain faces. Figures in open space have always been what film is all about. American film. (*N* 198)

This seems to confirm David Bell's claim in *Americana* that "the true subject of film" is "space itself, how to arrange it and people it" (*A* 240). That's why Volterra wants to film the cult, which, in its simplicity, in its singular focus on letters and murder, has pared things down to the minimum:

> You have a strong bare place. Four or five interesting and mysterious faces. A strange plot or scheme. A victim. A stalking. A murder. Pure and simple. I want to get back to that. It'll be an essay on film, on what film is, what it means. (*N* 199)

It is thus Volterra who gives one of the clearest expressions imaginable of the contraband principle: "We've come to a certain point in the history of film. If a thing can be filmed, film is implied in the thing itself. This is where we are. The twentieth century is *on film*. It's the filmed century" (*N* 200).

If a thing *can* be filmed, then film is *implied* in the thing; if a thing is *filmable*, then it has in a sense already been filmed. In short, when everything *can* be filmed, when everything is *virtually* on film, contrabanded in principle if not in fact, then there is no longer any stark difference between what is filmed and what is not. That's the logic that Volterra uses to try to convince the cult members to allow themselves to be filmed:

> The whole world is on film, all the time. Spy satellites, microscopic scanners, pictures of the uterus, embryos, sex, war, assassinations, everything. I can't believe these people won't instantly see they belong on film. Instantly. I want them to film some of it themselves. ... I want them to recite alphabets. Strange things. Whatever they do, whatever they say and do. It'll be like nothing you know. (*N* 200)

Film thus contrabands the world and, in a sense, begins to replace the world, becoming independent of it. That seems to be the final step in the argument and the process:

> Film is not part of the real world. This is why people will have sex on film, commit suicide on film, die of some wasting disease on film, commit murder on film. They're adding material to the public dream. There's a

sense in which film is independent of the filmmaker, independent of the people who appear. (*N* 203)

There are movie stars, moviemakers, and then moviegoers, Oswald, for example, on a "movie binge" in Atsugi, Japan, where he is stationed (*L* 112), or, when John Wayne is visiting the troops there, wanting "to get close to John Wayne, say something authentic" (*L* 93). Lee and Marina even name their second child Audrey after Audrey Hepburn in *War and Peace* (*L* 388)—you can't get more cinematic or more American or more American-Russian than that. There is Klara Sax's partner at the beginning of *Underworld*, Miles Lightman—a decent name for a movie buff—who "worked for a movie distributor part-time and also produced documentaries, or co-produced, or made phone calls" (*U* 378). He might not be the "catch" that Carlo Strasser will be, but he "saw everything, collected movie posters and lobby cards, could recite the filmographies of the obscurest directors because the more obscure the figure, of course, the more valuable the knowledge" (*U* 378). He would have probably gotten along well with Wendy Judd, a former classmate of David Bell, who would have given her left arm "to get the back of her head in a movie, her revolutionary fist raised in a Bastille crowd scene" (*A* 145).

"The Starveling" actually features a character who spends his whole waking life going to movies and taking notes in order "to dream away a grim memory of childhood, some misadventure of adolescence" ("S" 187; see 201). The character's life is marked not by major events like family births, marriages, and deaths but by film memories, like *Apocalypse Now*, "the day it opened, over thirty years ago, the nine-twenty a.m. show" ("S" 199) and then "the day, decades later, when Brando died" ("S" 199; see 208, *A* 315). In the course of the story, this character discovers and then follows, stalks, really, a young woman who seems to be doing the same thing, going to movies every day, all day, treating film like theatergoers in *The Day Room* treat the Arno Klein theater company or like collectors of Nazi memorabilia treat the rumored Hitler film: "She will devote her energies to finding and seeing the elusive masterwork, damaged print, missing footage, running time eleven hours, twelve hours, nobody seems sure, a privileged act, a blessing" ("S" 198). Obsessed, just like the main character, "she lies in bed, eyes open, and replays scenes from the day's films, shot by shot" ("S" 198). It sounds romantic, a relationship made in cinematic heaven, but it will turn pretty creepy by the end.

And then there's the Bronx connection: "Stanley Kubrick grew up in the Bronx. ... Tony Curtis, the Bronx" ("S" 209). Interestingly, those frozen and preserved in the Convergence would have their memories not only left intact but enhanced by means of these very films, through "nano-units implanted in the suitable receptors of the brain. ... the films of Bergman, Kubrick, Kurosawa, Tarkovsky" (*ZK* 72)—in addition, of course, while they're at all, to "classic works of art. Children reciting nursery rhymes in many languages. The propositions of Wittgenstein, an audiotext of logic and philosophy. ... the intertwined structures of music and mathematics ... the plays of Ibsen ... the rivers and streams of sentences in Hemingway" (*ZK* 72).

Such movies are—or at least were—part of our common culture. As such, our references to them often reveal more about ourselves than we might like. Here's a little exchange about film between Nick Shay, just back from seeing his coworker Brian Glassic, and his wife Marian, who happens to be having a secret affair with Brian. Marian asks off-handedly about Brian: "Did he recommend another movie where everybody ends up in a storm sewer shooting each other?" (*U* 115) The comment is meant to conceal the affair, to deflect attention from it, but the title of the film that Marian seems to be describing seems to point right back to it: *The Third Man*.

In addition to all these references to film in DeLillo, there are movies that are, as it were, "screened" in his novels, that is, described, narrated, sometimes frame by frame, the Hitler film in *Running Dog*, Eisenstein's *Unterwelt* and then *Cocksucker Blues* in *Underworld*, *Psycho* (as mediated by the *24 Hour Psycho* exhibit) in *Point Omega*, and, in the preface to *Players*, an in-flight movie playing in the background of a piano bar on the upper level of a jetliner.

The in-flight movie is itself, of course, an advanced form of contraband, "little floating memories of earth" in a metal container moving at some five hundred miles an hour (*M* 165). In *Players*, the eight-page preface, entitled simply "The Movie," is a sort of cameo that lays out the major themes of the novel—wealth, violence, terrorism—in a classic DeLillo back-and-forth between the grizzly scene in the film, terrorists attacking wealthy golfers on a golf course, and the pleasant banter of passengers in the piano bar of the luxury liner (*P* 8). It's a beautifully choreographed contrabanded narrative at 35,000 feet, neatly delimited in time and space, the movie within the plane and the plane within the novel. It's contraband as contrast and disruption, where "the simple innocence of this music"—you can almost hear the tinkling of the piano keys—"undermines the photogenic terror, reducing it to an empty swirl" (*P* 8). And in addition to all of that, it creates a kind of complicity between the camera and the audience, which can sometimes see coming what those in the film cannot, the camera bestowing upon the audience the status of "privileged onlookers" (*P* 6; see *P* 178).

This preface to *Players* is echoed in the novel's final pages, a sort of codicil entitled "The Motel," which narrates in very cinematographic terms what is happening to the main character. It is as if we were not reading what is happening but watching it on a screen or hearing the director as he tries to capture what he wants on film, right down to the final fade-out and "Cut!":

> We watch him stand by the bed. ... There's a splatter of brightness at one edge of the window. Minutes and inches later, sunlight fills the room. ... The angle of light is direct and severe, making the people on the bed appear to us in a special framework. ... The propped figure, for instance, is barely recognized as male. Shedding capabilities and traits by the second, he can still be described (but quickly) as well-formed, sentient and fair. We know nothing else about him. (*P* 210–212)

As we saw earlier in our discussion of "Erotica," *Running Dog* revolves around a rumored sex film of Hitler in his bunker during his last days in Berlin. This connection between film and the Nazis, and Hitler in particular, is, of course, hardly accidental. Jack Gladney would often screen Nazi propaganda films in his Nazism 101 classes, films with "no narrative voice. Only chants, songs, arias, speeches, cries, cheers, accusations, shrieks" (*WN* 26). For the Nazis, as we know, were film crazy. Lightborne recalls in *Running Dog*:

> You have the fact that movies were screened for him all the time in Berlin and Obersalzburg, sometimes two a day. Those Nazis had a thing for movies. They put everything on film. Executions, even, at his personal request. Film was essential to the Nazi era. Myth, dreams, memory. He liked lewd movies too, according to some. Even Hollywood stuff, girls with legs. (*RD* 52)

We eventually get an almost frame-by-frame description of that Hitler movie, which doesn't quite live up to its erotic billing but is nonetheless "compelling," "primitive and blunt, yet hypnotic, not without an element of mystery" (*RD* 227). At first we see children and adults in the bunker just sitting and talking, though there's an obvious attempt at a montage, with posing and props. Again, it is not completely un-David Bell-like: very simple, just people talking, "one and only take of each scene" (*RD* 228). As for the audience, it sees from the point of view of the camera and so sees things in the frame that those in the frame cannot, as if they were already meant for another time:

> This footage has the mysterious aura of an event that cuts across time. This is because the man, standing beyond the doorway, is not yet visible to the audience of adults and children in the immediate vicinity. The other audience, watching in a dark room in New York in the 1970s, is

aware of this, and they feel a curious sense of preview. They are seeing the man "first." (*RD* 234)

It is a filmic event that, by being doubled, is counterbanded in time, at once singular and plural, unique and yet immediately double-banded. For the film then shows Hitler, but Hitler imitating Chaplin—Hitler and Chaplin, born within just a day of one another, as chance would have it (*RD* 235): "He produces an expression, finally—a sweet, epicene, guilty little smile. Charlie's smile. An accurate reproduction" (*RD* 236). Hitler imitating Chaplin is thus the contraband to Chaplin contrabanding Hitler in *The Great Dictator*, a film described earlier in the novel: "*The dictator sits on his desk, holding a large globe in his left hand. A classic philosophical pose*" (*RD* 60). It is thus a movie capturing a figure imitating a movie depicting an imitation of that figure—a bit as if Hitler were the most photographed dictator in history because of "The Great Dictator." And talk about contrabanding, there is in DeLillo yet another "Chaplinesque figure, skating along the edges of vast and dangerous events" (*L* 194), another moviegoer who also imagines himself in the movies, and his name is Lee Harvey Oswald: "His peculiar smile appeared, the little smirk that made George think of a comedian in a silent film with the screen going dark around his head" (*L* 289).

But that's not all, for the screening of the Hitler film is itself interrupted by or juxtaposed with another narrative featuring Selvy in Texas, confronting his assassins in an abandoned training camp in what looks more and more like an American Western (see *RD* 229–234): "These bursts of unexpected color. The beauty of predators. / Strong sense of something being played out. Memory, a film. Rush of adolescent daydreams. He'd been through it in his mind a hundred times, although never to the end" (*RD* 239). All this seems to conform to what David Bell suggested in *Americana*: "Defeat is always glorious on film. The loser is ennobled by suffering and death. No camera can resist the man going down to defeat" (*A* 315).

In *Underworld* there is a semi-private screening of "a Robert Frank film, *Cocksucker Blues*, about the Rolling Stones on tour in America" (*U* 382). DeLillo puts his own description into the head of Klara Sax, a description that focuses, not surprisingly, on light: "She loved the washed blue light of the film, a kind of crepuscular light, a tunnel light that suggested an unreliable reality," and then "the concert footage that's gelled red, bodies bioluminescent, what we all love about rock, Klara thought, the backlit nimbus of higher dying" (*U* 382–383, 84).

Then there's the showing of the eponymous film of *Underworld* itself, not "the other *Underworld*, a 1927 gangster film and box office smash" (*U* 431), but "the legendary lost film of Sergei Eisenstein, called *Unterwelt*, recently found in East Germany, meticulously restored and brought to New York" (*U* 424). The screening thus itself becomes an event, with "tickets going for shocking sums and counterfeit tickets and people rushing back from the Vineyard and the Pines and the Cape to engineer a seat" (*U* 425–426). Like the Hitler film in *Running Dog*, it is made up by DeLillo not out of whole cloth but pieced together out of other Eisenstein films and things we know about the director, a film "probably shot in the midthirties, sporadically and in secret, during a period of acute depression for Eisenstein" (*U* 424–425). Of course, in the description of the film itself, the film that DeLillo is inventing, we learn as much about DeLillo as about Eisenstein:

> In Eisenstein you note that the camera angle is a kind of dialectic. Arguments are raised and made, theories drift across the screen and instantly shatter—there's a lot of opposition and conflict. / It seems that you are watching a movie about a mad scientist. … Figures move through crude rooms in some underground space. They are victims or prisoners, perhaps experimental subjects. … The plot was hard to follow. There was no plot. Just loneliness, barrenness, men hunted and ray-gunned, all happening in some netherland crevice. (*U* 429–430)

The film reminds Klara of "radiation monsters in Japanese science-fiction movies," and it causes her to ask: "Was Eisenstein being prescient about nuclear menace or about Japanese cinema?" (*U* 430) In retrospect, if one can say this about prescience, he seems to have been prescient about both, to say nothing about DeLillo's own *Underworld* and, why not, *Zero K*, for it is as if this were already a film about the Convergence: "You wonder if he shot these scenes in Mexico, or could it be Kazakhstan, where he went to shoot *Ivan the Terrible*, later, during the war? … These deformed faces, these were people who existed outside nationality and strict historical context" (*U* 443). Finally, there is a sort of summary statement about the film, one that sounds like the theory of band and contraband that we have been following throughout this work:

> All Eisenstein wants you to see, in the end, are the contradictions of being. You look at the faces on the screen and you see the mutilated yearning, the inner divisions of people and systems, and how forces will clash and fasten, compelling the swerve from evenness that marks a thing lastingly. (*U* 444)

Point Omega also features film, in this case a feature film, but one that is itself contrabanded in a work of art. The novel begins at an exhibit at the

MOMA in New York featuring a video projection of the classic film *Psycho* slowed down to 2 frames per second (rather than 24) so that it would run over the course of twenty-four hours. The slow motion reminds DeLillo's reader, of course, of the Zapruder film, another murder caught on screen, but here it's Douglas Gordon's 1993 video work *24 Hour Psycho*, "Not a movie but a conceptual art piece" (*PO* 47). It's the original film but "without dialogue or music, no soundtrack at all" (*PO* 4). Slowed down like this, it was close to "pure film, pure time" (*PO* 6). The original is something familiar, "a common experience to be relived on TV screens, at home, with dishes in the sink" (*PO* 12), but in the exhibit version one can see both sides of the screen, making right and left shift sides, allowing one to see the film from, as it were, the contrabanded side, though "what made this side of the screen any less truthful than the other side?" (*PO* 4; see *RS* 408) Slowed down, broken down, in this way, Anthony Perkins just "turning his head ... was like whole numbers. ... It was like bricks in a wall, clearly countable, not like the flight of an arrow or a bird" (*PO* 5). Through this surfeit of technology, "the action becomes something near to elemental life" (*PO* 10), "like watching the universe die over a period of about seven billion years" (*PO* 47). And then, to add one more band, because it's an exhibit one can watch not only the film but others watching the film or others watching the watching of others (*PO* 105).

We compare our lives to the lives of those in film, and we think of our lives as lives to be filmed. DeLillo's narrators tend to do this, and so do his characters. Throughout *End Zone*, for example, the language of cinema is used to describe everything from the movements of an individual ("I moved about not as myself but as some sequence from the idea of motion" (*EZ* 62)) to the action of a football game: "In slow motion the game's violence became almost tender, a series of lovely and sensual assaults. The camera held on the fallen men, on men about to be hit, on those who did the hitting" (*EZ* 98). Same thing in *Amazons*, where an original gesture is already doubled by what seems to be an even more "original" voice-over: "He picked up the glass with both hands, the way people hold steaming mugs of cocoa at ski resorts in movies made for TV" (*AZ* 124). Ditto for *Mao II*: "Everything around us tends to channel our lives toward some final reality in print or on film. Two lovers quarrel in the back of a taxi and a question becomes implicit in the event. Who will write the book and who will play the lovers in the movie?" (*M* 43–44; see 91).

The Body Artist is almost a study in the contrabanding of life and film, life as it is lived as life as it would be filmed: "When the phone rang she did not look at it the way they do in the movies. Real people don't look at ringing phones" (*BA* 34).

She thought of a man showing up unexpectedly. ... a man appearing suddenly, as in a movie, and he is shot from below. Not shot but photographed. Not shot-shot but captured on motion picture film, from below, so that he looms. ... [And] she saw herself in the scene, in the driveway, listening to the man. It was just a passing thing, a story she told herself, or screened, forgettably. (*BA* 78–79)

There are thus films throughout DeLillo's novels and then there are moments that are compared by either the narrator or characters to film. In *Falling Man* Lianne's mother "smoked a cigarette like a woman in the 1940s, in a gangster film, all nervous urgency, in black and white" (*FM* 114). And then there is Keith, returning to his building near the ruins of the World Trade Towers after the 9/11 attacks: "In the movie version, someone would be in the building, an emotionally damaged woman or a homeless old man, and there would be dialogue and close-ups" (*FM* 27). (If there ever is such a movie version, perhaps the emotionally damaged woman from *Great Jones Street* could be inserted here or, better, the woman in *Point Omega* who walks down stairs "backwards" (*PO* 37; see 81).) Same thing in *Underworld*: "In the movie version you'd freeze the frame with the dog in midleap about to snare the frisbee. A park on a summer's day somewhere in America—that would be the irony of the shot, with a solo guitar producing the bitter screech of feedback" (*U* 462). Each time, then, the movie is described in counterpoint or else is placed in counterpoint in the narrative—even if just for ironic effect: "And in the movie version of his life he imagined how everything is projected on a CinemaScope screen, all the secret things he did alone over the years" (*U* 517; see also 292–293, 338, 615).

Characters imagine themselves on screen. Oswald in Russia, suspected of being a US spy, imagines that the Russians "might shoot him in the courtyard, like a movie, to muffled drums" (*L* 191). Wayne Elko likes to think of himself as a character out of his favorite film, *Seven Samurai*, "in which free-lance warriors are selected one at a time to carry out a dangerous mission. In which men outside society are called on to save a helpless people from destruction. Swinging those two-handed swords" (*L* 178; see 145, 295). And as we saw earlier, Oswald not only watches movies on TV but even imagines that they are being screened just for him. So much does his life revolve around movies that he goes to the Texas Theater in Dallas just after the assassination in order, he thinks, to be spirited out of the country to Cuba, though Wayne Elko (like one of those Samurai) has been sent there to kill him—to shoot him when the sound in the theater got really loud. Why? "Because that's the way they do it in the movies" (*L* 412). And what was playing that afternoon, you might ask, because "whenever there's a famous finish in the vicinity of a movie house, it behooves you to know what's playing" (*L* 140): turns out to have been a double feature, *Cry of Battle*, with Van Heflin, and *War Is Hell* (*L* 411, 413).

Before turning to "home movies," a word has to be said about the home and movies, that is, about watching movies at home, a son, almost always, with his mother in front of the TV, or else mother and son leaving home for the movie theater. Just as he is about to confront the person who is trying to kill him, Eric Packer begins to think back and so begins to go back-and-forth, in typical DeLillo fashion, between the so-called present moment when he is about to kick down the door and confront his assassin and memories of the movies his mother took him to as a child, where, each time, a man with a gun drawn would kick down a door (*C* 183). And then there's little Billy Twillig's mother Faye, who seems also to have appreciated the obvious and yet frequently overlooked fact that movies take place in the dark—that is, in a sort of underworld:

> "Movies are the dreams I never had," Faye said. "I went everywhere and saw every picture, the greats and the stiffs, great and stiff alike. What's great is that they were all great, even the stiffs. Because they took place in the dark. ... Because it was like something you were remembering instead of seeing for the first time. We talked back to movies then. You could do that then." (*RS* 136; see *U* 711)

You watch movies with your mother and so movies will always remind you of your mother. Watching *24 Hour Psycho*, Jim Finley thinks about "the moment when Norman Bates will carry Mother down the stairs in her white bedgown," and that "makes him think of his own mother, how could it not, before she passed on, two of them contained in a small flat being consumed by rising towers" (*PO* 116). Film takes us back or takes us down, to the mother's room, to childhood. How else to explain the date chosen by David Bell to make his little home movie? "It was the eighth anniversary of my mother's death" (*A* 287).

All this to say that films take place always in some basement, some underworld, where another world materializes from out of the dark: "Movies take place in the dark. This seemed an obscure truth, just now stumbled upon" ("*S*" 206). It is a truth that DeLillo himself keeps on discovering or stumbling upon: "A two-dimensional city would materialize out of the darkness" (*RD* 225). It's not unlike the equally obscure truth that fictions take place through black letters on white pages, just a word or two and a person, a city, a landscape, or a world suddenly materializes.

Films thus transpire in a sort of underworld of their own, in their own time and space. When one comes out of that underworld, especially in the middle of the day, the effect can be disconcerting, the streets "all agitation and nasty glare, every surface intense and jarring, people in loud clothing that did not fit" (*U* 445). Same thing in *Running Dog*: "Movies in the afternoon. The rude surprise of sunlight when you emerge. What is this place? Why are these people so short and ugly? Look at the hard surfaces, the blatant flesh of things" (*RD* 244).

Much of *Americana* is the story of David Bell, who is supposed to be making a film for his TV network job, making instead a home movie as he drives out west with Pike and Sullivan, the latter a sort of surrogate mother: "We'll discover all the lost roads of America. I'm bringing my movie camera. We'll get it all on film" (*A* 49). Bell calls it "the strangest, darkest, most horrifying idea of my life," the "idea for a film I might make somewhere out there among the lost towns of America" (*A* 125). At the end of Part I of the novel, Bell takes his 16 mm Canon Scoopic and tape recorder and says, "West ... Aim her more or less to the west" (*A* 125). It's a home movie of sorts, but it has ambitions of being something more than that. It eventually turns into a long, elaborate quasi-autobiographical movie that uses the locals from a small town named Fort Curtis for its actors. Bell at one point films the quiet streets of Fort Curtis out the window of their moving car (see *A* 256), but most of the movie is a series of interviews with actors playing his advertising executive and Second World War veteran father, a POW in the Philippines, his sister and her mobster boyfriend, David Bell himself and his wife, and, especially, his mother. It's not unlike Bell's "Soliloquy" TV series, where "each show consisted, very simply, of an individual appearing before the camera for an hour and telling his life story" (*A* 24), and not unlike Jim Finley's projected film with Richard Elster in *Point Omega*. No plot, single camera positions, the entire film in black and white: "This whole thing is what is known in some circles as inspired amateurism" (*A* 240). And yet there is something deadly serious in the way the film brings mother, father, and son together. As Bell says:

> What I'm doing is kind of hard to talk about. It's a sort of first-person thing but without me in it in any physical sense, except fleetingly. ... Not quite autobiographical in the Jonas Mekas sense. ... The interview technique. The monologue. The anti-movie. The single camera position. The expressionless actor. The shot extended to its ultimate limit in time. (*A* 263)

As Bell later says, "The Fort Curtis episodes are only a small part of what eventually became a film in silence and darkness. ... I ended in silence and darkness, sitting still, a matter of objects that imitate my predilection"

(*A* 34–347). None of the objects are as large as the Empire State Building, the centerpiece of Warhol's film with Jonas Mekas, but they all are just as silent.

For Bell, film can be a way of capturing or dominating others, a way of getting a piece of them before they get a piece of you (see *A* 241). But it is also and especially a way of preserving others for the future, a way of assuring them a certain or uncertain—and always double-banded—survival:

> I took the camera from my lap, raised it to my eye, leaned out the window a bit, and trained it on the ladies as if I were shooting. ... Maybe they sensed that they were waving at themselves, waving in the hope that someday if evidence is demanded of their passage through time, demanded by their own doubts, a moment might be recalled when they stood in a dazzling plaza in the sun and were registered on the transparent plastic ribbon. ... there they stand, verified, in chemical reincarnation, waving at their own old age, smiling their reassurance to the decades, a race of eternal pilgrims in a marketplace in the dusty sunlight, seven arms extended in a fabulous salute to the forgetfulness of being. What better proof (if proof is ever needed) that they have truly been alive? Their happiness, I think, was made of this, the anticipation of incontestable evidence, and had nothing to do with the present moment, which would pass with all the others into whatever is the opposite of eternity. I pretended to keep shooting, gathering their wasted light, letting their smiles enter the lens and wander the camera-body seeking the magic spool, the gelatin which captures the image, the film which threads through the waiting gate. ... I could not help feeling that what I was discovering here was power of a sort. (*A* 254–255)

Bell doesn't film these seven ladies—they are all lost now (recuperated only in literature)—but he does film others and himself, and he imagines replaying the film some thirty years later after retrieving it from the underworld:

> The film is a sort of sub-species of the underground. What I'm shooting now is just a small segment of what will eventually include more general matter—funerals, traffic jams, furniture, real events, women, doors, windows. Auto-fiction. Actors, people playing themselves, lines of poetry. When I'm done I'd like to put the whole thing in a freezer and then run it uncut thirty years from now. (*A* 288–289)

Underground, funerals, traffic jams, auto-fiction: one hears already in 1971 at once *Underworld*, *Cosmopolis*, *The Body Artist*, and who knows what else ...

Bell's reference to "running" the film thirty years after gets taken to a new level later in the novel when David Bell, in the present, speaks to himself in the distant future, band and counterband superimposed upon one another. "It was his final scene. I sighted on him standing against the printed black words. Then I narrated, making it up as I went."

> The year is 1999. You are looking at a newsreel of an earlier time. A man is standing in a room in America. It is you, David, more or less. What can the two of you say to each other? How can you empty out the intervening decades? … You barely remember the man you're looking at. Ask him anything. He knows all the answers. That's why he's silent. (*A* 309)

It's a moment that seems to be anticipated much earlier in the novel, at a time when the narrator—now an author—looks back upon the events he will have narrated over the course of the novel:

> It's time now to run the film again. I mean that quite literally, for I still have in my possession a movie made in those years, and many tapes as well. There isn't much to do on an island this remote and I can kill (or rather redistribute) a fair amount of time by listening to the soundtrack and taking yet another look at some of the footage. (*A* 14)

The realization that movies take place in the dark seems to have as its correlate another stunningly obvious and yet easily overlooked truth: they happen because of light. Whether one is sitting at home or in a theater, something comes to light on the screen, something, more or less from nothing, just particles and pixels, somehow comes to light to make a world.

Videos, Home Movies, Newsreels

> *You know about families and their video cameras. You know how kids get involved, how the camera shows them that every subject is potentially charged, a million things they never see with the unaided eye. They investigate the meaning of inert objects and dumb pets and they poke at family privacy. They learn to see things twice.*
>
> *U* 155

> We're all on tape. All on tape. All of us.
>
> *A* 371

There are movies, therefore, the kind we see on TV or go to movie theaters for, and then there are, and more and more so, home movies, videos, and newsreels, amateur films made at little cost. Most of them are taken and watched once or twice, or else go unwatched altogether, only to disappear from memory and the archive. Some, however, survive and come to have an enduring power. Exhibit number one for this latter type is, hands down, the Zapruder film. Though *Libra* speaks about it and describes it, the film doesn't actually get "screened" until *Underworld*. It's 1974 and "a bootleg copy of an eight-millimeter home movie that ran about twenty seconds" has just emerged, "almost no one outside the government had seen it" (*U* 488). This is, of course, the little "home movie made by a dress manufacturer who stood on a concrete abutment above Elm Street as the shots were fired" (*L* 441; see also 400 for Zapruder, unnamed this time, unless it's not Zapruder but a newly discovered second cameraman on the abutment). More than a decade after it was shot, people are still shocked by what it captures:

> A woman seated on the floor spun away and covered her face because it was completely new, you see, suppressed all these years, this was the famous headshot and they had to contend with the impact. ... And oh shit, oh god it came from the front, didn't it? (*U* 488–489)

The film records in less than half a minute the entire assassination, all the shots from whatever angles. It is a film that captures one of the most important events in twentieth-century American history and yet it is also, at another level, a film about nothing other than light, a film about the capturing of light on film and the bringing to light of that light sometime in the future: "The footage seemed to advance some argument about the nature of film itself" (*U* 495–496).

The Zapruder film is an absolutely unique film about an absolutely unique and transformative event in US history. But in the theater of memory it plays right alongside another film, a newsreel this time, as if part of a double billing, Jack Ruby's killing of Lee Harvey Oswald on live TV just a couple of days later, an event that would be endlessly replayed in living rooms across America. As someone asks in *Libra*, "Why do they keep running it, over and over?" (*L* 446; see 414, 437) The answer is, of course, because of our fascination for the contraband, because of the tension between the band we recall in memory and the band we see being replayed, the one never completely overlapping with the other.

There's something similar in *Underworld* in the "famous videotape showing a driver being shot by the Texas Highway Killer," a video that one might watch on the TV news or else, by this time, on a personal computer, "enhanced and superslowed, trying to find some pixel in the data swarm that might provide a clue to the identity of the shooter" (*U* 118). The video, taken by a young girl "through the rear window of the family car at the windshield of the car behind her" (*U* 155), captures the moment the driver of another car is suddenly struck by a bullet. The tape is "jostled," "amateurish," but that's what gives it its "crude power" (*U* 156), and the camera itself inevitably puts the little girl "in the tale" (*U* 157), like the silent frame of a narrator's voice. There is the man driving the car, linked to the girl by the camera, the both of them unknowing, oblivious, the both of them about to be taken unawares by the thing we all now know is coming. That's why you cannot turn away, no matter how many times you've seen it:

> There's something here that speaks to you directly, saying terrible things about forces beyond your control, lines of intersection that cut through history and logic and every reasonable layer of human expectation. (*U* 157)

It's so engrossing, so irresistible, so real, that you want to share it with friends and family. When it's about to come on TV again you yell out, "Hur-ree u-up, here it co-omes" (*U* 217).

> You say to your wife, if you're at home and she is there, Now here is where he gets it. You say, Janet, hurry up, this is where it happens. ... It is awful and unremarkable at the same time. ... Here it comes all right. ... You want your wife to see it because it is real this time, not fancy movie violence. ... The way the camera reacts to the gunshot—a startle reaction that brings pity and terror into the frame, the girl's own shock, the girl's identification with the victim. (*U* 158)

There is the crime and there is the video of the crime; common sense would say that the second is simply there, accidentally, to record the first, the contraband there to repeat and archive the band. But DeLillo wonders whether the event's repetition is not somehow at the origin of the event itself. "This is a crime designed for random taping and immediate playing. You sit there and wonder if this kind of crime became more possible when the means of taping an event and playing it immediately ... became widely available" (*U* 159). And then, of course, there is not only the original crime and the endless repetition of it by video but also the inevitable "so-called copycat shooting" (*U* 272), because there is always someone who believes that contraband is the highest form of flattery.

The Zapruder film, the Texas Highway Killer video—those are just the two best known of the many videos in DeLillo's work, videos that are always more about the seeing than the seen. In *Mao II* we see kids in Beirut "looking at videos of the war in the streets." Why? Because "they wanted to see themselves in their scuffed khakis, the vivid streetwise troop, that's us, firing nervous bursts at the militia down the block" (*M* 110; see 143). In *The Body Artist* we see Lauren watching streaming video of a two-lane road in Kotka, a small town in Finland: "She didn't know the meaning of this feed but took it as an act of floating poetry. It was best in the dead times" (*BA* 38–39). It's an image prefigured in *Mao II*: "Cars run silently on the autobahns" (*M* 16). It's totally boring and absolutely absorbing, dull and yet oddly erotic: "She imagined that someone might masturbate to this, the appearance of a car on the road to Kotka in the middle of the night" (*BA* 38).

In *Cosmopolis* it's Eric Packer's own watch that begins to film his own end, allowing him—like Oswald—to watch himself die. But before that—still conscious after being shot—he is able to watch, in near real time, one final, radiant spectacle: "A zoom shot followed, showing a beetle on the wire, in slow transit. He studied the thing, mouthparts and forewings, absorbed by its beauty, so detailed and gleaming" (*C* 205).

Our century's interest in film and photography is, of course, of apiece with the themes of spycraft and surveillance that we looked at earlier. Is it paranoia or just very keen perception that makes a man in a NYC bar see "little cameras ... Tiny transmitters. ... everywhere" (*RD* 64), both inside the bar and out. (It could in fact be the very same guy in the very same bar, speaking of paranoia, who is heard in *Underworld* "moaning a bummed-out monologue that involved being followed wherever he went" (*U* 620).) Because they are indeed everywhere—cameras if not the people behind them:

> Go into a bank, you're filmed. Go into a department store, you're filmed. Increasingly we see this. Try on a dress in the changing room, someone's watching through a one-way glass. Not only customers, mind you. Employees are watched too, spied on with hidden cameras. Drive your car anywhere. Radar, computer traffic scans. They're looking into the uterus, taking pictures. Everywhere. What circles the earth constantly? Spy satellites, weather balloons, U-2 aircraft. What are they doing? Taking pictures. Putting the whole world on film. (*RD* 149–150)

This was written in 1978 or thereabouts, a time when there were powerful cameras (like the Minox, "the world-famous spy camera" (*L* 248)) but not yet security cameras on every corner or iPhones in every hand or live video feeds from more or less everywhere in the world (*C* 151). As for U-2s and other spy planes, we'll see them come back in *Libra*, and by the time we get to *Underworld* it will be satellites that are watching us, photographing us from space, perhaps already detecting "the unspoken emotions of the people in the rooms" (*U* 415).

Finally, there is *Zero K*, with its films or videos of natural disasters and wars, scenes of tornados, floods, and mass evacuations, projected onto large screens in the Convergence (*ZK* 11; see 121 and "S" 193). Jeffrey Lockhart, our narrator, feels he has to watch, "obligated to something or someone, the victims perhaps," himself the "lone witness, sworn to the task" (*ZK* 36). He eventually realizes, however, that he is watching not films or videos of real disasters but "a digital weave, every fragment manipulated and enhanced, all of it designed, edited, and redesigned. ... all of it computer-generated, none of it real" (*ZK* 152). Later there are scenes—this time maybe real or maybe not—of "troops in black-and-white ... striding out of the mist" (*ZK* 259), and then "masses of people carrying whatever possessions they can manage," and then "slaughtered men in a jungle clearing, vultures stepping among the corpses" (*ZK* 260). "It was awful and I watched," says Jeffrey (*ZK* 260), as if he were wandering around in Bruegel's *The Triumph of Death*, or a "worst of" retrospective of the evening news, things that could have happened centuries ago or just yesterday. Once again, it is not just the horror but the double-banded watching that seems to count:

> Hand-to-hand, six or seven men with knives and bayonets, some in camo jackets, concentrated bloodletting, up close. ... Facedown corpse on a potholed road, bomb debris everywhere. ... A woman in a chador, seen from the rear, stepping out of a car. ... camera pulling back, then the blast, purely visual, seeming to rip the screen apart and shred the air around us. All those watching. (*ZK* 261)

There's everything here from hand-to-hand combat to suicide bombings. We recognize all these images and scenarios: "It looks and sounds like traditional war, men in arms ... all the world wars embedded in these images, a soldier with a cigarette in his mouth, a soldier asleep in his bunker, a bearded soldier with a bandaged head" (*ZK* 262). It's like a replay of all the well-known scenes from all the old wars, all the "traditional wars," all motivated, it seems, by a kind of "warped nostalgia," because another, untraditional and even more apocalyptic war seems to be brewing on the horizon.

The films projected in the Convergence appear to be compilations of previous wars, classic war clips—films, videos, newsreel—juxtaposed with contemporary scenes of war, live or nearly live, for example, a young man fighting in Konstantinovka, Ukraine, "three times life size, here, above me, shot and bleeding, stain spreading across his chest ... eyes shut, surpassingly real." It could have been another war from another time but it's not this time: "It was Emma's son. It was Stak" (*ZK* 263). Jeffrey thus sees his girlfriend's son Stak, who had run away to join the Ukrainian forces, killed right there on the screen before his eyes, turning him from a mere spectator into a witness (*ZK* 272).

In *Americana*, the place from which we began this long look at film in DeLillo, there's a passage where Bell has the sense that everything he and others were doing had been done and experienced before. Instead of describing this in terms of déjà vu, however, he speaks of it all as having been on videotape, waiting to be rebroadcast (*A* 23). *Underworld* returns to this fantasy or this nightmare, the promise of a strange kind of witnessing or after-life footage that will reveal all the secrets of the past, all protections and prophylactics gone. It is Eric Deming who has the fantasy this time, imagining himself replaying the episode he starred in with Danny Anderson the day this latter gave him his first condom, "Danny Anderson ... who swore he'd never used it himself—a thing that wouldn't be fully established until both boys were dead and Eric had a chance to see the footage" (*U* 517). It's an amusing line, but it appears to be animated by the recognition, the dream or nightmare, that in the digitally visual age everything can be—and thus everything virtually is—filmable and archivable, repeatable or replayable. The whole world is watching, to be sure, and, today, the whole world is watched.

Music

Music is dangerous in so many ways. It's the most dangerous thing in the world.

GJ 46

It was the last techno-rave, the end of whatever it was the end of.

C 127

If, as we have seen, there are photographs and films and videos everywhere in DeLillo, there is also music, buskers in the New York Subway (*M* 187), a band playing "live Muzak" in *White Noise* (*WN* 84), a Kazakhstanian cult rock band in *Underworld* (*U* 785), music of all kinds and genres, therefore, beginning with jazz. For if there is one musical genre perfectly suited to describe the narrative contraband that is DeLillo's, it would have to be jazz, with its improvisations, riffs, jams, and instruments in counterpoint. Hence the references to Thelonious Monk (*L* 87), Sun Ra (*A* 350), Charles Mingus (*U* 205), Ornette Coleman (*A* 71), John Coltrane (*A* 144), and Charlie Parker (*U* 326), the same Charlie Parker who, in a sense, gets Ismael Muñoz started on graffiti:

> He saw a spray-paint scrawl, maybe five years ago, down under Eighth Avenue, *Bird Lives*. It made him wonder about graffiti, about who took the trouble and risk to walk down this tunnel and throw a piece across the wall, and how many years have gone by since then, and who is Bird, and why does he live? (*U* 435)

But there is also folk music and rock, Bob Dylan's "Subterranean Homesick Blues," for example—already, notice, the underworld theme—on a car radio (*A* 375; see *L* 124), and Sullivan, Bell's substitute mother, as his "sad-eyed lady of the lowlands" (*A* 289). There are the Beatles, of course, for how could there not be, and their "Revolution"—not Revolution Number 9, the one that repeats 9 for 9 minutes, but the one that speaks of carrying pictures of Chairman Mao (*M* 223)—and, again in *Mao II*, Louis Armstrong singing not "What a Wonderful World" or "Hello Dolly" but—an echo of that earlier contraband—"Mack the Knife" (*M* 211).

In *Underworld* there is, as we saw, the screening of both the Rolling Stones movie *Cocksucker Blues* (*U* 384) and, later, the Radio City Music Hall showing of Eisenstein's "Unterwelt," accompanied by a "tinny piano," then "patriotic music," "a medley of familiar marches with drum ruffles and sousaphones," with the Rockettes dancing or marching to the beat (*U* 427–428), and then, finally, "Prokofiev ... that Three Orange thing, whatever it's called. You've heard it a thousand times" (*U* 442).

But there is also in DeLillo, indeed even more vintage DeLillo, the music of crowds, the power and sway of music on crowds, the power of music beyond what it says, the power of sound beyond all meaning. "Music," says Hanes in *Great Jones Street*, "is dangerous in so many ways. It's the most dangerous thing in the world" (*GJ* 46). That's because it seems to exist "beyond the maps of language" (*GJ* 12; see 121). Bucky Wunderlick is even more eloquent about the power of his own music to go beyond all words and meaning:

> We're processing a natural force. Electricity is nature every bit as much as sex is nature. ... We process nature, which I personally regard as a hideous screeching bitch of a thing, being a city boy myself. ... The true artist makes people move. ... I'd like to injure people with my sound. Maybe actually kill some of them. (*GJ* 103–105)

Later in *Great Jones Street* there is a twenty-page narrative insert where DeLillo gets to try his hand at being a (mock) rock lyricist and critic, first coming up with the names of bands (like Schicklgruber (*GJ* 154)), band members, including Bucky Wunderlick, and song lyrics (like "Nothing turns from death as much as flesh" (*GJ* 101), or "It was love animal love" (*GJ* 108), or this one, from "Protestant Work Ethic Blues," "Waiting for the strength to take that existential leap" (*GJ* 110–111)). He, DeLillo, will thus pen the lyrics of Bucky's long-awaited Mountain Tapes (*GJ* 201–207) and then write stories and conduct interviews with Bucky about them, band contra Bucky's band.

In *Cosmopolis* the themes of music, repetition, crowds, and religion all converge as Eric Packer goes to a theater under restoration for what is billed as "The Last Techno-Rave." He watches the writhing bodies becoming one under the influence of music and the drug novo: "All the menace of electronica was in repetition itself. This was their music, loud, bland, bloodless and controlled, and he was beginning to like it" (*C* 127). But then comes something we see repeated elsewhere in DeLillo, a tendency for music in its most powerful incarnations to become not just celebration but lament, celebratory lament:

> The music took a turn toward dirge, with lyrical keyboard flourishes bridging every segment of regret. It was the last techno-rave, the end of whatever it was the end of. … It was tender and moving, to know them in their frailty, their wistfulness of being. (*C* 127–128)

After the rave, Eric leaves the theater district, enters Hell's Kitchen, and runs right into the funeral procession for Sufi rapper Brutha Fez with its thirty-six white stretch limos. Eric cannot help but see the connection, feel the proximity, between Fez and himself, the dead and the living: "It brought a clear emotion to the night, a joy of intoxicating wholeness, he and they, the dead and provisionally living. … There was rapture in this, fierce elation, and something else that was inexpressible, dropping off the edge" (*C* 135–136). Learning of the death of Fez, Eric says, "How can this be? I love his music. I have his music in my elevator. I know the man" (*C* 131). Yes, "He knew the man," and "the sadness, the plangency of this remark was echoed in the music itself, the *qawwali* model of devotional rhythms and improvisations, over a thousand years old" (*C* 131). We thus go from the death of a new musical form to death in an old one, and it all begins to have an effect on Packer, breaking him down, unpacking him, as it were, emptying him out. His "delight in going broke seemed blessed and authenticated here. He'd been emptied of everything but a sense of surpassing stillness, a fatedness that felt disinterested and free" (*C* 136). In the midst of the funeral procession for

Brutha Fez we thus get sentences that sound like fragments from the pre-Socratics, on the verge of Western philosophy, sentences like: "Because whirl is all. Whirl is the drama of shedding everything" (*C* 138). As always, the newest is contrabanded with the oldest, the one somehow in the other.

Music and mourning, then: two essential elements of Greek tragedy. Already in *The Names* we are given a taste of such mourning in an impromptu duo in an Athenian restaurant between a guitarist and a random customer who cannot resist adding his voice to the lament:

> The song gathered force, a spirited lament. Its tone evoked inevitable things. Time was passing, love was fading, grief was deep and total. ... Their subjects were memory and tragic narrative and men who put their voices to song. ... For the rest of the song they looked at each other, strangers, to something beyond. A blood recollection, a shared past. I didn't know. (*N* 64)

6

Double Takes

I felt a breath of estrangement in the room and thought she might be a voyeur of her own experience, living at an angle to the moment and recording in some state of future-mind.

U 300

It's an event all right.

WN 151

Retrospection and Memory

Standing in someone's kitchen, slicing a lemon, she understood that the knife would slip and she would cut herself and she did.

U 387

Writing is memory, she thought, and memory is the fictional self, the powdery calcium ash waiting to be stirred by a pointed stick.

RS 362

Are you saying you saw a chance to use the real event in order to rehearse the simulation?

WN 139; see 204

In the world of DeLillo, the outside world is perpetually doubled or repeated—contrabanded, as I have been calling it—by media such as radio, television, video, and film. It is easy to think that what we then have is the thing or the event itself, followed by its repetition or its contrabanding in various forms or by various media, and that after a number of repetitions the reproduction ends up replacing the event itself. But that's not exactly it. The truth is that it is often the repetition or reproduction that tells us what the event or the thing is in the first place, the second moment that, at the extreme, makes the first what it was.

Here, for example, is how Bucky Wunderlick's bandmate learns that their band has finally broken up: he "heard it on the radio," and "it sounded pretty official" (*GJ* 181). According to this logic, if you want to know it's raining outside, you don't ask a friend, and you certainly don't look outside; you just turn on the radio—or take a look at your iPhone. Here's a brief father-son conversation about the weather where the father has direct perception on his side and his son the media. Anyone with direct a knowledge of fathers and sons can guess who will have the final word:

"It's going to rain tonight."
"It's raining now," I said.
"The radio said tonight." (*WN* 22; see *RS* 422)

The contraband, the repetition, produces the reality; what is outside comes round to invent an inside; truth is then nothing without its mediatization since it is the media that teaches us who we are and what we are becoming. When Eric Packer's limo, inching through Manhattan, is suddenly surrounded by protesters during the antiglobalization demonstration, Packer takes a peek outside but then quickly ducks back in, not to protect himself from what was happening but to see exactly what's going on. "It made more sense on TV. He poured two vodkas and they watched, trusting what they saw. It was a protest all right" (*C* 89). Packer thus really only hears what the antiglobalization protesters around him are chanting when he is able to hear it on TV. He is finally able to see what's happening and, most incredibly, what's happening to *him*, only through his own image on a screen: "His own image caught his eye, live on the oval screen beneath the spycam" (*C* 93). When a bomb suddenly goes off, Packer sees himself recoil on the screen, sees himself recoil in shock, and *then* hears the blast, the reaction to the event preceding the event itself, as it were. Having recoiled on the screen, therefore, he "recoiled for real," "whatever that might possibly mean" (*C* 95).

It's quite a scene, this combination of reality and replay, this double-banded scene, though it is itself already a replay or restaging of a scene from another novel, a do-over of the scene in *Libra* where Oswald, having himself become a fictional character in his own life, sees himself shot on TV: "He could see himself shot as the camera caught it. Through the pain he watched TV. ... Lee watched himself react to the augering heat of the bullet" (*L* 439). Grimacing and doubled over, Oswald could have said to himself or said looking into the camera what Packer will say to himself near the end of *Cosmopolis*, "O shit I am dead" (*C* 206; see *GJ* 91)—DeLillo's repetition or reinscription of that most impossible of all speech acts from Edgar Allan

Poe's *The Strange Case of M. Valdemar*. For this is also the time, the doubled or contrabanded time, of literature.

Things are recognized for what they are, they become what they are—yup, it's a protest, all right, it's a toxic event all right—only in retrospect, through their repetition and mediatization. In *Valparaiso* Michael says: "The plane is taking off outside the cabin and the plane is taking off inside the cabin. I look at the monitor, I look at the earth" (*V* 32; see 104). He might have gone on to say, after a second look at the monitor: "We're taking off all right." Jack in *White Noise* seems to recognize Babette—or at least certain aspects of Babette—only through her appearance on TV: "It was her all right, the face, the hair, the way she blinks in rapid twos and threes" (*WN* 104; see *RS* 290 and 409). Retrospection thus comes before -spection, the doubling of the self before the self itself. Even self-identity seems to appear only retrospectively, coming to us through the outside, through the second band or track that allows us to reflect upon ourselves. Our most real, "shitmost self," seems only ever possible, then, as a contraband effect.

We thus recognize ourselves or even first become ourselves only by means of a passage through a second band or second track, through our doubling or repetition, our recording or our mediatization. This second track or band can be rather low-tech, nothing more than that other voice running inside us—call it conscience or superego or, better, a *contrabande sonore*—the voice that brings the outside inside in order to tell us how to be and how to act. That's the lesson of the UN worker held hostage in Beirut in *Mao II*: "Be alert and note the details said the conscientious tape running in his head, the voice that whispers you are smarter than your captors" (*M* 107).

It's not just individuals, of course, but groups, fringe or terrorist groups, for example, that know that they can become themselves only through their mediatization. In *Mao II* everyone is aware that the UN hostage has value only insofar as his capture and release receive media attention. In short, "his freedom is tied to the public announcement of his freedom" (*M* 129). Even the prisoner knows that he has value, that he has meaning, only to the extent that he can be translated into wavelengths, "wavebands" of a certain kind:

> They were putting him together, storing his data in starfish satellites, bouncing his image off the moon. He saw himself floating to the far shores of space, past his own death and back again. But he sensed they'd forgotten his body by now. He was lost in the wavebands, one more code for the computer mesh, for the memory of crimes too pointless to be solved. (*M* 112)

But it's not just the hostage who has this fate in our world. In the end, nothing is unmediated; everything is itself and its waveband, its counterband or its mediatization. We read earlier in the novel, "News of disaster is the only narrative people need. The darker the news, the grander the narrative" (*M* 42). In Bucky Wunderlick's words of wisdom: "Be willing to die for your beliefs, or computer printouts of your beliefs" (*GJ* 133). Again, it's not that those printouts are mere reproductions or translations of beliefs on the inside. They are what help produce the inside. We read in *Running Dog*: "Devices make us pliant. If *they* issue a print-out saying we're guilty, then we're guilty" (*RD* 93). Same thing in *White Noise*, where Jack Gladney becomes convinced of his own impending death not because he feels worse but because of test results and data interpretation—not blood samples and X-rays so much as computer simulations, indeed, as in *The Names*, risk assessment, actuarial tables, mega-data.

Or take guns. It's obvious that they operate at a distance, through the mediation of a relatively sophisticated technology. They extend what can be done with the hand far beyond the reach of any hand, pretty much as far as the eye can see. But when you add a scope to a gun, you introduce a whole other layer of mediation. You end up trying to shoot not the man a hundred meters away but the man right there in the scope. And if your aim is good and you get the man in the scope, then the man a hundred yards away will suddenly, quasi-miraculously, fall down as well:

> He shot a government scout, aiming through a telescopic sight. It was uncanny. You press a button and a man drops dead a hundred meters away. It seemed hollow and remote, falsifying everything. It was a trick of the lenses. The man is an accurate picture. Then he is upside down. Then he is right side up. You shoot at a series of images conveyed to you through a metal tube. (*L* 297; see *C* 90, 171)

But there's another way or another sense in which we ourselves become both band and contraband. This happens when we incorporate another voice inside ourselves, counterbanding within us a discourse that comes from without. It could be a song or slogan or jingle or just a piece of language that has become lodged within us as contraband, an external band, a headband, precisely, now running in our own head, turning us into the medium if not the message for something besides us: "I sat on the front steps alone, waiting for a sense of ease and peace to settle in the air around me. / A woman passing on the street said, 'A decongestant, an antihistamine, a cough suppressant, a pain reliever'" (*WN* 262). What is heard enters us like linguistic shrapnel, as we will see, and we become its double band. "She leaned over the pot, looking for an egg. / A jingle for a product called Ray-Ban Wayfarer began running through my head" (*WN* 212). We thus become the radio or the TV, at once the advertiser and the audience. As a stage direction for *The Day Room* puts it: "In the motel sequence, an actor in a straitjacket functions as the TV set" (*DR* 58). Sometimes what we receive are precise words, literal slogans, exact instructions, and sometimes it's just a recognizable pattern or plan picked up from who knows what TV show or film. When, for example, the sound of the radio or TV contraband goes mute in Jack Gladney's private world, the band inside his head picks up the slack and begins telling him how to proceed:

> I was ready to kill him now. But I didn't want to compromise the plan. The plan was elaborate. Drive past the scene several times, approach the motel on foot, swivel my head to look peripherally into rooms, locate Mr. Gray under his real name, enter unannounced ... (*WN* 311)

> This was part of my plan. My plan was this. Tell him who I am, let him know the reason for his slow and agonizing death. (*WN* 312)

More effective, sometimes, than an external recording of some kind, easier to misread or to forget, to be sure, but also harder to turn off, the headband can play and replay whatever message has taken hold within us—for example, the image of Babette with Mink and then the plan or plot to get revenge. It is, in the end, the most effective band of all, for even "in the dark the mind runs on like a devouring machine, the only thing awake in the universe" (*WN* 224), the only thing to survive blackouts, energy surges, and solar flares.

Before all the gadgets and technology, then, there is simply memory, which is one of the most common ways of facilitating narrative contraband in DeLillo's novels. There is, for example, in *Ratner's Star* a narrative back-and-forth between Billy's memories of early childhood with Babe and Faye and his time at Field Experiment Number One (see *RS* 69, 131), or, in *Zero K*, the back-and-forth between Jeffrey Lockhart at the Convergence with his father and stepmother and his teenage or childhood memories of being with his mother (*ZK* 56), or, in *The Names*, the back-and-forth between Owen Brademas as an older man traveling through Greece, India, and Pakistan and his early childhood memories in Kansas, memories that can themselves be compared—a secondary contrabanding—to fiction or to film: "In his memory he was a character in a story, a colored light" (*N* 304). It should thus come as no surprise that memory itself would be described in terms of "playback" (*RD* 222, 229; see 239), or film, "a day now gone to black and white in the film fade of memory" (*U* 134), or film frames, "a series of still images, a film broken down to components" (*L* 72).

Memory is everywhere in DeLillo, memory of various kinds and modalities, rote memory as opposed to interpretation (*RS* 206), lapses and losses of memory brought on by excessive drinking—David Bell in Chicago (*A* 265) or Bill Gray in Cyprus (*M* 211–212)—or Dylar (*WN* 53, 116) or, in *Falling Man*, Alzheimer's, which causes the mind "to slide away from the adhesive friction that makes an individual possible" (*FM* 30). There are even speculations about the possibility of transgenerational memory, "common memories drifting across the generations" (*N* 279), even the possibility of memories detached from individual persons altogether (*N* 113), speculations about the way memories are triggered and so facilitate the transition from one narrative band to another (*FM* 205, 246), body memories (*A* 199, *M* 90, 129–130), for example, or the way memories seem to reside in things (*P* 204). Certain words are also, of course, attached to memory, oftentimes childhood memories: "He had walked out the door, rejecting his wife and son while the kid was doing his homework. *Sine cosine tangent*. These were the mystical words I would associate with the episode from that point on" (*ZK* 234; *RS* 7).

But then there is the case of events or memories that border on the traumatic, the kind of memory that seems to accompany or to double every experience with its shadow. In "Baader-Meinhof," that's the effect of being stalked and threatened, every waking moment haunted by its contrabanded double: "She saw everything twice now. She was where she wanted to be, and alone, but nothing was the same. Bastard. Nearly everything in the room had a double effect—what it was and the association it carried in her mind" ("BM" 117).

"Live" Perception

She climbed the stairs, hearing the sound a person makes who is climbing stairs.

BA 33

She climbed the stairs, hearing herself from other parts of the house somehow.

BA 35

You can tell something about a woman by listening to her footsteps on a flight of stairs. ... It is interesting to speculate on the curve of her ankles, how her apartment is furnished, whether or not she believes in a supreme being.

A 54

Granting all these mediated, contraband formations in DeLillo, what, we might want to ask, is not contrabanded or doubled? Well, one might be tempted to think, *perception*, direct, unmediated perception. But one would need to think again because even in perception there is, it seems, a certain repetition, a retrospective thinking or perceiving that seems to make perception possible in the first place. As paradoxical as it may seem, even perception, what we take to be original, unmediated, unrepeatable perception, seems to require mediation and repetition.

The Names is a novel about language, as we will see, but it is also one about perception, about seeing things anew or seeing them for the first time. "Owen Brademas used to say that even random things take ideal shapes and come to us in painterly forms. It's a matter of seeing what is there. He saw patterns there, moments in the flow" (*N* 19; see 172, 209). The novel is thus an apprenticeship or a journey in perception. James Axton, who is following in the tracks of both Brademas and the language cult, is the first to take up this apprenticeship when his travels through the southern Peloponnese become "something like a pure rite of seeing" (*N* 182). But it's a pure or heightened perception that does not come without effort. One can be looking right at something—a landscape or a person or a painting—and not really see it. "I realize now that the first day I was only barely looking. I thought I was looking but I was only getting a bare inkling of what's in these paintings. I'm only just starting to look" ("BM" 109). In other words, a sort of second sight is required to see what is right there, a second sight that requires an undoing of our first sight. The same goes for hearing what is right there in the background, the sound of poker chips in a casino, for example: "It surprised him every time to find what an effort it takes to hear what is always there. The chips were there. Behind the ambient noise and stray voices, there was the sound of tossed chips ... like insect friction" (*FM* 225).

> But how do we do this? How do we break through habit in order to see or to hear? You have to break through the structure of your own stonework habit just to make yourself listen. There it is, the clink of chips, the toss and scatter, players and dealers, mass and stack, a light ringing sound so native to the occasion it lies outside the aural surround, in its own current of air, and no one hears it but you. (*FM* 229)

The Body Artist is also a novel about perception, about becoming aware of things for the first time, the initial clearness of water in a sink faucet before it turns opaque (*BA* 8), the brightness of the day after a storm (*BA* 7), birds at a feeder (*BA* 8, 13), a "leaf in midair, turning" (*BA* 41), even a carton containing bread-crumbs: "She looked at the bread-crumb carton for the first true time, really seeing it and understanding what was in it, and it was bread crumbs" (*BA* 34). Seeing for the first time thus means seeing what one has always been seeing or seeing what one thought one already knew: "Things she saw seemed doubtful—not doubtful but ever changing, plunged into metamorphosis, something that is also something else" (*BA* 36; see 11). Things happen so quickly that it is difficult to see them for what they are, difficult "to notice the details" (*BA* 11). But when one looks very closely, one begins to see that what is perceived is not grasped all at once, in one go, in a singular moment of perception that must then be slowly analyzed or unfolded in a second time that is beyond or outside the event of perception itself. No, the moment of perception is itself already divided, already repeated, belated, at once behind and ahead of itself, the result of an *après coup* that is the very time of contraband. Lauren, for example, sees a bird out of the corner of her eye "mostly in retrospect because she didn't know what she was seeing at first and had to re-create the ghostly moment, write it like a line in a piece of fiction" (*BA* 91). Birds are exemplary in this regard; one often sees them only in retrospect, after the flurry (*BA* 91), not the bird in the cage, of course, or a bird in free flight, but a bird or birds in sudden flutter, all flash and sound. Something similar happens earlier in the novel with something said by Rey: "She reached in for the milk, realizing what it was he'd said that she hadn't heard about eight seconds ago" (*BA* 9). Later in the same novel, DeLillo treats us to what could not be a more banal and, thus, a more telling or illuminating example of retrospective perception, the phenomenology, if one will allow me the big term, of a paper clip dropping:

> You stand at the table shuffling papers and you drop something. Only you don't know it. It takes a second or two before you know it and even then you know it only as a formless distortion of the teeming space around your body. But once you know you've dropped something, you hear it hit the floor, belatedly. The sound makes its way through an immense web of distances. You hear the thing fall and know what it is at the same time, more or less, and it's a paperclip. ... Now that you know you dropped it, you remember how it happened, or half remember, or sort of see it maybe, or something else ... but when you bend to pick it up, it isn't there. (*BA* 89–90)

A paper clip drops and it takes a moment to realize what has happened—a moment to hear it in the first place. One recognizes it, or actually hears it for the first time, after the fact. And that's how memory sometimes works as well: one realizes *that* one has forgotten something only after recalling what was forgotten. DeLillo's work is full of such lapses of memory, for example, in

Falling Man, with sentences like this one, which really should be committed to memory by the members of writing workshops from coast to coast:

> It was the kind of day in which you forget words and drop things and wonder what it is you came into the room to get because you are standing here for a reason and you have to tell yourself it is just a question of sooner or later before you remember because you always remember once you are here. (*BA* 83)

The second moment confirms or actually allows us to perceive the first. The second moment leads one to recognize the first, to recognize, then, not simply what the first already was but we didn't know it, not what the first was in our experience though we couldn't express it, but what the first *will have been*, in retrospect. It takes a second moment, a moment of retrospect at the sound of a mousetrap being sprung, for example, to recognize that there will have been something else in the house, that "there were three of us now" (*PO* 31). That is also what happened in Dallas on November 22, 1963, to a woman watching the motorcade: "She didn't really hear the first noise until she heard the second" (*L* 397). Or to the woman with the Polaroid who saw the whole thing through her camera but "realized" only later that "she'd just seen someone shot in her own viewfinder" (*L* 401; see 405). And that's what happened in NYC on September 11, 2001, with the two planes and the two towers: it was the second that helped us to perceive the first: "In time he heard the sound of the second fall" (*FM* 5). Two towers, two planes, two shots, two bombs dropped, first Hiroshima, then Nagasaki, because it seems we couldn't quite recognize what was going on after just one.

Between the first time and the second time there is thus not only time but language, culture, knowledge, and other people, an entire education in the ways of the world that tell us what a paper clip is, what a gunshot is, that a tower is falling. The contraband, the things we carry, the implications, are first and foremost in us and in our language. We return to ourselves in this second take in order to make sense of what we suppose to be our immediate perception. And, oftentimes, we try to make sense of our perceptions by appealing to others and the perceptions of others. We try to verify or even inform our own perceptions and experiences through others. It is not just our own perception, then, but our perception of another's perception, the glance of another, that confirms our reality, that tells us who we are, or that there is nothing to be afraid of, or something to be very afraid of. From the very beginning, DeLillo has been particularly attentive to the way we seek confirmation of what we think we feel or experience by looking to others. "We sat around the living room, plates on knees, and searched each other's raincloud faces for some clue to our dilemma" (*A* 105; see *RD* 117).

We may not know, in the end, who others really are, but we do look to others to tell us who *we* are, how we should react. *White Noise* is itself an entire study in the phenomenon—funny and yet all-too-telling to be only funny. When Wilder's seven-hour-long crying fit suddenly stopped on the drive back home from the Congregational Church where they had just picked up Babette, Jack looks to Babette in order to know what to think and how to react: "I waited for Babette to glance at me behind his back, over his head, to show relief, happiness, hopeful suspense. I didn't know how I felt and wanted a clue" (*WN* 79). Later, Babette looks at Jack with a similar intention: "She seemed to study my face for the hidden meaning of the message she was receiving" (*WN* 113; see 121).

We need a second to see the first; or we need to see what we think others have seen in order to see it ourselves. Throughout DeLillo's novels characters try to find out what they think or feel or see by appealing to the thoughts, feelings, or perceptions of others. It is not just confirmation of what they already know that they are looking for but knowledge itself. It happens most frequently in moments of danger or distress, the glance searching for the glance of another to tell it what it is seeing—a sort of perceptual feedback loop. The first minutes and hours of the airborne toxic event are full of such glances or such attempts to exchange them. "We looked at people in other cars, trying to work out from their faces how frightened we should be" (*WN* 120). It makes sense because "in a crisis the true facts are whatever other people say they are. No one's knowledge is less secure than your own" (*WN* 120; see 121). Jack's girls thus "look at each other" to confirm their "dark suspicion" (*WN* 118), while Jack's teenage son Heinrich searches his father's face "for some reassurance against the possibility of real danger—a reassurance he," as the son, "would immediately reject as phony" (*WN* 117). It's a form of communication that goes beyond any particular perception or form of knowledge. In *Falling Man*, Lianne "looked around for someone, just to exchange a glance" (*FM* 163). During the Cuban Missile Crisis, people were so desperate to learn how to think and what to feel that they went to hear "the infamous sick comic, Lenny Bruce, and they waited for him to tell them how they felt" (*U* 504; see 574).

We find similar attempts to get confirmation of what we should think and feel in the faces of others in the short story "The Ivory Acrobat." In the hours and days after an earthquake in Athens, the main character "looked for something in people's faces that might tell her their experience was just like hers, down to the smallest strangest turn of thought" ("IA" 70; see 55). Same thing in *Mao II*: "There's a lot of looking back and forth. Nobody knows how to feel and they're checking around for hints" (*M* 4). The reassuring glances of people on the street, of the locals, the "signs and portents" of taxi drivers (*U* 793), or else doctors—especially doctors (see *DR* 8–9)—these are what tell us who we are or at least what the hell is going on in our world or in the depths of our body.

We look not just to confirm our own impressions, then, but to see what others see so that we may see ourselves. Sometimes it helps and sometimes, for example for Keith in the burning towers, it does not: "He was a client or consulting attorney and Keith knew him slightly and they exchanged a look. No telling what it meant, this look" (*FM* 240). Indeed when the look goes totally unreturned, when one seeks reassurance in an identity that is itself being undone, then the whole world seems on the verge of collapse, on the brink of what systems people call catastrophic failure:

> He looked at Rumsey, who'd fallen away from him, upper body lax, face barely belonging. The whole business of being Rumsey was in shambles now. … He stood and looked at him and the man opened his eyes and died.
> This is when he wondered what was happening here. (*FM* 243)

One thus comes to recognize oneself or what is happening to oneself through an external perception, a perception that is itself always double-banded. Perception is always like that, but there are moments when it is heightened, like just after an earthquake, when one's hearing develops "a cleanness, a discriminating rigor" ("*IA*" 60), or when one suddenly becomes aware of not just *what* one is seeing but *that* one is seeing. Jack Gladney's confrontation with Mink in the motel is a study in such heightened perception and self-perception:

> I was advancing in consciousness. I watched myself take each separate step. With each separate step, I became aware of processes, components, things relating to other things. Water fell to earth in drops. I saw things new. (*WN* 304)

As his plan advances Jack begins sensing not only the things around him in a heightened way but what seems like the very process of perception itself:

> I could feel the pressure and density of things. So much was happening. I sensed molecules active in my brain, moving along neural pathways. (*WN* 306)

In this heightened state, attuned to "a heightened reality," things become at once more and less solid or stable than they once were, endowed with "a denseness that was also a transparency. Surfaces gleamed. Water struck the roof in spherical masses, globules, splashing drams. Close to a violence, close to a death" (*WN* 307). Broken down into individual elements, particles and rays, sights and sounds become more and more vivid: "Things in their actual state. ... White noise everywhere" (*WN* 310).

The correlate of the contrabanded perception would thus seem to be the thing becoming itself doubled in order to become itself, not as thing and image (see *RS* 264), or the thing as it is and as it appears, but the thing itself—only doubled, the thing shining through its name and the name giving access to the thing. It is, as it were, a contrabanded transcendence, not a false transcendence but a double-edged one, luminous and illuminating, the only transcendence in town.

White Noise, The World Hum

The highway was almost empty but a roar filled the interior of the car, an air blast so integral to travel on major routes that he couldn't break it down to component sounds. So much his own car. So much the sparse additional traffic. So much the power of night.

RD 108

The world hum. Do you hear it, yourself, ever?

ZK 132

When an author's best-known and most celebrated novel goes by the name *White Noise* (a title in contraband from the get-go), a few words about *sound* would seem to be in order. For sounds are everywhere in DeLillo, individual, identifiable sounds, like the haunting sound of a voice (*N* 177), or clanging radiators (*BA* 113), or birds at a feeder, or an animal in the walls of an old house (*BA* 39), sounds that can take you out and away from yourself, that can prevent you from folding back in on yourself, like Lauren, after Rey's death. In *White Noise* itself there are all the comforting or exciting or annoying sounds of household appliances, the trash compactor with its "whining metal, exploding bottles, plastic smashed flat," a well-known "mangling din" (*WN* 34), or the massive "throbbling" of the refrigerator (*WN* 101), or the sounds of the washer and dryer, "vibrating nicely" (*WN* 109; see 225 and *FM* 151). In each case, the task is to hear—and for the author to describe—what is right there on the surface, sounds that can go unnoticed unless they are localized and identified.

But then there are the sounds—or there is the sound—of something just below the surface, the sound of a television without words or message, just sound, or the sound of a NYC traffic jam, "noise for the sake of noise, overwhelming the details of time and place" (*ZK* 174), "the sound of car horns building, the dinosaur death of stalled traffic at rush hour" (*U* 623; see "IA" 55 and *WN* 118), or the muted sound of planes taking off in the distance, a sound that is "mysterious, full of anxious gatherings, a charged rumble that seemed a long time in defining itself as something besides a derangement of nature, some onrushing nameless event" (*N* 6).

There are individual sounds, then, and indistinguishable sounds, the sound of sound itself. But then there seems to be the buzz or the hum below all that, just below the threshold of identification, the indistinguishable, barely audible white noise beneath all the individual, recognizable sounds. You can often "hear" it, sort of, in your local supermarket:

> People tore filmy bags off racks and tried to figure out which end opened. I realized the place was awash in noise. ... And over it all, or under it all, a dull and unlocatable roar, as of some form of swarming life just outside the range of human apprehension. (*WN* 36)

It's like the first intimations of a world hum, a sound below or before all sound. Just as there is a secret world or a world of secrets below the world of messages and information, and an underground beneath the city, so there is another level of sound—a "world hum"—beneath the identifiable sounds on the surface of the world. Sometimes one can hear or sense this level of sound as one approaches the horizon or limits of the world itself, on an airplane, for example, the sound of "the systems running through the aircraft" there at "the edge of the stratosphere, world hum, the sudden night" (*N* 90). But sometimes one can hear it before even getting on the airplane, already on one's way to the airport:

> There was a noise that started, a world hum—you began to hear it when you left your carpeted house and rode out to the airport. He wanted something friendly to read in the single sustained drone that marks every mile in a business traveler's day. (*U* 252)

Sometimes one can even hear it beneath the everyday traffic, perhaps not only in cities but especially in cities, the hum beneath every identifiable sound.

Taxis, trucks and buses. The noise persists even when traffic is stopped. I hear this from my rooftop, heat beating into my head. This is the noise that hangs in the air, nonstop, whatever time of day or night, if you know how to listen. (*ZK* 222)

And sometimes one doesn't need to go anywhere to hear it, since it seems to be the sound of simply *being*—the sound of world in the making:

I wanted to hear what Ben-Ezra had described, the oceanic sound of people living and thinking and talking, billions, everywhere, waiting for trains, marching to war, licking food off their fingers. Or simply being who they are. / The world hum. (*ZK* 135)

World hum: the ultimate *contrabande sonore*.

Double Vision

It was late afternoon and almost dark on the floor of the ballroom. But there were still rays of gorgeous, dusty pink light striking the upper walls, the upper sections of one of the murals—a huge sky full of clouds and birds. In other words, the real sky was pouring delicate, late, winter light onto the painted sky on the wall. It was a small moment in a day crowded with impressions, but the sight was so glowing and full of unexpected poetry that I had to stop in my tracks and just stand looking at that twice-made sky.

AZ 122

We saw earlier Lee Harvey Oswald's doubleness, his duplicity, his penchant for secrets and secret names: none of this is unrelated to his double vision of himself, to the distance he always seems to take with regard to himself, seeing himself always from afar, as if he were another. He sees himself as if were being spied upon, even when doing unspectacular things—like walking down a street: "He saw himself go inside, a fellow on a quiet street doing ordinary things, unafraid of being watched" (*L* 51). Or drinking a glass of water: "He drinks his water slowly, almost formally, aware of himself, holding himself in a correct and serious way, as anyone does who knows he is being watched" (*L* 358). The experience is heightened, it seems, when he sees himself doing exceptional things—like getting laid for the first time:

> He saw himself having sex with her. He was partly outside the scene. He had sex with her and monitored the scene, waiting for the pleasure to grip him, blow over him like surf, bend the trees. He thought about what was happening rather than saw it, although he saw it too. (*L* 84–85)

Though everything having to do with Oswald's involvement in the assassination is murky, overdetermined, complex, at the moment of the shooting itself everything appears to him with stunning clarity. He is the shooter and he is the one watching the shooter, and this distance does not trouble but actually clarifies his vision:

> There was so much clarity Lee could watch himself in the huge room of stacked cartons, scattered books, old brick walls, bare light bulbs, a small figure in a corner, partly hidden. He fired off a second shot. (*L* 398)

This quality of seeing oneself from afar or being away from oneself at the moment of the event seems to be contagious when it comes to the assassination. Oswald shares this quality with one of the two men behind the grassy knoll, as this latter jumps into the getaway car right after no doubt firing that fatal head shot. "He felt there was someone sitting inside his body making these moves and turns. ... He didn't know how he'd feel when he was back in his body again" (*L* 403). The same thing happens to Jack Ruby as he steps forward to shoot Oswald: "Jack came out of the crowd, seeing everything happen in advance" (*L* 437). It's as if everything has been filmed in advance and Jack is simply doing what he has already done—while Oswald, on the other side of the bullet but in the same newsreel, sees what has already happened to him, not reliving it but seeing what has just happened so he can know how to react. He "could see himself shot as the camera caught it. ... Lee watched himself react to the augering heat of the bullet" (*L* 439). As Oswald might have said, imitating Eric Packer before the fact, "I've been shot all right."

DeLillo's characters thus not only reflect upon themselves but see themselves, from afar, from a distance, as if they were at once themselves and another, themselves and their own contrabanded selves. In *The Body Artist*, Lauren spends much of her time "more or less seeing herself from the edge of the room or standing precisely where she was and being who she was and seeing a smaller hovering her in the air somewhere, already thinking it's tomorrow" (*BA* 34; see *U* 379; see *N* 230). Then there's Keith in *Falling Man*, who, talking with Florence, thinks of himself not as himself but as someone like himself: "He thought this kind of conversation was for other people. People have these conversations all the time, he thought, in rooms like this one, sitting, looking" (*FM* 108).

Consider in the same vein this moment from *Zero K*, where it becomes clear that the ultimate contraband would be a second, future, contraband life:

> His name was Ben-Ezra and he liked to come out here, he said, and think about the time, many years away, when he would return to the garden and sit on the same bench, reborn, and think about the time when he used to sit here, usually alone, and imagine that very moment. (*ZK* 123)

It's hard to know how far to take this seeing oneself from afar, but in *Mao II* DeLillo seems to suggest that it is not completely unrelated to all those twentieth-century technologies of film and space travel that have made us what we are—at once band and contraband, unsynthesizable, irresolvable:

> We've gone too far into space to insist on our differences. Like those people you talk about on the Great Wall, a man and a woman walking toward each other across China. ... We've learned to see ourselves as if from space, as if from satellite cameras, all the time, all the same. As if from the moon, even. We're all Moonies, or should learn to be. (*M* 89)

As Brita says of this contrabanded vision that seems to come to us so easily and unbidden: "It's strange how I construct an aerial view so naturally" (*M* 70; see 161). We see ourselves from afar, from an aerial view, as if we were already being narrated or filmed. Here's a passage in which a very young Matt Shay is going by himself to the movies in NYC, seeing himself as if he were already watching a movie, at once character and spectator, actor and director:

> He sees himself from this distance in the white sands standing across the street looking at the great Italianate façade of the Paradise. He sees himself staring up at the clock ... He sees himself buying a ticket ... He sees himself sitting in the balcony at the Paradise. (*U* 407–408; see 387, 719–720)

One sees oneself and sometimes even hears oneself from a distance, as another. As Artis says in *Zero K*: "I feel artificially myself. I'm someone who's supposed to be me. ... My voice is different. ... It seems to be coming from outside me. Not all the time but sometimes. It's like I'm twins, joined at the hip, and my sister is speaking" (*ZK* 52). Art, Artis, Artifice—the one in the other, the one counterbanded by the other.

Finally, here is a passage from *Ratner's Star* where the contraband effect is illustrated by nothing other than a band aid, a double-banded band aid, peeled off by little Billy Twillig in an airplane toilet:

A bandage covered a small cut on his thumb and he peeled it off now ... flushing the bandage down the germless well, imagining for a moment an identical plastic strip floating to the surface of the water that filled a stainless-steel wash basin in a toilet on an airliner above an anti-podal point. He double-checked his zipper. For the mirror he poured forth a stereotyped Oriental smile, an antismile really, one he'd learned from old movies on TV. (*RS* 8)

It's hard to imagine a more poignant example to make the point stick. There is the doubling of imagination and then the contrabanded narrative, marked by a double-checked zipper and a face doubled in a mirror, a face that itself comes from a movie. Bandage and counterbandage, then, and sometimes the counterbandage is so convincing, so vivid, sometimes it sticks so well, that it just dissolves into the skin of the real.

Repetitions and Mirror Images

The moment seemed false to her, a scene in a movie when a character tries to understand what is going on in her life by looking in the mirror.
FM 47; see 104

The universe, the multiverse, so many cosmic infinities that the idea of repeatability becomes unavoidable.
ZK 130

I was fascinated by the way the state troopers copied from each other's little books. ... There couldn't possibly be a mistake if they all had the same information.
EZ 72

Every real event breaks with routine, with habit, and yet the event can be produced only by the repetition of routine: "Do something over and over and soon little irregularities show up in the routine. Unconscious, unbidden" (*GJ* 26). Take the Moonie wedding in Yankee Stadium. It's not just a single, ordinary wedding multiplied by seven thousand; it's something else entirely, a mass wedding, a crowd-sourced event: "They take a time-honored event and repeat it, repeat it, repeat it until something new enters the world. ... The bridegrooms in identical blue suits, the brides in lace-and-satin gowns" (*M* 4).

In "The Power of History" DeLillo speaks of the game in the Polo Grounds in 1951 as "an example of some unrepeatable social phenomenon." "We had the real Dodgers and Giants. Now we have the holograms" (*U* 95). There is, then, still a sense of the original, the irreplaceable in DeLillo, but that original never seems to come without its repetition, without anticipation or memory or narrative. For the doubling of the original will have always been there, since even perception, as we have seen, depends on a sort of original duplicity. It can be the unexpected or the exceptional that is repeated, or else the most everyday, someone entirely new and unknown or else someone or something one has known all one's life.

In the culture—particularly the American culture—in which DeLillo is writing and to which he is reacting, this original duplicity is itself doubled by all sorts of simulacra and simulations, holographs and holograms, rip-offs and knockoffs, mirror images and mirroring effects. That is why DeLillo's novels are always about seeing oneself and seeing oneself seeing (in a mirror, for example), about specularity and speculation, about what I continue to call narrative contraband. These are the tools and tricks of DeLillo's narrative trade, and they determine both the form of his narratives and the themes and images within them.

Throughout *Libra*, for example, Oswald doubles are everywhere. Aboard a freighter bound for Le Havre, Lee Harvey, trying to make it to Finland and then Russia, meets "a boy just out of high school and on his way to France to study French. He is a Texas boy and just close enough to Lee outwardly to be the world's preferred vision of the type" (*L* 133). That's just the first of a whole host of nearly identical Oswalds, dead ringers for Oswald, "Oswald doubles who were active for almost two months, mainly in and around Dallas but also in other Texas cities" (*L* 377), identifiable in photographs before, during, and after the assassination: "They all look like Oswald. Branch thinks they look more like Oswald than the figure in profile, officially identified as him" (*L* 300): "Isn't that *him* in a photograph of a crowd of people on the front steps of the Book Depository just as the shooting begins?" (*L* 300)

There are the doubles and then there are the resemblances and coincidences, some of which Oswald himself sees and some of which others see for him (see *L* 318), such as the double that Branch sees when he "thinks of the day and month of the assassination in strictly numerical terms—11/22" (*L* 377; see 318). Or the fact that Lee would be born a Libra, "capable of seeing the other side," a "man who harbors contradictions," a "boy sitting on the scales, ready to be tilted either way" (*L* 319; see *L* 175, 263, 315). Or the fact that Lee and DeLeello (as it is pronounced in French) are doubles of a kind; born just a couple years apart, they could have played street games together in the Bronx.

Or consider J. Edgar Hoover in *Underworld*, who has an unlikely double in the person of Sister Edgar, his soul sister in paranoia and germophobia, J. Edgar who has the uncanny experience in a New York hotel of catching himself "unexpectedly in a full-length mirror, across the room, in his white robe and soft slippers, ... startled by the image" (*U* 564). He catches himself unexpectedly and then, a minute later, poses there intentionally, in front of the mirror, "a seventy-one-year-old man wearing nothing but his sequined biker's mask and his wool-lined slippers, listening to the voices in the street" (*U* 565).

We become who we are, it seems, through this doubling, "watching ourselves age in the bathroom mirror, next to the toilet where we evacuate and the shower where we purify" (*ZK* 247; see *BA* 63, 84). When we look in the mirror what we see is indeed our double, which means not exactly *ourselves* but ourselves as contraband. It gets to the point where we cannot really tell where the reflected ends and the reflection begins:

> I looked at my face in the bathroom mirror, double-checking the effectiveness of the close shave I'd given myself twenty minutes earlier. I recalled something Ross had said about his right ear in the mirror being his real right ear instead of the mirror-image left ear. I had to concentrate hard to convince myself that this was not the case. (*ZK* 209)

The mirror can confirm something about ourselves in the present, or it can take us back, for example, to a time, as in *Cosmopolis*, when we would go to a barbershop with our father for a haircut. In the familiar simplicity of Anthony's barbershop, after a long, sleepless day and night, Eric Packer finally dozes off, only to awaken a moment later to a strangely familiar image: "He opened his eyes and saw himself in the mirror, the room massing around him. He lingered on the image" (*C* 165). One looks at Packer (a name recycled from *Amazons*, by the way, just as Murray Jay Siskind gets reused in *White Noise*) looking at himself but thinking of his father and one sees the reflection of Jeffrey Lockhart from *Zero K* looking back: "I looked in the mirror over the sink and said my name aloud. Then I went looking for my father" (*ZK* 96).

7

Writing in Tongues

All the letters and numbers are here, all the colors of the spectrum, all the voices and sounds, all the code words and ceremonial phrases. It is just a question of deciphering, rearranging, peeling off the layers of unspeakability.

WN 38

It was a sinister thing to discover at such an age, that words can escape their meaning.

EZ 17

Literature

"What would you read?"
"Lord, I don't know. Something in hard cover. I suppose I'd begin with the classics. One usually does. Then the neoclassics."

AZ 129

I wanted to be bookish and failed. I wanted to steep myself in European literature. There I was in our modest garden apartment, in a nondescript part of Queens, steeping myself in European literature. The word steep was the whole point. Once I decided to steep myself, there was no need to read the work.

ZK 102

When you strip away all the surfaces, when you see into it, what's left is terror. This is the thing that literature was meant to cure. The epic poem, the bedtime story.

PO 45

When a writer writes about or even just mentions another writer in his writing, it is never completely without purpose, never completely disinterested. For literature then itself becomes a place of reflection for the novelist or the novel being written. In short, it becomes a place of contraband.

There are many writers mentioned in DeLillo, but—an interesting symptom—there are probably more writers cited, named, alluded to, or echoed in *Americana* than in *all* of DeLillo's subsequent novels put together. Indeed there are probably as many writers in *Americana* as there are mathematicians in *Ratner's Star*, and that's a lot. We there find, in order of appearance—and I've surely missed more than a few—William Blake (*A* 21, 265, 322), Charles Olson (*A* 21), Walt Whitman (*A* 27), Kafka (*A* 73), Rilke and Chekhov (*A* 21), Tolstoy (*A* 85), Yeats (*A* 116), Swift (*A* 143, 322), O'Casey (*A* 161), Milton (*A* 171), Beckett (*A* 220), Rimbaud (*A* 265), Coleridge, Melville, and Conrad (*A* 322), Proust and Faulkner (*A* 326), and, of course, perhaps first and foremost, Joyce (*A* 95, 220, 321, 326). We have already cited Warren Beasley's radio monologue recalling Kinch, whose mother is "beastly dead" (see *A* 231-232, 234). Earlier, David Bell describes himself and his old friend Wild as having "committed the usual collegiate blasphemies of word and deed, using as our text the gleeful God-baiting of Buck Mulligan in the first few pages of *Ulysses*" (*A* 145). Later, Bell calls the same Wild with this special Joycean offer: "You are cordially invited to a black mass at your local martello tower. Roman collar. R.S.V.P." (*A* 246). And later still, we hear Sullivan, an exemplary storyteller and figure of a writer (see *A* 322-331), speak in a *Finnegans Wake* sort of way of her Irish heritage and of an uncle who "hated my father like plague, like incense. Brothers they were, stem and stern, Shem and Shaun" (*A* 321). We thus get little tastes from the beginning to the end of *Americana* of "Buckmulliganism in its bowl" (*A* 368).

There are far fewer explicit references to literature in the novels that follow, though there are always some, an occasional reference to Kafka (*GJ* 155, *P* 122), Orwell (*GJ* 155), Hemingway (*L* 160, *ZK* 72), Shelley (*FM* 8), or Dostoevsky ("MD" 134, *L* 150—not *Crime and Punishment*, even though we are talking about Oswald, but *The Idiot* (*L* 179))—Tolstoy (*WN* 282, *L* 388), Whitman (*L* 94), George Orwell and Big Brother in *Nineteen Eighty-Four* (*L* 100, 106), H.G. Wells (*L* 269), whom Oswald is reading—"The Invisible Man," we might speculate—and Edgar Allan Poe, the namesake of Sister Edgar in *Underworld* (*U* 572, 775). As for Beckett, he makes a return appearance in *Mao II*, when Bill Gray, the writer, says: "Beckett is the last writer to shape the way we think and see. After him, the major work involves midair explosions and crumbled buildings. This is the new tragic narrative" (*M* 157). In *White Noise* there is reference to another kind of literature, better-selling but surely not better written, the kind sold in the checkout line in American grocery stores: "The paperback books in spindly racks, the books with shiny metallic print, raised letters, vivid illustrations of cult violence and windswept romance" (*WN* 37).

Then there are references to the genre, at least, of science fiction (*EZ* 66, *BA* 56, *FM* 18), and, in *End Zone*, to a fictional science fiction writer, Tudev Nemkhu (*EZ* 169). And, of course, there's *Ratner's Star*, DeLillo's own attempt at science fiction, whose setting, not coincidentally, is the desert, a place that lends itself to speculation about life on other planets and facilitates encounters with UFOs (*A* 357, *PO* 20). But what seems to interest DeLillo most about science fiction is the way in which it returns us, often ominously, to the most familiar or else the most ancient, to what is happening today or to what has already happened here on earth. Professor Zapalac in *End Zone* already gives us this principle of science fiction:

> Science fiction is just beginning to catch up with the Old Testament. ... See carbon dioxide melt the polar ice caps. See the world's mineral reserves dwindle. See war, famine and plague. See barbaric hordes defile the temple of the virgins. ... I said science fiction but I guess I meant science. Anyway there's some kind of mythical and/or historic circle-thing being completed here. (*EZ* 160)

Given this convergence of the ancient and the contemporary, it is not surprising that the theory of evolution proposed in *Ratner's Star* would be a story not of uninterrupted progress but of great advances, ancient civilizations of great refinement, followed by a fall, a devolution, and then a progressive return to those ancient accomplishments.

Hence writing, the activity, the craft or even the profession of writing, is often in the vicinity, if not at the center, of DeLillo's writing. On the one hand, DeLillo's novels are about all kinds of things—9/11, the Kennedy assassination, fame, college life, baseball, nuclear war, and so on. On the other hand, they are about nothing other than writing. There are from the very beginning characters who are writers or would-be writers, people with stories but perhaps not the "staying power" to write them (*A* 194). First among these would be, in *Americana*, David Bell's friend Bobby Brand, who is "writing the novel that would detonate in the gut of America like a fiery bacterial bombshell" (*A* 112), a novel about a former US president, a man, who turns into a woman, while the new president, "patterned after Sonny Liston," is black—a scenario that really must have sounded like science fiction in 1971 (*A* 205). Though still completely unknown and, indeed, unaccomplished, Brand already imagines adoring disciples from Europe making pilgrimages to see him, the great American writer. He says, and one has to wonder how prescient or prophetic these words, which are echoed to some extent in *Mao II* with regard to Bill Gray, will have been in the life of Don DeLillo.

> I see myself as one of those unique old writers who's still respected for his daring ideas and style. Young disciples make pilgrimages to visit me. They come hiking to my house carrying knapsacks and copies of my books. There are no roads in the area. It's like Big Sur, only more lonely and remote. ... I see myself as lean and craggy. The young disciples come from every corner of the world. Sometimes they come in groups, a bunch of young Frenchmen and their girlfriends bringing greetings from famous old French philosophers and writers, guys I shared symposiums with and signed petitions with, famous old French intellectuals who haven't given up their revolutionary ideas and who still exert a profound influence on French foreign policy. (*A* 290–291)

Brand is also confident about what writing can offer others: "Who wants to be in my novel?" he asks. "It'll cost you fifty dollars and I'm in a position to guarantee immortality" (*A* 255).

The only problem with all of this is that Brand is a writer who does not write. "There is no book, Davy. There's eleven pages and seven of them don't have any words on them. And I'm not making any great claims for the other four" (*A* 307). He's the author, in the end, of "The Great American Sheaf of Blank Paper" (*A* 337). As Bell says, Brand is "definitely a novelist, by all means a craftsman of high talent—but one who chose words of the same color as the paper on which they were written" (*A* 347). A writer of blank pages—like a painter who paints blank canvases (see *U* 386)—Brand is at once a colossal failure and the image of a certain success.

Americana is, among many other things, the story of David Bell, who is working for a TV network at the beginning of the novel, becoming the novelist that Brand never became. By the end of the novel, Bell has a sheaf of paper with actual words on them, black words on white paper, we imagine, presumably the novel that is *Americana*:

> Every so often I move the manuscript to another room in order to be surprised by it as I enter that room. It never fails to be a touching thing, my book on a pinewood table, poetic in its loneliness, today still, Cézannesque in the timeless light it emits, a simple object, the box-shaped equivalent of the reels which sit in my small air-conditioned storage vault. (*A* 346)

We have spoken a couple of times of the radiance that certain objects emit; here it is a manuscript in its paper-whiteness that gives off such a light.

Like Joyce, yet again, Bell's becoming a writer seems to be in some way related to the impending death of the mother, to a memory of those intimations, between junior and senior year in high school, and the recognition that something else, something momentous, was on the brink of happening. The mother's death is indeed linked to the beginning of writing, but then so is her life. For if it is Bell's mother who, as we have seen, first gives him a taste for film, it is also she who first turns him toward language:

> I was playing baseball one day, or hardball as we called it, standing out in center field, when I saw her coming across the grass toward me.
> "Good little boys do not pick their nose," she said.
> "Do not pick their noses. Boys is plural so noses has to be plural."
> "Boys *are* plural," she said. "I was quite a brilliant little grammarian as a girl. I also played the harpsichord." (*A* 138)

Language used versus language mentioned—just that is enough, perhaps, to set one on a path. By the end of *Americana*, David Bell seems to suggest that language—writing—is what has helped him to order if not to make sense of the chaos of it all: "Our lives were the shortest distance between two points, birth and chaos, but what appears on these pages represents, in its orderly proportions, almost a delivery from chaos" (*A* 345).

After *Americana*, DeLillo will seem to follow his own aesthetic model in his references to literature, that is, the idea that "less is best." If *Americana* is the story of becoming a writer, a portrait of the American artist as young man, or a portrait of the artist as an American young man, then by the end of the novel he will have shed or overcome a certain literary tradition—mostly but not exclusively European—in order to develop a more uniquely American voice. "At Leighton Gage College," says David Bell, "I wanted to be known as Kinch. This is Stephen Dedalus' nickname in *Ulysses*, which I was reading at the time" (*A* 143). Bell thus reads literature, writes poetry, tries to write jazz, and makes little experimental films (*A* 145), trying out different art forms before settling, it seems, on writing. The movie Bell makes over the course of the novel, filmed out of the death of his mother, eventually gives way, in the latter parts of the novel, to literature, to a kind of American literature. The narrator says, for example, as he describes his trip out west, "Literature is what we passed and left behind, that more than men and cactus" (*A* 349; see 364, 376). And then, on the final page of the novel:

> I drove all night, northeast, and once again I felt it was literature I had been confronting these past days, the archetypes of the dismal mystery, sons and daughters of the archetypes … I drove at insane speeds. (*A* 377)

The book ends with Bell—who had already given someone an autograph earlier in the novel, in New York, simply because someone thought he looked famous—giving an autograph to someone on his flight back to New York (*A* 377). He is, it seems, becoming an author, that is, someone who will not only write but publish, sign, perhaps even autograph and dedicate books.

Brand and Bell are the first two in a fairly long line of writers in DeLillo's work. In *Great Jones Street* we meet the writer or the anti-writer Fenig, who spends as much time gauging the literary market as actually writing: "Knowing the market. Spotting its fluctuations. Measuring its temperament" (*GJ* 29)—that would be Fenig's advice to the would-be writer. At least he is not without a sense of humor: "The market is rejecting me but I'm not blind to the cruel poetry in it" (*GJ* 141). And then there's Murray Jay Siskind—not the professor of Elvis Studies at College-on-the-Hill in *White Noise* but his avatar in *Amazons*, a sportswriter with other, grander literary ambitions. When we meet him on the road covering the New York Rangers he is carrying with him an "eight-hundred-page manuscript" (*AZ* 152, 193), his "Work in Progress" (*AZ* 90): "It has a nice heft to it," he says, and he has "great hopes for it," "but it's not light reading. It's harrowing, brutal stuff" (*AZ* 271). We soon come to find out that "it's investigative reporting of the most sensitive kind," an in-depth report on how the mob has "muscled in on a particular industry," namely, are you ready for it, snowmobiles (*AZ* 272). When he pops back up a few years later at College-on-the-Hill it is not at all clear what has happened to this tale "of violence and extortion running from the northeast U.S. clear to the Rockies," unclear whether Murray has indeed blown the lid off of corruption in the snowmobile industry (*AZ* 272–273; see 365) or just spent his time, after separating from his wife, "trying to develop a vulnerability that women will find attractive" (*AZ* 263, see *WN* 21).

Then there is Bill Gray in *Mao II*, who also fits rather well Bobby Brand's self-image, a sort of cult writer, reclusive, sought out by admirers with backpacks, like Scott, and photographers, like Brita, who makes a living tracking down and photographing writers living in self-imposed exile (see *M* 25). If *Americana* is the story of a young man becoming a writer, *Mao II* depicts an already successful writer who is worried about his next book and is being driven toward his own demise. Bill says of his reclusive life: "It's an irrational way of life that has a powerful inner logic. The way religion takes over a life. The way disease takes over a life" (*M* 45).

Mao II is a novel that gives us a rather different portrait of the artist, a middle-aged novelist who has had commercial success even though his total output consists of "two lean novels in their latest trade editions" (*M* 20). What we have here, then, is an author who, "afraid and hemmed in by doubt" (*M* 121), has retreated from the world because of his celebrity and success and fears returning to that world because his work may not meet with the same success. In the figure of Bill Gray we are thus treated to many reflections on the trials and tribulations of the writer, the uncertainties and self-doubts, the reticence to let a work go:

> There is the epic and bendable space-time of the theoretical physicist, time detached from human experience, the pure curve of nature, and there is the haunted time of the novelist, intimate, pressing, stale and sad. (*M* 54)

Bill Gray likes to exaggerate, as he himself confesses, "I exaggerate the pain of writing, the pain of solitude, the failure, the rage, the confusion, the helplessness, the fear, the humiliation" (*M* 37). And he can always console himself by the thought that "the most successful writers make the biggest complainers" (*M* 101). But then he says, "I'll tell you what I don't exaggerate. The doubt. Every minute of every day. It's what I smell in my bed. Loss of faith. That's what this is all about" (*M* 38). "I'm between novels, he used to say, so I don't mind dying" (*M* 55). It's enough to make one think that maybe "the withheld work of art is the only eloquence left" (*M* 67), that, in the end, the writer who does not write is the best kind of writer to be. Maybe there is something after all to Brand's brand of the great American novel, the kind without words, or to this "visionary insight" from *Ratner's Star*: "It is not necessary to fill in the blank pages, to entrust any kind of writing at all to these pages. ... To express what is expressible isn't why you write if you're in this class of writers. To be understood is faintly embarrassing. What you want to express is the violence of your desire not to be read" (*RS* 398, 410–411).

Mao II seems both to invite and to reject comparisons between Bill Gray, the pen name of Willard Skansey Jr., and Don DeLillo himself, who, according to all accounts, writes under his own name (except that once, by all accounts, as Cleo Birdwell). One could be tempted to read these sentences from *Mao II*, "Bill was not an autobiographical novelist. You could not glean the makings of a life-shape by searching his works for clues" (*M* 144), as implying something similar about DeLillo himself. But DeLillo is, of course, an autobiographical novelist. It is impossible *not* to be to some extent. As proof of that we might cite the following lines from DeLillo's essay "The Power of History," though they could have been uttered by Bill Gray himself: "The novel itself, the old, slow water-torture business of invention and doubt and self-correction, may seem to be wearing an expiration date that takes effect tomorrow" ("PH"). And while this is not exactly the profile of Bill Gray, Gray would have recognized this truth of blank white paper: "[The writer] has his teaching job, his middling reputation and the one radical idea he has been waiting for all his life. The other thing he has is a flat surface that he will decorate, fitfully, with words" ("PH").

Mao II is the novel that devotes the most space, the most words, to the craft of writing, the craft of crafting sentences, and it sounds in places very much like DeLillo's craft:

> I've always seen myself in sentences. I begin to recognize myself, word by word, as I work through a sentence. … The deeper I become entangled in the process of getting a sentence right in its syllables and rhythms, the more I learn about myself. … I've forgotten what it means to write. Forgotten my own first rule. Keep it simple, Bill. (*M* 48)

"Keep it simple": that would seem to be Bill Gray's translation of "least is best" (*GJ* 5), DeLillo's rewriting of Mies van der Rohe's "less is more," a phrase one can find in one form or another in many DeLillo novels and a description of writing that seems to characterize both DeLillo's writing in general and the development of it, a writing that has become more and more spare, even when, as with *Underworld*, the books are long. The narrator says of Bill's writing: "He thought sentences lost their heft and edge when they were stretched too far" (*M* 140). There are also indications of the kinds of stories Bill Gray likes to write—Bill says at one point, "Stories have no point if they don't absorb our terror" (*M* 140)—but it is, for the most part, the craft of writing not stories but *sentences* that seems to be the focus. As Bill tells George, "I'm a sentence-maker, like a donut-maker only slower" (*M* 162). If Bill Gray is—has to be, in part—the shadow or counterband of Don DeLillo, it is first of all because they are both writers of sentences—words and names as well, as we will see shortly, but perhaps first of all sentences, sentences with "heft" and "edge."

"Least is best" (*GJ* 87): As rock star Bucky Wunderlick says of his anticipated return to the music scene: "One thing's sure. I can't go out there and sing pretty lyrics or striking lyrics and I can't go out there and make new and louder and more controversial sounds. … Maybe what I want is less. To become the least of what I was" (*GJ* 87). Less is better and least is best: that's an aesthetic touted in several places in DeLillo's work, from *Great Jones Street* to *Running Dog*: "The less there is, Glen, the more you're tested to find the things that do exist. Within and without. It works. If you limit yourself to the narrowest subject" (*RD* 231). And then in *The Body Artist*: "I am Lauren. But less and less" (*BA* 117).

Least is best: this is perhaps another way of saying, "It takes centuries to invent the primitive" (*A* 238). These words, spoken by David Bell of the simple home movie he made in Fort Curtis, could well apply to DeLillo's work as a whole—and particularly to the winnowing down of language that takes place between *Americana* and later novels. Bell says later in *Americana* in a sort of self-interview between himself and his future self: "I've spent twenty-eight years in the movies. ... I'm inventing the primitive" (*A* 283). And later: "The movie functions best as a sort of ultimate schizogram, an exercise in diametrics which attempts to unmake meaning" (*A* 347).

By the time of *Cosmopolis* this aesthetics of the primitive, or at least of the sparse, the minimal, is on display in everything from the epigraph from Zbigniew Herbert to Packer's preference for "spare poems situated minutely in white space, ranks of alphabetical strokes burnt into paper" (*C* 5). *Underworld* testifies at one point to a similar aesthetic:

> Louise told me once, Nevelson, that she looked at a canvas or a piece of wood and it was white and pure and virginal and no matter how much she marked it up, how many strokes and colors and images, the whole point was to return it to its virgin state, and this was the great and frightening thing. (*U* 386)

If literature is a place of contraband par excellence, a place where one has the right to rewrite or reinvent everything, then it would not be surprising if the writer wanted to *represent* this contraband in his or her work in the form of reflections on writing, writers, and characters who, while not writers themselves, double or contraband the moment or the process of writing itself. Here's a moment from *Mao II*, initially a very funny one, when Bill consults some British veterinarians at a conference in Cyprus on the medical symptoms he would like to give one of his characters in a work (it's himself, actually, a literary version of the old "I have a friend who ... "): "All right. My character is hit by a car on a city street. He is able to walk away unassisted. Bruises on his body. Feels twinges and aches. But he's generally okay. ... Let me add one thing. My character has a tendency to drink" (*M* 206–207). The diagnosis turns out to be a "lacerated liver" (*M* 208) and the veterinarians' recommendation the following: "If you give him the symptoms we've agreed upon, the only plausible recourse is a doctor" (*M* 209). Bill thus gets the diagnosis, sees what his character should be doing, and then himself does just the opposite. As we will see in a moment, this tendency for characters *in* DeLillo's novels to get involved in the techniques and process *of* writing them will be one of the hallmarks of DeLillo's contraband writing, especially in later works.

Reflections on what seem to be the craft of writing or storytelling are thus everywhere in DeLillo, not only helpful or unhelpful tips that seem to have been lifted from some writing workshop—"The best place to begin a story is as close to the end as possible" (*RS* 144)—but reflections on the materials or the materiality, the accoutrements of writing. Once again, *Mao II* would have written the book on this subject, with numerous references to Bill Gray's "corrected drafts, notes, fragments, recorrections, throwaways, updates, tentative revisions, final revisions," and so on (*M* 31), as well as a long contrabanded back-and-forth between Bill and George Haddad about global terrorism, on the one hand, and the virtues of using a word processor rather than a typewriter, on the other. It's the end of the 1980s, and George is trying to convince Bill to adopt this new writing technology—at the same time as he is trying to get him to go to Beirut to meet with a terrorist organization:

> Do you use a word processor? ... Because I find I couldn't conceivably operate without one. Move words, paragraphs, move a hundred pages, plus instant corrections. When I prepare material for lectures, I find the machine helps me organize my thoughts, gives me a text susceptible to revision. I would think for a man who clearly reworks and refines as much as you do, a word processor would be a major blessing. (*M* 137–138)

But—and who knows who is speaking on whose behalf here—Bill "missed his typewriter. ... He could see the words better in type, construct sentences that entered the character-world at once, free of his own disfiguring hand" (*M* 160). And yet George remains relentless right to the very end, passionate about both his politics and his processor:

> Go home, Bill, and do your work. ... And think about what I told you. A word processor. The keyboard action is effortless. I promise you. This is something you dearly need. (*M* 170)

There are, when you start doing an inventory, all sorts of word processors, computers, and, especially, typewriters in DeLillo—like the "old Royal portable" in *Ratner's Star* (*RS* 405) or the Panasonic in *Mao II* (*M* 164) and, especially, *White Noise* (*WN* 241), whose original title was, supposedly, "Panasonic." Even Oswald, who wanted to become a writer, as we will see in a moment, feels the satisfaction of typing, seeing "the sentences emerge so clear and solid with the authority his handwriting could not convey" (*L* 375).

And then there are, of course, all the people in the publishing industry, Bill Gray's agent in *Mao II*, Grace Delaney, the editor of *Running Dog*—to be compared, just for kicks, to Floss Penrose in *Amazons*—Toinette in *Love-Lies-Bleeding*, who "edits children's books for a small shaky imprint" (*LL* 54), and Lianne in *Falling Man*, working for a university press, editing a "book on ancient alphabets" and forms of writing (*FM* 149; see "BM" 111), information that would have been useful for the author of *The Names* or *Ratner's Star* (*FM* 22, 217).

Falling Man is also, in a sense, a novel about writing. In addition to Lianne's occupation and her attempts to write poetry (*FM* 151), not to mention her son Justin's adolescent attempts "to speak in monosyllables only, for extended stretches," because, as he says, it helps him to think, "measuring each word, noting the syllable count" (*FM* 66), a little experiment in writing-thinking that might have interested—that obviously did interest—DeLillo himself, there are Lianne's writing workshops, her "story sessions" with elderly patients suffering from Alzheimer's. Identified only by their first name and the first letter of their last name (Rosellen S., for example), the workshop members are encouraged by Lauren with prompts like "Remembering my father, that sort of thing, or What I always wanted to do but never did, or Do my children know who I am" (*FM* 29). They are hardly innocuous examples for Lianne, who is herself trying to remember, her mother for starters, but then also her time with Keith, and then her father, diagnosed with the very same disease, Alzheimer's, before he took his own life. We thus see the gradual silence and distance into which Lianne's workshop members fade, their "loss of memory, personality and identity, the lapse into eventual protein stupor" (*FM* 125). "These people were the living breath of the thing that killed her father" (*FM* 62; see 68). These sessions thus seem to bring along with them all the problems of memory and trauma of *Falling Man* itself (see *FM* 93–94), especially when Lianne decides to use this as a prompt: "Where were you when it happened?" (*FM* 126) Then, "for the first time since the sessions began, she is afraid to hear what they will say" (*FM* 142). And she is right to be afraid, for "they wrote about the planes. They wrote about where they were when it happened. They wrote about people they knew who were in the towers, or nearby, and they wrote about God. / How could God let this happen" (*FM* 60; see 31). *Falling Man* they no doubt were not, these little stories written by patients on the road to remembering less and less, but they too were attempts, perhaps therapeutic, perhaps not, to recover or to lose what happened on 9/11. One big difference, however, between the writing in *Falling Man* and that of the workshop members is that "no one wrote a word about the terrorists" (*FM* 63–64), no one, in short, followed that other band that DeLillo would interweave with the story of Keith Neudecker and his fellow New Yorkers.

Even *Libra*, a novel ostensibly about the Kennedy assassination, is also a novel about writing. We saw earlier how *Libra* consists of two narrative bands or strands that intersect or get telescoped together on November 22, 1963. Actually, there are at least three different strands: Oswald growing up in the

Bronx, in Texas, his time in the Soviet Union, etc., then Win Everett and others, beginning in April 1963, plotting what will become the assassination of JFK, and then, finally, Nicholas Branch, at least fifteen years later, writing the secret history of the JFK assassination, those "six point nine seconds of heat and light" (*L* 15; see 181). Branch too, then, Branch especially, is the shadow or double of DeLillo the writer writing his own secret history, as it were, of the assassination. Branch's task, like DeLillo's, is in effect to "follow the bullet trajectories backwards to the lives that occupy the shadows" (*L* 15). When Jack Ruby prophetically declares, with a phrase that DeLillo uses as the epigraph to Part II of the novel, "somebody will have to piece me together," we know that that is precisely the work of Branch as well as DeLillo (*L* 215). And one can imagine the following phrase about Branch mocking DeLillo himself in retrospect, at one of those times, months or maybe even years into the research for *Libra*, he had become bogged down somewhere in volume 13 of the Warren Report: "The truth is he hasn't written all that much. He has exhaustive and overlapping notes—notes in three foot drifts, all these years of notes" (*L* 59). One can imagine DeLillo commiserating, thinking that his results are not much better than Branch's, which resemble "a kind of mind-spatter, a poetry of lives muddied and dripping in language" (*L* 181).

And then there is Win Everett, former CIA agent, who has charged himself with creating not just a profile for a potential assassin but a full-blown character, someone who would, in effect, go by the name Lee Harvey Oswald. In other words, on the basis of "fingerprints, a handwriting sample, a photograph" (*L* 51; see 180), and not much more, Everett has to create for his plot a plausible character to assassinate—or, before the plot changes, shoot and miss—the President of the United States: "He would script a gunman out of ordinary dog-eared paper. ... They wanted a name, a face, a bodily frame they might use to extend their fiction into the world" (*L* 50). His plan is to create everything for Oswald, including false names, and he even "looked forward to coming up with names" (*L* 147). It is as if DeLillo were sharing some of his anxiety—as well as his pleasure—with one of his own characters.

So there is Branch, Everett, but then also Oswald himself, who declared on his application to a Swiss college—a ruse to travel to Europe and defect to Russia—that his "vocational interest" was "*To be a short story writer on contemporary American life*" (*L* 134; see 160, 408). Later, "he saw himself writing this story for Life or Look, the tale of an ex-Marine who has penetrated the heart of the Soviet Union" (*L* 206; see 213). This penchant for narration is in fact there from the beginning, indeed already in childhood: "He had a little vision of himself. He saw himself narrating the story to Robert Sproul, relishing his own broad manner of description even as the moment was unfolding in the present, in the larger scheme ... and he felt singularly superior in the telling" (*L* 45). Much later, he sees himself again telling the story of his time in Russia to "someone who resembled Robert Sproul, his high-school friend in New Orleans" (*L* 159). Even after the assassination, in a holding cell in Dallas for those few hours before he himself is killed, Oswald still dreams of being a writer, no longer of American life in general but of himself, for "his life had a single clear subject now, called Lee Harvey Oswald" (*L* 435). (Even Oswald's mother imagines herself getting into the act at one point, "writing a book, she said, about his defection" (*L* 227).)

Oswald-Everett-Branch-DeLillo: Oswald himself as a shadow or double of DeLillo? It seems somewhat implausible given their highly divergent fates, and yet how could it be otherwise? There is a world inside the world and a writer inside the writer.

In *The Names* it is not the main character, James Axton, who is the writer—at least not yet—but Tap, Axton's nine-year-old son. Tap is writing "a prairie epic" (*N* 14; see 197), a novel about "rural life during the Depression" (*N* 32). Despite the "flamboyant prose," the "lurid emotions," and the "atrocious" spelling (*N* 32), there is something compelling about his writing, both his epic narrative and his letters to his father. When Tap moves with his mother to British Columbia, James asks his son to put into his letters the same kind of details that James's own father once asked of him: "A detailed picture in which to place the small figure," for "the only safety is in details. ... I had to give him names, numbers, colors, whatever I could collect of particular things. These helped him see me as real" (*N* 311). And when James finally reads Tap's narrative, presented as the final chapter of *The Names*, entitled, precisely, "The Prairie," the "flamboyant prose" and "atrocious" spelling get a much more generous read. Axton says of his son's "spirited misspellings":

> I found these mangled words exhilarating. He'd made them new again, made me see how they worked, what they really were. They were ancient things, secret, reshapeable. ... His other misrenderings were wilder, freedom-seeking, and seemed to contain curious perceptions about the words themselves, second and deeper meanings, original meanings. It pleased me to believe he was not wholly innocent of these mistakes. (*N* 313)

But Axton himself is also a figure of the writer even if he does not actually write. He is, after all, the narrator, though there are many other suggestions that he is a writer-in-waiting or a writer-the-making, and the members of the alphabet cult take him for a writer (*N* 212). We thus see him engaged at various points in a kind of virtual or imagined narration not unlike that of a writer (see *N* 239; see 293–295, 300), and there are even a few places where he is given a certain self-consciousness about his own narration, as if he *were* in fact a writer. Here, for example, on the second page of the novel: "One night (as we enter narrative time) I was driving ... " (*N* 4).

But then Owen Brademas is also a writer of sorts, telling Axton in Pakistan what happened to him in India, recounting this recent history and then thinking back, in contraband, to his childhood in Kansas. It all becomes so vivid that, as Axton says, "the telling had merged with the event. I had to think a moment to remember where we were" (*N* 308). And then there is this comment of Axton's on Brademas's curious way of ending his story: "It was interesting how he'd chosen to finish, impersonally" (*N* 309; see 149).

Axton himself denies being a writer throughout *The Names*, but his encounters with Owen Brademas, with the cult obsessed by the alphabet, and even his reception of his own son's writing, seem to awaken him to narrative and to language:

> I moved slowly, feeling a need to remember all this, and I ... noted the colors of the stone as if some importance might attach to my describing them precisely someday, the unmellowed tone of this particular biscuit brown, this rust, this sky gray. (*N* 196)

At the end of the novel, after his resignation as a risk analyst, he thinks about turning to "some kind of higher typing, a return to the freelance life" (*N* 318). Only by writing, he thinks, will he ever be able to give the people he has met in Greece a "second life":

> These are among the people I've tried to know twice, the second time in memory and language. Through them, myself. They are what I've become, in ways I don't understand but which I believe will accrue to a rounded truth, a second life for me as well as for them. (*N* 329)

Only by writing will these people live in memory or in language. Only by writing will they gain renown, *cleos*, as those Greeks would call it, which may explain why *Amazons*, published just two years before *The Names*, was written under the pseudonym Cleo Birdwell. The novel begins, most appropriately, with an epigraph from a totally made-up author, Wadi Assad, a Kahlil Gibranish sort of writer with books like *The Mystic Prince I*, *The Barefoot Rose*, *The Romance of Being* (*AZ* 5; see 7, 22), *The Immortal Peacock* (*AZ* 32), *The Desert Nectar of Wadi Assad* (*AZ* 174), *The Heart-Shaped Moment* (*AZ* 238), and so on, books that are not only referred to but cited— sometimes at length—throughout the novel. Cleo Birdwell considers Wadi Assad to be a refined taste, a "private pleasure" (*AZ* 131) for the elite few

(*AZ* 131), so that "when you meet someone who reads Wadi Assad, you've found a friend for life" (*AZ* 29; see 323). But it turns out that pretty much everyone in the NHL—including management—has been reading him for years, unbeknownst to everyone else. For Wadi Assad is not just literature; he's a way of life, he's self-help of a higher order. For "there is a pattern, a plan, a design, a lesson, a principle, a truth. ... Above all, there is an inner calm. ... We are comforted, reassured, quietly invigorated. The appeal is spiritual" (*AZ* 323; see 349). Wadi Assad is, in short, "pseudo profound," and "this is the whole point," "this is the man's charm" (*AZ* 378). "Wadi Assad makes sense, even when he sounds like a fortune cookie" (*AZ* 379). It sounds like a put-down but someone in the novel puts a pretty good face on it:

> Isn't pseudo profundity exactly what we need in these terrible times? Don't all our problems arise from true profundity? Isn't the failure of our age a failure of profound men with profound ideas? What was Marx if not profound? Or Freud or Gandhi or Bertie Russell. Yet all we have to do is look around us to discover the fruits of this deep, true, genuine profundity. (*AZ* 327)

Of course, wherever there are writers there are critics, and DeLillo's novels are full of these as well. And when an author such as DeLillo includes a critic in one of his novels, or a film, music, or art review from a critic, it can never be wholly without purpose, that is, it can never not cast a shadow upon the novel in which it is found. In short, it can never escape—indeed it always seems to court—a contraband effect. The reviews of Bucky Wunderlick's new music, of Bill Gray's new but unpublished novel, of Lauren Hartke's performance piece, all these are, inevitably, self-reviews of a kind, reflections on the whole process or phenomenon of reviews but also, inevitably, reviews real or imagined, anticipated or feared, of the novel in which they are found. Of course, a review about some work, or an interview about a performance, can itself turn into a performance and can become central to the novel or script in which it is featured. (DeLillo's script of the movie *Game 6* revolves around precisely this.)

In *The Body Artist*, the film critic Philip Stansky—close to Skansey (but with a more back-loaded *k*), the real name of Bill Gray in *Mao II*—says of the films of Rey Robles: "His subject is people in landscapes of estrangement," "he found a spiritual knife-edge in the poetry of alien places, where extreme situations become inevitable and characters are forced toward life-defining moments" (*BA* 29)—not a bad description or self-description of certain aspects of DeLillo. Then, later in the novel, there is a review of Lauren Hartke's body work piece that seems to function as an implicit review, or even defense, of DeLillo's own novel. One might imagine a fan of the fast-clipped prose of *White Noise* or *Libra* coming upon *The Body Artist* and wondering what in the world has happened. For such a person or critic, the description of Lauren Hartke's performance piece sounds like an appropriate counterband: "Hartke clearly wanted her audience to feel time go by, viscerally, even painfully. This is what happened, causing walkouts among the less committed. / They missed the best stuff" (*BA* 104). As Hartke then says in an interview about her own work: "I know there are people who think the piece was too slow and repetitious, I guess, and uneventful. But it's probably too eventful. I put too much into it. It ought to be sparer, even slower than it is, even longer than it is. It ought to be three fucking hours" (*BA* 106).

In *Ratner's Star* there is even a clue—or maybe a false clue—about how to read the novel itself: "Reading my book will be a game with specific rules that have to be learned. I'm free to make whatever rules I want as long as there's an inner firmness and cohesion, right? Just like mathematics, excuse the comparison" (*RS* 352).

Numbers

Names tell stories and so do numbers. Zahl and tale. One coils continuously into the other.

RS 156

I have a head for numbers. Numbers fascinate me. Numbers have power. The whole country runs on numbers. ... Everybody has numbers. Everybody is a number. Is that so terrible? Maybe it is.

A 121

It may seem like a sidestep, like an irrational number within a set of wholes, but DeLillo's fascination with language and writing is almost equaled by his fascination with numbers and mathematics. Both, it seems, are ways of giving order to our world. In *Ratner's Star* they form a pair: "Words and numbers. Writing and calculating" (*RS* 7–8). But this interest in mathematics, often paired with language, runs throughout DeLillo's work. Already in *Americana*, radio-ranter Warren Beasley speaks of the "pure mathematics of the desert" (*A* 368), and, earlier, there is speculation, inspired by a strip of bacon, regarding the significance or insignificance of numbers: "With her fork she bisected a crisp slice of bacon ... Did the bacon represent the insignificance of numbers; the futile quest for infinity; the indivisible nature of God as opposed to the fractional promiscuity of numbers?" (*A* 123) In *Zero K* there is not only Jeffrey, whose father walked out the door when he was doing trigonometry homework, but Emma's son Stak who, like Jeffrey, is "interested in numbers. High, medium, low. Place-names and numbers. Shanghai, he will say. Zero point zero one inches precipitation. Mumbai, he will say. He loves to say Mumbai" (*ZK* 177).

Between these two novels, the first and the last or the latest, there are mathematicians and reflections upon mathematics more or less everywhere. There is Matt Shay, a numbers guy who works for a time in weapons research and before that as an analyst in the military in Vietnam: "When he found a dot on the film he translated it into letters, numbers, coordinates, grids and entire systems of knowledge" (*U* 463). Matt may have gotten his head for numbers from his father, a bookie who had a legendary memory, even if the legend may have been more of Nick's making than a reflection of reality. In any case, memory and numbers, memory and math, link father to son in more than one DeLillo narrative: "He left when I was thirteen. ... I kept doing my homework while he spoke. I examined the formulas on the page and wrote in my notebook, over and over: *sine cosine tangent*" (*ZK* 14).

Numbers, like words, equations, like narratives, help us make sense of the world, giving it an order and an orientation, a shape and a direction: "Carrying the fetus to term. Nine months. Seven pounds two ounces. We need numbers to make sense of the world. We think in numbers. We think in decades. Because we need organizing principles" (*U* 735).

There can thus be great meaning in numbers, but there can also be secrets, just as inscrutable as the secrets in texts: "Intoxicating theorems. Nagging little symmetries. The secrets hidden deep inside the great big primes" (*RS* 67). Lyle of *Players* was attracted to the stock market because he "saw in the numbers and stock symbols an artful reduction of the external world to printed output, the machine's coded model of exactitude" (*P* 70); he had "a feel for numbers" as "secret mnemonic devices" (*P* 156) and so used numbers to "pull things into a systematic pattern or the illusion of a systematic pattern" (*P* 211). *White Noise* returns to this relationship between numbers and systems, to the way they define our interactions and, thus, our lives. "The system was invisible, which made it all the more impressive, all the more disquieting to deal with" (*WN* 46). Micro-dots and mega-data: DeLillo seems to have been talking about both for a very long time: "Terrifying data is now an industry in itself. Different firms compete to see how badly they can scare us" (*WN* 175).

Finally, there is *Ratner's Star*, a great book about numbers, about language, and about the relationship between the two. The novel is filled with reflections about mathematics and astronomy, beginning with Kepler's

Somnium, "A beautiful and extremely rare book. Written in Latin with a smidgen of Hebrew and Greek." It's "an experimental novel," "an allegory, a lunar geography, an artful autobiography, a cryptic scientific tract, a work of science fiction" (*RS* 57)—a description that sounds like a review of *Ratner's Star*. But Kepler is just the first in an astonishingly long list of mathematicians, physicists, and astronomers, not just Pythagoras, Aristotle, Copernicus, Brahe, Galileo, Pascal, Newton, Leibniz, Cantor, and Einstein but also, in alphabetical order, Niels Henrik Abel, Girolamo Cardano, Arthur Cayley, Richard Dedekind, Charles Dodgson, Gottlob Frege, Évariste Galois, Carl Friedrich Gauss, Sophie Germain, William Rowan Hamilton, Charles Hermite, David Hilbert, Jacob Jacobi, Sonja Kowalewski, Leopold Kronecker, Nicolai Lobachevsky, John Napier, Giuseppe Peano, Henri Poincaré, Jean-Victor Poncelet, Srinivasa Ramanujan, Bernhard Riemann, James Sylvester, Karl Weierstrass, and others still.

We find in *Ratner's Star* discussions of everything from a screaming lady in the Bronx who made cryptic mathematical notations (*RS* 249; see 73) to peoples who "can count only as far as one" and who "don't understand the multiple form at all. Beyond one, everything is considered a heap" (*RS* 103). And then there's Billy Twillig, math prodigy, world-famous at the age of fourteen for his work with "zorgs" (*RS* 4, 20), the kind of kid who is interested in "imaginary quantities (the square root of minus-one, for instance)" (*RS* 3), and who, right after a NYC subway accident, "realized there is at least one prime between a given number and its double" (*RS* 5), the kind of kid who appreciates "the arch-reality of pure mathematics, its austere disposition, its links to simplicity and permanence; the formal balances it maintains, inevitability adjacent to surprise … its precision as a language; its claim to necessary conclusions; its pursuit of connective patterns and significant form; the manifold freedom it offers in the very strictures it persistently upholds" (*RS* 13), the kind of kid who undertook mathematics "solely to advance the art" (*RS* 33) and who is recruited to decode a message from extraterrestrials and then, because of his "fantastic grasp of connective patterns, of relationships and forms" (*RS* 274), is asked to construct a "logistic cosmic language based on mathematical principles" (*RS* 273), "a transgalactic language," a "pure and perfect mathematical logic," to respond to these extraterrestrials. He's the kind of kid who understands so well the mathematical properties of zorgs that he began "to learn to view zorgs as events rather than numbers, just as particles are events rather than things" (*RS* 418). He's that kind of kid—a dime a dozen.

Ratner's Star also explores the relationship, as old as Pythagoras and Kabbalah, between numbers and creation: "Numbers as the basis of creation" (*RS* 44; see 429), "the emanations of the *en-sof* are numbers. … *Sefiroth* comes from the infinitive 'to count.' The power of counting, of finger-numbers, of one-to-ten" (*RS* 223). There are the intricate patterns in nature but then also those in man-made things, for example, in a Middle Eastern rug: "A contained and intricate rapture, the desert universe made shapely and complete. … Geometry, nature and God" (*N* 219).

But inasmuch as numbers undergird all living systems, they also ultimately refer to death. "When I read obituaries I always note the age of the deceased" (*WN* 99). "The power of numbers is never more evident than when we use them to speculate on the time of our dying" (*WN* 99). Numbers themselves are thus related to death, both in and of themselves and through our instruments of measurement, that is, our technological uses of them: "If I were on my deathbed today, and did not know the date, my cells would probably refuse to surrender. Without a calculator, a stopwatch, a measuring cup on the night table, I couldn't possibly know how to die" (*A* 159).

In *The Names* the Maitlands' mathematician son gives a lesson in the usefulness—and uselessness—of mathematics: "The only test is mathematics. You've got to know the secrets. … It makes no sense if you don't know the secrets, the codes. It means nothing, says nothing, refers to nothing, is in fact absolutely useless" (*N* 164; see 41). But the fact that it is useless in this way makes it interesting, like a self-referring language, a language with no outside: "It's interesting in itself, you see. It refers to itself and only itself. It's the pure exercise of the mind. It's Rosicrucianism, druids in hoods. The formal balances, that's what counts. The patterns, the structures" (*N* 164). But then the language of mathematics may not be that different from any language, a language that seems to refer to what is before or beyond it but can always be heard as referring only to itself. As someone says in *Ratner's Star*, "You never heard my name—only my name's name" (*RS* 145).

But there is, of course, an interface between mathematics and the world, a way of translating the one into the other. It can all seem perfectly innocent or purely academic, up until the moment someone tries to turn abstract numbers into a physical force, a series of numbers and symbols into, say, a guided missile:

> It was a splendid mystery in a way, a source of wonder, how a brief equation that you tentatively enter on your screen might alter the course of many lives, might cause the blood to rush through the body of a woman on a tram many thousands of miles away, and how do you define this kind of relationship? (*U* 408–409)

There is a power in numbers, not just when they are raised to a certain power, squared, for example, but already in themselves, in the equations that express them:

E equals MC squared. ... How is it that a few marks chalked on a blackboard, a few little squiggly signs can change the shape of human history? ... Never mind what happens when we split the atom and release this energy. ... Never mind the energy packed in the atom. What about the energy contained in this equation? This is the real power. How the mind operates. How the mind identifies, analyzes and represents. (*U* 735)

In *Zero K* there is even the thought that a particular equation in the Convergence—"a cracked clay tablet ... bearing a tightly compressed line of numbers, letters, square roots, cube roots, plus and minus signs, and there were parentheses, infinities and other symbols with an equal sign in the midst of it all, an indication of logical or mathematical equality" (*ZK* 255)—might somehow express "the merger, breath to breath, of end and beginning. ... a scientific expression of what happens to a single human body when the forces of death and life join" (*ZK* 255). This equation would be the ultimate contraband, the ultimate interface or convergence, the one that connects beginning to end, life to death, band to contraband. It would be like the pineal gland of mathematics.

Mathematics, then, is imagined here as bringing opposites together, opposites—or seeming opposites—like "experience and pure thought. The mind and the world. External reality and independent abstract deduction" (*RS* 418). Once again, what seems furthest away, most abstract, can lead us back to ourselves. However abstract Billy Twillig's work may seem to be, its "natural tendency was to provide a model of his own mind" (*RS* 238).

In addition to all these reflections on mathematics in this more abstract sense, on the purity and power of numbers (*RS* 272, 285, 318), on mathematical "axioms" and "curved space" (*L* 164), numerical connections and coincidences ("MD" 143–144), odd numbers and prime numbers ("MD" 136), there is DeLillo's repeated interest in particular numbers, like 1, 13, 51, and 101 (prime numbers all—except 51, though it sure looks prime). As we might expect, the interest in primes revolves not just around the numbers themselves but around the way we *define* them:

> We stood in the veer, gliding out of Zero K, out of the numbered levels. I thought of prime numbers. I thought, Define a prime. The veer was an environment, I thought, suited to rigorous thinking. I was always good at math. I felt sure of myself when I dealt with numbers. Numbers were the language of science. And now I needed to find the precise and perpetual and more or less mandatory wording that would constitute the definition of a prime. ... Prime number.

A positive integer not divisible. But what was the rest of it? What else about primes? What else about integers? (*ZK* 151)

For the number 13, there's *Underworld*, a novel that mushrooms out of its ground-zero setting in NYC's Polo Grounds as the New York Giants, who began their pennant drive thirteen and a half games behind the Dodgers, win the playoff game that puts them in the World Series when Bobby Thompson (thirteen letters) of the Giants hits a baseball off Brooklyn Dodgers pitcher Ralph Branca, who "wears the number thirteen blazoned on his back" (*U* 31) and who had won thirteen games that year (*U* 678; see 95), into the stands on October 3—that is, "ten three. Add the digits, you get thirteen" (*U* 678; see 95)—1951, all of this immortalized by the Giants radio voice Russell Hodges—also thirteen letters (*U* 133; see *RS* 134 and 262 for further speculations on numbers, names, and letters). And then, as Nick Shay reminds us, there's

> "the time of the home run. Three fifty-eight. Add the digits of the minutes. Thirteen," and then "the name Branca. The *B* is two. The *r* is eighteen. And so on and so on. You end up with thirty-nine. What is thirty-nine? It is the number which, when you divide it by the day of the month of the game, gives you thirteen." (*U* 679; see 307)

And this treiskaidekamania goes well beyond Nick; indeed it's catchy and even the narrator comes down with a bout of it: "Moonman 157. Add the digits and you get thirteen" (*U* 439). And what inspired Moonman 157 to become a graffiti artist in the first place? Some subway graffiti about Bird, aka Charlie Parker—another name with thirteen letters. And then there's the isotope Uranium-238, "add the digits and you get thirteen" (*U* 122), and talk of a bomb of "fifty-eight megatons—add the digits and you get thirteen" (*U* 826), and the famous headshot of the Zapruder film, turns out to be "frame 313," for "there had to be a thirteen somewhere in the case" (*U* 488–489).

As for 51, as in October 3, 1951, it is not as omnipresent as 13, but it is there, oddly, well before *Underworld*: "Sweat trickled down my ribs. The digital reading on the clock-radio was 3:51. Always odd numbers at times like this. What does it mean? Is death odd-numbered? ... 'I'll be fifty-one next week.'" (*WN* 47; see *EZ* 183 and then *C* 189 for the number 41, which not only looks like a prime but is one.)

Of course we mustn't forget zero, zero first of all, as a name or synonym for what is nothing or less than nothing, something of no value, like a person, 0swald, for example, in the eyes of those who are planning the assassination,

"A zero in the system" (*L* 151, 357), which is why people will be forever trying to figure out "how a complete nothing, a zero person in a T-shirt, could decide out of nowhere to shoot our President" (*L* 421).

There is the zero that seems to be a zero all by itself and then there's the zero that is paired with 1, its opposite—as in "the binary black-white yes-no zero-one hero-goat" (*U* 466)—but also its partner in programming, the two of them responsible for the whole "zero-oneness of the world" (*C* 24). Already in *Ratner's Star* there is a lot about zero, about the number, if it is a number, zero.

> The history of zero is both interesting and informative. It is thought that zero was discovered in India by a Hindu many, many years ago. It is the shadow of pure quantity. ... Zero is an element of a set that when added to any other element in the set produces a sum identical with the element to which it is added. (*RS* 266)

Zero, then, because you don't need to be a math whiz to know that if you add the first part of *Ratner's Star*, "Field Experiment Number One," to the second part, "Logicon Project Minus-One," what you get is zero, the place, it seems, where all life begins and is in danger of coming to an end, there at "ground zero" (*U* 793), at the "zero point" (*U* 84).

Then there's 101, the number that is central to *Ratner's Star*, a prime number that, to state the obvious, is made up of nothing but a 0 and two 1s. It initially appears in the novel that earthlings have been "contacted by someone or something in outer space," "an extraterrestrial civilization" (*RS* 46), by means of a message or code consisting of fourteen pulses, one gap, twenty-eight pulses, a gap, and fifty seven pulses—101 pulses in all with two gaps: "one hundred and one," "the lowest three-digit prime" (*RS* 47), "indivisible except by itself and the number one" (*RS* 77). "One zero one. Not only the lowest three-digit prime but the smallest three-digit palindrome. Not only reads the same forward and back but right side up and upside down" (*RS* 99). Billy Twillig's mentor Endor first thought that "the Ratnerians might be offering us a simple declarative sentence or a neat cluster of numbers that would tell us why the universe is so big" (*RS* 85; see 101, 163). But it is eventually discovered that the message didn't come at all from Ratner's Star or from one of the planets around it but from the earth itself, sometime in its distant past (*RS* 179). It turns out to be not "notation by sixty," that is, a number of base sixty, but—not wholly unrelated—a time, in hours, minutes, and seconds (see also *ZK* 234).

So, 0, 1, 13, 51, 101 (add all the digits and you again get 13): those are just some of the numbers (we saw 17 earlier when we looked at the internet) that populate the literary universe of Donald DeLillo.

Writing

"What's it like to weigh three hundred pounds?" "It's like being an overwritten paragraph."

EZ 48

When the novelist loses his talent, he dies democratically, there it is for everyone to see, wide open to the world, the shitpile of hopeless prose.

M 159

I'm not a great big visionary, George. I'm a sentence-maker, like a donut-maker only slower.

M 162

Back to language, to words and to names, to writing: there are many places in a DeLillo work where the narrative seems to be about the process of writing itself. Someone says in *Players*, for example: "Don't believe what he says necessarily. He likes to make up a character as he goes along" (*P* 185). Much earlier in the same novel, we read this about the protagonist, Lyle Wynant, who is observing others as if he were an informant, or a witness, or, indeed, a narrator, though he is in fact a broker on the Stock Exchange:

> He went east on John Street, enumerating these facts as though he were conversing with someone who sought a description of the woman. This was something he did only on buses as a rule. His attention would wander to someone across the aisle and he'd find himself putting together a physical description of the man or woman. (*P* 45)

There are thus moments when the writer or the tropes of writing appear to intervene in the writing itself or when the narrator stops simply commenting on the action and begins commenting on the narration itself. Elsewhere called irony or self-reference, one of the marks or hallmarks, it is often thought, of what is called the postmodern, it is perhaps best understood as a contraband effect. Here is a moment in *End Zone* when the narrator addresses his reader—his "spectator": "The spectator, at this point, is certain to wonder whether he must now endure a football game in print" (*EZ* 111). And that is, in fact, just what the spectator or reader will get, a thirty-page account of a football game. In *Libra* there is a similar address to the reader, from inside, as it were, the narrative memory of Lee Harvey Oswald—who seems to be assuming that we have read the rest of DeLillo's *Libra*: "Remember the ambulance in Atsugi, camouflage-green" (*L* 439; see *U* 57). Here is another example, from near the end of *White Noise*: "How literary, I thought peevishly. Streets thick with the details of impulsive life as the hero ponders the latest phase in his dying" (*WN* 281). We see something less explicit but just as intriguing in the sudden appearance a bit earlier of Babette's father in the backyard. "A white-haired man sitting erect in the old wicker chair, a figure of eerie stillness and composure. At first, dazed and sleepy, I didn't know what to make of the sight. ... I thought one thing, that he'd been *inserted* there for some purpose" (*WN* 242). Inserted like an incongruous detail or passage in a book, Babette's father appears in the backyard unexpectedly, an appearance and a paragraph in contraband. We get something similar in *Amazons*, when Cleo Birdwell remarks, "I've always thought that simultaneous talk was a sign that an event was going well. Aside from everything else, it means no one is listening. Listening is deadly to a sense of good times" (*AZ* 267). It's a remark about good dinner parties, not about good writing, but it becomes something different just after when her agent—with whom she is going to "do a book"—calls it "overlapping dialogue" (*AZ* 267). That's a lesson not in having good parties but in constructing contrabanded narratives.

Elsewhere, characters—not the writer or the narrator but *characters*—come to ask themselves about certain words and meanings, suggesting a kind of double band between themselves and the writer. Take the way, for example, Brita in *Mao II* "waited for Scott to call this room the bunker. He never did" (*M* 31–32) or the way Lauren in *The Body Artist* "refrains, in her imagining ... from using the lost dog analogy as it pertains to Mr. Tuttle, out of whatever scruple and so on" (*BA* 79). Hence Lauren refrains but DeLillo does not or at least he doesn't refrain from mentioning Lauren's refrain. Or Jim Finley in *Point Omega*, out on the porch with Jessie, surprised to find himself using the phrase DeLillo whispered in his ear: "I asked her to come over and sit with me. I used that phrase, sit with me" (*PO* 69). And then, just a couple of pages later: "One day soon all our talk, his and mine, will be like hers, just talk, self-contained, unreferring" (*PO* 72). And Bill Gray in a taxi after a long drunken night in a Cyprian nightclub, surprised to find himself not just feeling in a certain way but thinking of a certain word to describe his feeling: "Bill sat jammed in a corner of the taxi feeling muddled and blurred. Muzzy. This was a word he hadn't heard or thought of in many years" (*M* 210).

But then there's the fact that characters in DeLillo's narratives not only reflect upon names, and, as we saw, pay attention to them, but try to recall or find a right name, much like what the writer himself or herself must do on a daily basis. For example, in *Mao II*: "Now there's a crack all of a sudden. What's it called, a fissure" (*M* 57). Or in *Cosmopolis*: "A man lay dead or sleeping in the vestibule, if this is still a word" (*C* 182). Or in *Amazons*: "Sidney Glass lived in a sprawling apartment that overlooked the East River. Houses are rambling, according to my mother. Apartments sprawl" (*AZ* 99). It's as if the narrator, if not the novelist, were using a character—or a character's mother—to recall the right word for something. Once again, there is a world inside the world and, sometimes, it talks back.

If writers make their sentences with words, these words are not just there for the taking. They must be found—the right ones at the right moment. It is thus not just any gesture of writing when a writer has one of his characters actively search, himself or herself, for a particular word. Sometimes, more rarely, a character searches for an analogy: "It's an effort. It's like what. It's like pushing a boulder" (*BA* 17). Much more frequently it's a question of a character looking for a word. Martin Manx, for example, looks for a particular word to support his argument for selling the Bobby Thomson home run ball. "He tries to think of the word that means a thing will increase in value over the years. ... The baseball's bound to appreciate is the word. And the cash be worth less by the minute" (*U* 653–654). Benno Levin says in *Cosmopolis*: "I'm what's the word, pervious to visible light" (*C* 195). And Delfina in *Valparaiso*: "What is the word that describes the condition of a man who advances bravely toward his own grueling truth? ... Perishability" (*V* 103). And then there's "The Starveling": "There was a word he wanted to apply to her. It was a medical or psychological term and it took a long moment before he was able to think of it, *anorexic*, one of those words that carries its meaning with a vengeance" ("S" 196; see 202). In *Underworld* Sister Gracie tries to come up with "abdication" (*U* 819; "AE" 95). And then there's Jeffrey in *Zero K*, who gives us a prime example of a word that seems to refer to itself before anything else:

> I kept looking into his face, thinking of a certain word. I think of words that lead me into dense realities, clarifying a situation or a circumstance, at least in theory. Here was Ross, eyes tired and shoulders hunched, right hand trembling slightly, and the word was *desuetude*. (*ZK* 201; see 204)

It's already an interesting list: pervious, perishability, anorexic, desuetude, fissure, abdication. Anyone see a family resemblance?

It is never without interest when a writer, who seeks his words and tries to choose them carefully, wisely, involves his characters in the same activity. For example, at breakfast, barely awake: "What's it called, the lever. She'd pressed down the lever to get his bread to go brown" (*BA* 9). This is followed, just a page later, with a bit of uncertainty, whether genuine or feigned, regarding the tense of that same lever's activity: "The lever sprang or sprung" (*BA* 10). Thirty pages later, we are back to where we were before the lever was remembered as a "lever": "You had to flip the thing twice to get the bread to toast properly" (*BA* 44). Trying to find the right word for the flip thing is like looking "under the lampshade for the on-off thing, the knob, the switch that will turn on the light" (*ZK* 19). Making toast, then, or turning on a light, or doing laundry, where one has to "put the filter pan back on the agitator or activator or whatever it was called" (*FM* 150), these everyday household words elude many of DeLillo's characters, both wives and husbands: "She believes he is growing into it, a husbandman, even though she knows this is another word completely" (*FM* 70). In *Libra* it's the word *lair* rather than *lever* that momentarily escapes the mother of Lee: "This is a boy who studies the lives of animals, the eating and sleeping habits of animals, animals in their burrows and caves. What is it called, lairs?" (*L* 10; see *DR* 18)

But Marvin Lundy is the undisputed king of such word searching. He does it repeatedly, not only trying to find certain words himself but enlisting the help of others in his search for words like "obliterate" (*U* 171–172) or "lineage": Lundy says of the Bobby Thomson home run baseball he is trying to sell: "I have to tell you first thing. I don't have the what-do-you-call completely established." "The lineage." "The lineage. I don't have the lineage all the way" (*U* 192; see *U* 307–308).

There are words, then, sitting there in the dictionary, waiting to be found, and then there are attempts to find these words, right or precise words, in everyday conversation. A character might search for a word—like a narrator or a writer: "I've always been—what have I been? Disoriented. Like where is the man that uses my name?" (*V* 57) Or what is it that a crowd does when it's coming apart, "what is the word, dispersed?" (*M* 177) Or that whole idea of souls going elsewhere, "What's the word I'm looking for? … The word is *metempsychosis*" (*ZK* 48). Or what's the word to describe a part of the Convergence: "I searched for the word. There was a word I wanted, not *crypt* or *grotto* … I walked along … and the sight was overwhelming and the place itself, the word itself—the word was *catacomb*" (*ZK* 133).

Zero K takes this peculiar process of inscribing writers and the process of writing within narrative to its logical conclusion. First of all, there is Stak, Emma's teenage son, learning Pashto, talking to cabdrivers in the language and then inventing stories about what they talked about: "He invented the Taliban story. … He improvises now and then, inflates something, expands something, takes a story to a limit in a way that may or may not test your standards of belief" (*ZK* 178). But then it is the narrator, Jeffrey Lockhart, who imagines the narration of Stak, his unofficial stepson: "I found myself imagining that the man at the wheel of the taxi we hailed would have a Ukrainian name and accent and would be glad to speak the language with Stak, giving the boy another chance to turn a stranger's scant life into lavish fiction" (*ZK* 181). Fiction inside fictions inside fiction—and that's just the beginning of Jeffrey Lockhart's tale-telling. First, he does voices:

> I described the details of several job interviews to Emma, who enjoyed my accounts of the proceedings—voice imitations, sometimes verbatim, of the interviewers' remarks. She understood that I was not ridiculing these men and women. This was a documentary approach to a special kind of dialogue and we both knew that the performer himself, still jobless, was the subject of the piece. (*ZK* 198)

But then, because there are lots of people who tell stories, and even do voices, Jeffrey goes that extra mile by giving fictional names to the people he meets. This tendency has been in DeLillo's work pretty much from the beginning, but it has become even more pronounced in recent works like *Zero K*, where the narrator, Jeffrey Lockhart (a name with *k*), gives names (many with *k*'s) to those he meets in the Convergence (no *k*, though it has a *k* sound):

> I decided to give him a name. I would give them names, both of them, just for the hell of it, and to stay involved, expand the tenuous role of the concealed man, the surreptitious witness. ... I thought of several names and rejected them. Then I came up with Szabo. I didn't know if this name was a product of his country of origin but it didn't matter. There were no countries of origin here. I liked the name. It suited his bulging body. Miklos Szabo. (*ZK* 66–67)

And it doesn't stop there. "I named them the Stenmark twins. They were the Stenmark twins. Jan and Lars, or Nils and Sven" (*ZK* 71; see 241). And then, after giving them a name, he provides them with a background—just as a fiction writer would: "I decided that they were street anarchists of an earlier era" (*ZK* 75). Much later in the novel, Jeffrey decides he needs "a name for Stak's father, Emma's ex, in Denver, mile-high" (*ZK* 195; see 217). "I'd more or less settled on a first name for the man. Volodymyr" (*ZK* 223).

Even when no proper name seems appropriate, the common name can sometimes do—especially if it has a *k*: "It occurred to me that I might give him a name, as I'd done with the speakers in the stone room. But a name, in his case a fictitious birth name, would be dead weight. He was the Monk" (*ZK* 95). Not all names have *k*'s, of course, because *k* doesn't always suit the character. Sometimes Jeffrey needs an *l*, or more than one, like for some long and lanky man he has never met but who is perhaps his mother's lover: "I tried to find a name for her friend that was suited to his height, weight and personality. Rick Linville was a skinny name. She listened to my alternatives" (*ZK* 103).

Jeffrey cannot help giving people fictitious names, for it's a way to make them real: "I looked again at the woman in the headscarf, unnamed still. She would not be real until I gave her a name" (*ZK* 72; see 95). Even those whose names are already known seem to require a renaming: "The name Ben-Ezra was itself an invention, so I decided. The name suited the man, suggesting a composite of biblical and futuristic themes ... I was sorry he'd told me his name, sorry he'd named himself before I could do it for him" (*ZK* 125). And certain names, those he likes, like the name of his partner, Emma Breslow, seem to him to have been, in retrospect, of his own invention: "I liked to say the name. I liked to tell myself that I would have guessed the name, or invented it, if she hadn't told me what it is at the wedding of mutual friends on a horse farm in Connecticut, where we first met" (*ZK* 176). And once in a while, Jeffrey decides *not* to give someone a name, though, even there, the reasons seem to be aesthetic, dictated by the setting or the plot: "I watched her dress, slowly, and decided not to give her a name. She blended better, nameless, with the room" (*ZK* 79).

Characters not only make up names for other characters—just as a narrator or writer would—but they make up names for themselves. We learn in *Zero K*, for example, that "Ross Lockhart is a fake name" (*ZK* 81), a name that Ross, "born Nicholas Satterswaite" (*Z* 82), had given to himself and so had to grow into: "In time he would become the man he'd only glimpsed when *Ross Lockhart* was a series of alphabet strokes on a sheet of paper" (*Z* 81). As for Jeffrey, the son, once he realizes that he is someone he was "not supposed to be" (*ZK* 82) he can begin to comment, like an author or an editor, like the "better maker," on the appropriateness of his own name: "The name Lockhart was all wrong for me. Too tight, too clenched" (*ZK* 82–83). This is precisely a writer's sensibility, a writer's need, "the need," says Jeffrey, "to get inside the name, work it, wedge myself into it" (*Z* 82). It's as if Jeffrey understands what the narrator of *Falling Man* has understood, namely, that names define who we are within certain limits, that they have implications. Rumsey, for example, would have been different if "he'd been born a Ramsey," that is, given the name Ramsey by the author (*FM* 150)—and, fun fact, not only is Rumsey not Ramsey, he is not even the only Rumsey in DeLillo (see *L* 43).

On his second trip to the Convergence, this time to accompany his father, Jeffrey continues to play this novel or novelist's game, looking for a name in *Z*, this time, rather than *K*:

> I needed a name for her. I hadn't named anyone on this visit. A name would add dimension to the lithe body, suggest a place of origin ... She needed a name that started with the letter Z. ... A clipped voice, authoritative, slightly accented, and the tension in her body, the

stretched energy. I could call her Zina. Or Zara. The way the capital letter Z dominates a word or name. (*ZK* 238, 240)

But shortly thereafter Jeffrey suddenly decides to change Zara's name; or rather, he decides that Zara is not her name: "She was Nadya Hrabal. That was her name" (*ZK* 246). Neither a K-name nor a Z-name, we get the sense that the novel *Zero K* is nearing an end. And that gets reinforced when Jeffrey says of yet another woman: "I would not ask her name or create one for her. This was my version of progress. Time to go home" (*ZK* 254).

Back in New York, Jeffrey says that "invented names belong to the strafed landscape of the desert" (*ZK* 223). Perhaps it is no coincidence, then, that by far the greatest number of invented names in DeLillo's work are to be found in *Ratner's Star*, a desert setting in some unidentified part of what seems to be China. Here's a partial list of the rather extraordinary cast, all of them from Field Experiment Number One, none from Billy's home in the Bronx, though the last is from Brooklyn:

> Ottum, Hof, Byron Dyne, Endor, Cyril and Myriad Kyriakos, Una Braun, Mimsy Mope Grimmer, J. Graham Hummer, Howie Weeden, Robert Hopper Softly, U. F. O. Schwarz, Olin Nyquist, Rahada Hamadryad, Peregrine FitzRoy-Tapps, Viverrine Gentian, Shirl Trumpy, LoQuadro, Soma Tobias, Kidder, Hoad, Othmar Poebbels, Simeon Goldfloss, Gerald Pence (aka Mutuka), Beveridge Kettle, Celeste Dessau, Desilu Espy, Timur Nût, Hoy Hing Toy, Burris and Calliope Shrub, Haroun Farad, Elux Troxl, Grbk, Shlomo Glottle, Siba Isten-Esru, Armand Verbene, S. J., Thorkild, Harry Braniff, Maidengut, Lepro, Bhang Pao, Masha Simjian, Melcher-Speidell, Kyzyl, Orang Mohole, Evinrude, Pitkin, Fish, Dr. Bonwit, LaMar T. Sandow, Georgette Bottomley, Cheops Feeley, Dr. Skip Wismer, Hercule Leduc, Robert Hopper Softly, Knobloch, D' Arco, Edna Lown, Lester Bolin, Jean Sweet Venable, Walter Mainwaring, Maurice Xavier Wu, Chester Greylag Dent, Jumulu Nobo, Bö, Skia Mantikos, and Shazar Lazarus Ratner.

That's a pretty impressive list, and it must have cost DeLillo a good bit of effort, though also given him a good bit of pleasure. Other novels would be much sparer, *The Body Artist*, for example, which is basically limited to Lauren Hartke, a friend of hers from New York, Rey Robles, a critic, the pseudonymous Mr. Tuttle, and the owner of the house Lauren is renting in Maine.

Once a character has been given a name, other qualities can be assigned, a whole narrative built, a past, a bearing, a way of being, things the character would or would not say or do. This is traditionally the work of the author of narratives. In DeLillo, however, this work sometimes gets delegated to, repeated or contrabanded by, the narrator or the characters in the narrative. Remember Rick Linville, Jeffrey Lockhart's mother's lover? Once Jeffrey has invented a name for him, an entire destiny is not long in coming: "I decided to terminate the man in the crash of a small plane off the coast of Sri Lanka, formerly Ceylon, body unrecovered" (*ZK* 107).

The short story "Midnight in Dostoevsky" is another perfect case in point. The two main characters, college students, begin speculating, just like a narrator might, about an old man who lives in their little college town: "He's not from here," Todd (the character named Todd) said. "He's from somewhere in Europe" ("MD" 127). "I thought of the Baltic states and the Balkan states, briefly confused—which was which and which was where" ("MD" 129). "Todd said that Russia was too big for the man. He'd get lost in the vast expanse. Think about Romania, Bulgaria. Better yet, Albania" ("MD" 140). They speculate about his name—just as Jeffrey Lockhart does throughout *Zero K*: "German names. Names with umlauts" ("MD" 130). And then they put the past together with the name, which, wouldn't you know it, will have a *k*: "His son lives in this town because he teaches at the college. His name is Ilgauskas" ("MD" 137). Hence they give him a fictive name taken from the real name, if that makes sense, of the logic teacher in DeLillo's fiction. Finally, one begins to get something like a full-blown character: "He drinks coffee black, from a small cup, and spoons cereal out of a child's bowl. His head practically rests in the bowl when he bends to eat. He never looks at the newspaper. He goes back to his room after breakfast, where he sits and thinks" ("MD" 139). It is as if the two college students were writing a novel like *The Body Artist*: "Do we make him dead? Do we keep assembling the life posthumously? Or do we end it now, tomorrow, the next day, stop coming to town, stop looking for him?" ("MD" 141) Though the two boys seem to agree that it is not "a matter of literal answers" ("MD" 143), that finding out exactly who the man really is was never the point of their exercise, the short story ends with an argument, a fight even, over whether to talk to the man, over to what extent this character—this person—should remain imaginary or fictional (see "MD" 145), that is, whether he should become "literal" or remain simply "literary."

Something similar happens in "The Starveling," as the main character becomes so obsessed by a young woman he has seen in movie theaters but never spoken to that he begins imagining—or inventing—everything about her: "He thought about her name. He needed a name, a way to claim her, something to know her by. When he opened his eyes a house stood onscreen, alone in a wintry field. He thought of her as the Starveling. That was her name" ("S" 199). "She almost never speaks. When she speaks, is there a stutter, an accent?" ("S" 202) "Was she eating while he was eating? Did the Starveling eat?" ("S" 204; see 210) *The Starveling* is thus the name that Leo of "The Starveling" gives her, the name becoming the title of the story in which the name is given or invented. It is a form of literary speculation not unlike the one we just saw in "Midnight in Dostoevsky," only even creepier and seemingly more dangerous. It leads one to want to ask: is there a stalker lurking in the heart of every great writer? (see *N* 147, *DR* 81, and *AZ* 233)

The point is that DeLillo involves his fictional characters in the process of creating fiction. Characters invent other characters and narrators stalk the characters their characters have invented. But then there are narrators or narrations within the narration. Lauren Hartke in *The Body Artist*, for example, seems to have the imagination of a novelist. While driving she sees paint cans on a plank between chairs and begins imagining a man, an entire life, out of this configuration: "His life flew open to her passing glance. A lazy and manipulative man, in real estate, in fairview condos by a mosquito lake. She knew him. She saw into him" (*BA* 70; see *WN* 18, 91). Lauren thus finds herself inside stories, finds herself telling herself stories, though this time they are not from the newspaper, as others will be, as we will soon see, blooming inside her—like organic shrapnel (*BA* 115).

Throughout *Amazons* there are many signs of Cleo Birdwell, the narrator, not just as the first woman ever to play in the NHL telling her unique story but as a writer, a narrator *reflecting* upon her writing, creating a distance between what she is narrating and the narration itself. Early on in her memoir she notes: "This is the second straight chapter that ends with sex and intimate lighting. ... Not that there isn't something right about a chapter that ends with sex. ... Sex is the thing that nothing can follow. It asks for blank space. We wish for a silence that will last at least for the turning of a page" (*AZ* 36). At the end of Part I we find a similar reflection upon writing: "I thought this would be a little book of meditations. ... I know I don't have the discipline for that. But now and then I'd like to develop a theme or find a shape for events" (*AZ* 146). Finally, at the very beginning of the book's final section: "This will be the meaningful part of the book, my last chance to find a theme in all the space junk that's been floating through these pages" (*AZ* 347). And then, near the very end of Birdwell's memoir, that is, of her—DeLillo's—novel: "In the last of the scenes that I imagine, I am scribbling in my notebook one day and I see ... " (*AZ* 389).

There are thus characters who act like writers in DeLillo's novels, characters who act like writers because they are writers, and then, to return to some of the forms of contraband we saw earlier, characters who fulfill a certain narrative function, announcing things or else making them up as they go. In *End Zone* there is Raymond Toon, college student and aspiring sportscaster, announcing games in his dorm room (*EZ* 23, 138) and, in *Libra*, Win Everett, mastermind of the Kennedy assassination, amusing his daughter at bedtime by doing imaginary play-by-play of a football game: "He broadcast the run in an urgent voice, described missed tackles and downfield blocks, added the roar of the crowd, became the official who signaled touchdown when the toy spun backwards into a pillow" (*L* 223). In *Mao II* the writer Bill Gray seems to equate announcing games with the purest form of writing: "When I was a kid I used to announce ballgames to myself. I sat in a room and made up the games and described the play-by-play out loud. ... I do batting orders in my head all the time. And I've been trying to write toward that kind of innocence ever since" (*M* 45–46; see 136). Later, we see him actually doing the play-by-play: "He looked up and said aloud, 'Keltner takes his time, tipping a glance at the baseball. Hey what a toss. Like a trolley wire, folks'" (*M* 198; see *WN* 269). In this case, the narration does not end with the game but the game with the narration: "I used to imagine, listening to a ballgame, as a kid, on the radio, that when I turned the radio off, in the seventh inning, say, with two out, men on first and third, that everything sort of shut down at that point. It simply stopped" (*DR* 43). Hence the game ends when the narration ends, though when it is recorded the narration—and thus the game—can live on pretty much for forever, like "radioactive waste" (*AZ* 89; see 22). Later then, after childhood, the adult will try to imitate or double the child and the writer (Bill Gray, Don DeLillo) the non-writer who was already imitating the writer (the radio or sports announcer). Here is how the announcer of all announcers, Russ Hodges, "the voice of the Giants" on WMCA (*U* 15), describes the time when he used to narrate games on the basis of teletype, all those "years in a studio doing re-creations of big league games":

> Somebody hands you a piece of paper filled with letters and numbers and you have to make a ball game out of it. You create the weather, flesh out the players, you make them sweat and grouse and hitch up their pants, and it is remarkable, thinks Russ, how much earthly disturbance, how much summer and dust the mind can manage to order up from a single Latin letter lying flat. (*U* 25)

It sounds like reading and it sounds like writing, or maybe both at once, because at this level of things it's contraband all the way down.

Foreign Languages

In the subways she read the Spanish emergency even if the English was right next to it. She reasoned that in an actual emergency she could switch to the English if needs be and in the meantime she was trying out voices in her head.

M 176

"There's something about German names, the German language, German things. I don't know what it is exactly. It's just there. In the middle of it all is Hitler, of course."

WN 63

"Andreas, is it absolutely necessary to know verbs? Must we know verbs?"
"I think it will help," he said.

N 63

In *The Names* the first question the members of the cult on the island of Kouros ask Owen Brademas is: "How many languages do you speak?" (*N* 28) It's a rather common question asked of American expats. But it's also a question we might pose DeLillo. How many languages does DeLillo smuggle into his novels, that is, into his American English novels? How many languages do his characters speak? For if language is, as we have seen throughout, the ultimate contraband for DeLillo, the inclusion of a foreign language within language is never completely arbitrary and always seems to serve some purpose.

Underworld's Nick Shay is able to say, "I studied Latin for a while. In school, then on my own, pretty intensively. And dabbled in German and Italian" (*U* 281). That's not bad, as Americans go, but elsewhere there are some much more serious people language-wise. Vosdanik, for example, in *The Names*: "He spoke seven languages. His father had walked across the Syrian desert as a boy, a forced march, the Turks, 1916" (*N* 148). He makes a good contrast with Del, Volterra's traveling companion in the same novel, "who calls the Arabs rag-heads. Another big help" (*N* 141), Del who recalls when talking with Jim Axton that "there's an Arabic letter called *jim*," but when asked what it looks like she has to admit, "Don't recall. I gave the language about an hour's study" (*N* 144). Living in Athens, it is not just Greek, of course, that surrounds Axton but languages of all kinds, guides speaking "German, French, Japanese, accented English" (*N* 330), in short, the languages of all the "major museum nations" (*PO* 116). There are thus long conversations about language itself throughout *The Names*, this title itself a translation of the Greek name of the religious cult at the center of the novel, *Ta Onómata* (*N* 188). DeLillo is thus a very American author who often speaks or has his characters speak of or in foreign languages. Part of that is New York, of course, where one hears foreign languages on almost every street corner. But much of it is DeLillo's interest in language itself and in the possibilities for a sort of linguistic contraband that consists in smuggling different languages across borders and epochs—starting with dead languages, and the ancient Greek word for "Word," *Logos*, as in Logos College in *End Zone*, but then also *crisis* ("*Crisis* is a Greek word" ("HS" 163)), and *chaos* ("*Chaos* is a Greek word" ("HS" 164)), and the Greek greeting that sounds like the name of an American accounting firm ("How do they say thank you in Greek?" "*Efharisto*." "Say it again, slowly." "F. Harry Stowe" ("HS" 172; see "S" 204)), and *amen* ("She made the sign of the cross, murmuring the congruous words. Amen, an olden word, back to Greek and Hebrew" (*U* 237; "AE" 73)).

After Greek, there's a little bit of Latin ("Fascinating, yes. An interesting word. From the Latin *fascinus*. An amulet shaped like a phallus. A word progressing from the same root as the word 'fascism'" (*RD* 151; see "MD" 124)), the well-known phrase "*Festina lente*," for example, "Make haste slowly" (*U* 235), or else "*Nostra aetate*, as the popes like to say. In our time" (*U* 805). In *Ratner's Star* someone recalls that the Latin *pupilla* means both pupil and "little orphan girl," "a connection based on the fact that when a child looks at her own miniature reflection in another person's eye, she sees a female figure locked inside concentric rings, a lone doll in a coiled room, a little orphan girl ... confined in the pupil of someone else's eye" (*RS* 398–399). It's hardly a gratuitous example, this embedding or contrabanding of the big (the girl) in the small (the pupil), the one *pupilla* at the eye of the other. It's a serious linguistic observation, though nothing prevents it or other Latin phrases from being remembered in more playful ways: "*Dominus vobiscum*, the priest used to say ... Dominick go frisk' em. What was Latin for if you couldn't reduce the formal codes to the jostled argot of the street?" (*U* 107) Of course, as everyone knows, Latin is also good for English etymologies and vocabulary. As Cleo Birdwell, the narrator and pseudonymous author of *Amazons: An Intimate Memoir by the First Woman Ever to Play in the National Hockey League* reminds us, "Memoir ... comes from the Latin for memory" (*AZ* 2), a little factoid she knows because her mother "taught Latin three days a week at the Catholic school" (*AZ* 80), convinced, as she was, that "Latin was something to be preserved, like good manners or elm trees" (*AZ* 81). That helps explain Cleo's many erudite etymological remarks throughout her memoir (*AZ* see 11, 284), for example, when she recalls how one of her lovers "licked me everywhere, nuzzled my labia, from the Latin" (*AZ* 72), and that "no one had ever shown such expertise with my Latinate parts before" (*AZ* 143). And just to show that she knows the Latinate parts for both genders: "That's my penis." "I know what it is. It's from the Latin" (*AZ* 27; see 65)

In *Underworld* there are also bits of Italian. Nick says, "There's a word in Italian. *Dietrologia*. It means the science of what is behind something. ... The science of dark forces" (*U* 280). As a writer of conspiracies, secrets, and secret organizations, a writer of secret or hidden forces, DeLillo is a first-class dietrologist, and that is no insult.

In *Valparaiso* there is Michael, or Miquel, "learning Spanish on tape" (*V* 34, 50, 103) after flying to the wrong Valparaiso. Elsewhere, there's the Spanish one speaks or hears in prison—"He called me *maricón*. He whispered to me, *maricón*, with a little sweet smile" (*L* 97; see *U* 439)—or the Spanish that Jackie Kennedy spoke, *muy bien* and much appreciated, to brigade members after the Bay of Pigs fiasco (*L* 51), or the Spanish that Keith Neudecker hears on the morning of 9/11 as he is evacuating the towers, "someone praying back in the line somewhere, in Spanish" (*FM* 245), or the kind Lee Harvey Oswald tries to learn: "He wrote in Spanish in his notebook the numbers one to seventeen, leaving out five and six" (*L* 203). (There's that seventeen yet again ...)

There is Chinese, Mandarin, to be exact, in *Zero K*, since Artis, the stepmother, had done archaeological work in China (*ZK* 17, 212), and a smattering of Japanese in *Libra* ("Ten thousand years of happiness, or whatever it means when they say *banzai*" (*L* 90)). There is even a Tibetan phrase, famous the world over—probably not the origin of the "world *hum*" we saw DeLillo speak of earlier, but it's a nice connection:

> They sent him to Vietnam, to Phu Bai, and the first thing he saw when he entered the compound was a flourish of spray-paint graffiti on the wall of a supply shed. *Om mani padme hum.* Matt knew this was some kind of mantra, a thing hippies chanted in Central Park, but could it also be the motto of the 131st Aviation Company? (*U* 462)

Om mani padme hum: the jewel in the heart of the lotus ...

In *Libra* we find Lee Harvey Oswald, intending to defect to Russia, spending "serious time at the base library" in Atsugi, Japan, "learning Russian verbs" (*L* 112). Later he picks up a few names to go with those verbs, "Stalin's name was Dzhugashvili. Kremlin means citadel" (*L* 155). "They have a phrase they use in Russian for assassinations that involve blood being spilled. *Mokrie dela*. Which is wet affairs. Like the ice pick used on Trotsky" (*L* 276). Emma's son Stak in *Zero K* studies "Pashto, privately, in his spare time" (*ZK* 169), speaking "Pashto to people in the street who look as though they might be native speakers" (*ZK* 195). And, of course, one woman's foreign language is another's mother tongue; for Marina Oswald, Lee Harvey's Russian wife, it was English that was foreign: "She'd rarely heard English, didn't know a word except song lyrics, Tarzan, Spam" (*L* 201). Same thing for Mohammed Atta in Hamburg, who needed to learn a little English and so troubled a woman friend "for lessons, for words and phrases and we can skip the grammar" (*FM* 82).

In a few DeLillo works, such as *The Names* again, the question of learning or not learning a foreign language is central to the lives of spies and expats. The latter group is a curious breed. As Kyle, an American expat living in Athens, says in "The Ivory Acrobat": "I'm sort of stranded but in a more or less willing way" ("IA" 65). That could be said by or about most expats and being stranded in that way means that one ultimately has to accept not understanding and not being understood in some if not most circumstances (see *N* 55, 189; see *L* 133). James Axton's near-daily confrontations with his concierge in Athens make for a good case study in such incomprehension: "Understanding him, answering correctly, was like making my way through a dream" (*N* 102). Axton is thus reduced on an almost daily basis to "a childlike fear and guilt," unable to express what he wants, unable to pronounce correctly what he knows how to express, and, on those rare occasions he can do both, wary of the political implications of what he is saying and how he is saying it (*N* 102–103). At the very least, then, one should do like Charles Maitland and learn the essentials of the language spoken in the country: "To Charles it was a mark of one's respect for other cultures to know the local terms of abuse and the words for sex acts and natural wastes" (*N* 4).

Languages too, then, are political, as George de Mohrenschildt from *Libra* well knew, "a charming and worldly man able to converse fluently in Russian, English, French, Spanish, probably Togo as well, or whatever they spoke in Togoland" (*L* 53). For people like him, people in the foreign service—okay, spies—learning languages is essential to the job:

> I will learn Croatian in Yugoslavia. I will learn the French patois as the Haitians speak it. This is how I survive as someone who has come through a revolution and a world war and so on. I am always willing to cooperate. I take on the coloration. It is my message to them that I am not the enemy. (*L* 237)

That's one strategy. Another is the one expressed by Charles Maitland in *The Names*: "The idea is to learn the language, but not to let them know" (*N* 41).

But then there are languages that are not quite languages, languages unlike the others. In the Convergence of *Zero K* one would learn Global English, and other languages as well, but also a metalanguage, as it were, a language for all peoples and generations, not unlike the language that scientists are trying to come up with in *Ratner's Star*, a global or even interplanetary, intergalactic language. As one of the guides in the Convergence explains, "There are philologists designing an advanced language unique to the Convergence. Word roots, inflections, even gestures" (*ZK* 33). Those who eventually emerge from the Convergence will thus be fluent in a "language system far more expressive and precise than any of the world's existing forms of discourse" (*ZK* 233), "a set of voice sounds and gestures" that makes the narrator think of "dolphins communicating in mid-ocean" (*ZK* 244), a language so pure it will resemble mathematics: "We will know ourselves as never before, blood, brain and skin. / We will approximate the logic and beauty of pure mathematics in everyday speech. / No similes, metaphors, analogies" (*ZK* 130).

Among all the languages spoken in DeLillo's novels, French is probably the most present and the most *problématique* (see *A* 7, *N* 20, *U* 34, 319). It is, reputedly, the language of a certain sophistication, but it is often avoided rather than coveted. Richard Spector, the former government worker walking across the United States in *Americana*, sets the tone:

> I no longer have any anxiety about not being able to speak French. It used to worry me. My father speaks French very well. He was always inviting people to dinner and speaking French with them. It was his way of maintaining power over me. ... They try to keep us down by speaking French and knowing how to mix whiskey sours ... But a lot of us have broken out. We don't care if we don't know how to pronounce the names of French wines. What's wrong with California wine anyway? (*A* 219–220)

Spector seems to prefigure Jeffrey Lockhart in *Zero K* in this regard: "My father on TV, an obscure channel, poor reception, Ross in Geneva, sort of double-imaged, speaking French. Did I know that my father spoke French? Was I sure that this man was my father?" (*ZK* 14; see 55, 229, *M* 100, and *BA* 81) It is a language of sophistication though also, sometimes, a sophisticated façade, a way of hiding one's insecurities, like "well-to-do people who have painted over their fear with graduate school and being able to order in French" (*AZ* 169).

If French is a language to be appreciated though also, sometimes, mocked—and just the accent is often enough, "It is the donjaire, he said. I liked the way that sounded. I am steef with terrour. It is the donjaire" (*AZ* 173; see 184–187, 306)—German is a language to be feared and mocked. In *End Zone* there is a course at Logos College on the untellable, featuring Rilke, where "knowledge of German was a prerequisite for being refused admission" (*EZ* 73; see 64, 181, *RD* 4). In *Ratner's Star* there is Little Billy Twillig, math superstar, who receives at the age of fourteen several offers from high-level research institutions across the world and decides which to take or reject on the basis of language: "The final bid came from the Institut für mathematische Logik und Grundlagenforschung in Münster. The name of the place scared him so much he never even replied" (*RS* 27–28; see *N* 189). In *Underworld* we hear Lenny Bruce, taking a cue from DeLillo's own brand of contraband, sprinkling in a bit of German just to show that he can get as high into high culture as he can sink down into the low:

> One of the college profs smiled invitingly and Lenny obliged with, "Fuck suck fag hag gimme a nickel bag." ... Many people had never heard these words spoken before an audience ... Lenny followed this flurry with an erudite riff on the German word *Sprachgefühl*, a feel for language, for what is idiomatically hip—he reads up on things like this in hotels and on planes and back home in the smoky dawn of L.A. while he's waiting for a woman or a pusher. (*U* 585)

And then there is Jack Gladney's attempt to learn German. Though he was founder and head of the Hitler Studies program at College-on-the-Hill, he had been faking it for years, doing what he could to conceal the shortcoming, walking around campus and town with a copy of *Mein Kampf* tucked under his arm like a shield (*WN* 244) and going so far as to give his son a very German name in order to mask the lack: "He was born shortly after I started the department and I guess I wanted to acknowledge my good fortune. I wanted to do something German. I felt a gesture was called for." "Heinrich Gerhardt Gladney?" "I thought it had an authority that might cling to him" (*WN* 63). But as the Hitler conference that Jack is hosting approaches, a conference with many native Germans in attendance, the lack becomes a genuine source of embarrassment or anxiety, then a source of motivation and amusement, and finally the object of ruse or subterfuge, right up to the final pages of the novel. Here's the embarrassment:

> I had long tried to conceal the fact that I did not know German. ... I'd made several attempts to learn German, serious probes into origins, structures, roots. I sensed the deathly power of the language. (*WN* 31)

And then the motivation:

> I asked my German teacher to add half an hour to each lesson. It seemed more urgent than ever that I learn the language. (*WN* 173)

And the amusement—provided by the same German teacher in three lessons:

> When he switched from English to German, it was as though a cord had been twisted in his larynx. ... He was only demonstrating certain basic pronunciation patterns but the transformation in his face and voice made me think he was making a passage between levels of being. (*WN* 32)
>
> Then the warping began. It was an eerie thing to see, shamefully fascinating, as a seizure might be if witnessed in a controlled environment. ... it must have sounded like a sudden bending of the natural law, a stone or tree struggling to speak. (*WN* 54)
>
> He stared into my mouth as I did my exercises in pronunciation. Once he reached in with his right hand to adjust my tongue. (*WN* 173)

And then, finally, the ruses or the subterfuge of Jack's German lecture and opening remarks:

> I talked mainly about Hitler's mother, brother and dog. His dog's name was Wolf. This word is the same in English and German. Most of the words I used in my address were the same or nearly the same in both languages. ... Of course there was Hitler himself. I spoke the name often, hoping it would overpower my insecure sentence structure. / The rest of the time I tried to avoid the Germans in the group. (*WN* 274)

But there is something more, something a bit more "religious" than that, something about a foreign language that brings us to the origin of language itself. We see this at the end of *White Noise*, as Jack and his would-be victim enter a hospital run by nuns speaking German, the very German he had been pursuing and avoiding throughout the novel: "I asked my nun her name. Sister Hermann Marie. I told her I knew some German, trying to gain her favor ... '*Gut, besser, best*,' I said" (*WN* 316–317).

> She said something in German. I failed to understand. ... She was spraying me with German. A storm of words. ... I began to detect a cadence, a measured beat. She was reciting something, I decided. Litanies, hymns, catechisms. The mysteries of the rosary perhaps. Taunting me with scornful prayer. / The odd thing is I found it beautiful. (*WN* 320; see "C" 17, 23)

The nun responds with words Jack cannot understand, though this time it doesn't seem to matter. The forerunner, it seems, of Sister Edgar in "The

Angel Esmeralda" and *Underworld*, another nun with an oddly masculine name who seems to participate in something like a miracle, Sister Hermann Marie also seems to anticipate the two brothers of *Zero K* who recite "a series of Swedish or Norwegian words" and then "a list, a litany of German words. ... words in most cases beginning with the syllables *welt*, *wort*, or *tod*" (*ZK* 77). In this case, Jeffrey understands the words—at least parts of them—and it turns out that all three are serious DeLillo words: *world*, *word*, *death*.

In addition, finally, to all these foreign and imagined languages, there is Ob, a language spoken by James Axton's son Tap; it's "a coded jargon" (*N* 10), "a kind of pig Latin. You insert *o-b* in certain parts of words" (*N* 42). It's a silly game but the syllable is less so, for *Ob* are the initials of Owen Brademas, an expert in foreign languages, at once ancient and modern, and a specialist in epigraphs who is directing the archaeological dig on the island of Kouros. In addition to speaking all the better-known languages, he had "learned a few words of Tamil and Bengali and was able to ask for food and lodging in Hindi when necessary" (*N* 278). He is thus "a man who knows languages. A calm man, very humane," with "a wide and tolerant understanding, a capacity for civilized thought," for "this is what it means to know languages" (*N* 207). And yet Brademas failed to speak the one language he dreamed of speaking, the one his parents spoke, the one related to a childhood trauma, a single, inspired language, the ultimate contraband language, even though it sometimes goes by a plural name: "speaking in tongues."

Glossolalia

They had to evacuate the grade school on Tuesday. Kids were getting headaches and eye irritations, tasting metal in their mouths. A teacher rolled on the floor and spoke foreign languages.

WN 35

I was born with all languages in my mouth.

GJ 204

They chant for one language, one word, for the time when names are lost.

M 16

DeLillo's interest in language, beginning with his native English, presumably, and then foreign languages of various kinds, inevitably takes him to the limits of language, to the question of what a "lost language" might have sounded like (*RS* 148) or what an "invented tongue" might try to say (*L* 144). It also leads him to what, in a Pentecostal tradition, is called speaking in tongues, glossolalia. As the preacher of Owen Brademas's youth says (echoing St. Paul), "Seal the old language and loose the new one" (*N* 336).

Speaking in tongues is thus one of DeLillo's favorite and favored tropes (*P* 70, *RS* 193, 397, *V* 49, *WN* 319), used to describe everything from the sounds of sexual ecstasy (*RS* 320) to a gaggle of shouting reporters (*L* 417), to people witnessing what they take to be a miracle—people in "trance utterance ... singing of things outside the known deliriums" (*U* 822, "AE" 99; see *U* 411). But in *The Names* speaking in tongues is not just a passing reference or trope but a central theme. The narrative revolves in large part around Owen Brademas's attempt to recall his early childhood experiences in a Pentecostal church in Kansas and to explain to himself why he was never able to speak in tongues as his mother and father could: "A congregation of poor people and most of them spoke in tongues. This was an awesome thing to see and hear. His father fell away to some distant place, his mother clapped and wept. ... The insideoutness of this sound, the tumbling out of found words, the arms raised, the tremble" (*N* 173; see 284, 335–336). All this at once fascinates and repels Brademas. Though he knows the critique or the rational explanation— "it is a learned behavior, fabricated speech, meaningless speech," "a life focus for depressed people, according to the clinical psychologists" (*N* 173)—this language has a force that grips him, especially when it's an experienced preacher who is stirring up the congregation:

> Paul to the Corinthians said men can speak with the tongues of angels. In our time we can do the same.
> Do whatever your tongue finds to do. Seal the old language and loose the new. ... I want to hear that beautiful babbling brook. ...
> *Time to get wet*, he says. *Get wet time*. (*N* 306–307)

Even if it is a fabricated speech and not the voice of God, speaking in tongues interests Brademas for the kind of innocence it seems to provide, for the way in which "normal understanding is surpassed, the self and its machinery obliterated" (*N* 307). But Brademas finally had to recognize that "the gift was not his"; it was the one language that "was not to be seized in his pityfull mouth. His tongue was a rock, his ears were rocks" (*N* 338).

This interest in speaking in tongues is not unrelated, of course, to stuttering or stammering or being tongue-tied in some way. In *Ratner's Star* there are several famous reputed stutterers and stammerers, from Moses, Aesop, Aristotle, and Virgil to Darwin and Dodgson (*RS* 397). It's interesting, it's DeLillo, because a stutter contrabands fluent speech like a limp contrabands normal walking. And both can be faked—just to give one's life a bit of "texture." In *Underworld*, for example, Eric Deming developed "a fake stutter," just "to texture the conversation" (*U* 417; see 422 and 519). In *Libra* there's a kid Lee Oswald knew from the Bronx who "walked around in hippity-hop limp, carrying a crab he'd stolen from the Italian market" (*L* 5; see *RS* 252–253), while Nick Shay in *Underworld* limped for a time ("I corrected my foot-drag step" (*U* 301; see 137)), to say nothing of Carlo Strasser, whom Klara Sax first sees limping only on their wedding day, and she was "amused to think she'd never noticed—felt free to be amused, felt what the hell it's only marriage" (*U* 497). The narrator of *Zero K* also takes on a limp as a sort of affectation that he hopes will make him appear to himself and others: "When I was fourteen I developed a limp. ... It was a limp set between quotation marks and I wasn't sure whether it was intended to make me visible to others or just to myself. ... I saw myself in the limp, in the way I refined and nurtured it" (*ZK* 101–102, 107). In short, Jeffrey developed a limp like Eric developed a stutter. It is no surprise, then, that Jeffrey's mother, when she has had enough of the limp, turns her son's interest to language:

> She said that it was time for me to resume a normal stride. She said that the limp is a heartless perversion of true infirmity. She told me that that pale crescent at the base of the fingernail is called the lunula, the *loon-ya-la*. She told me that the indentation in skin between the nose and the upper lip is called the philtrum. (*ZK* 108)

A limp is like a stutter except that a stutter, unlike a limp, is a thing of language. That is why Jeffrey's mother says to him, in essence, drop the limp, learn the lunula.

Linguistic Shrapnel

Cherish the language, I thought. Let the language reflect the search for ever more obscure methods, down into subatomic levels.

ZK 141

Royals in their pajamas eating mutton. Have I ever used the word mutton in my life? Came into my head, out of nowhere, mutton.

C 203; see ZK 39, 41

Glossolalia uniquely reveals what is common to all language, the fact that it comes to us from without, as a gift or a curse, as something from beyond that takes hold of us from within. It is here that DeLillo, especially in later novels, begins to think contraband in terms of the intersection of not only self and other, inside and outside, but the technological and the organic, the way the technological makes itself organic, as it were, while the organic, with its little machines and mechanisms of repetition and reproduction, provides some of our most exquisite images of technology. And all that as a key to understanding how DeLillo writes and how we read him—or rather how we write and how we read *in general*. Images or impressions enter us, like contraband—those images of the planes, for example, entering the towers, entering us, on 9/11. They are swallowed whole, incorporated into our bodies, becoming flesh and tissue, a contraband that now runs continually just below the surface of our skin. DeLillo writes in *Falling Man*:

> The second plane coming out of that ice blue sky, this was the footage that entered the body, that seemed to run beneath the skin, the fleeting sprint that carried lives and histories, theirs and hers, everyone's, into some other distance, out beyond the towers. (*FM* 134)

It is as if the image of the event had become a piece of the event itself, a weapon or the shard of a weapon, something akin to what is earlier called in *Falling Man* "organic shrapnel," the phenomenon by which "tiny fragments of the suicide bomber's body" come to be embedded in the flesh of survivors:

> Do you believe it? A student is sitting in a café. She survives the attack. Then, months later, they find these little, like, pellets of flesh, human flesh that got driven into the skin. They call this organic shrapnel. (*FM* 16)

The notion of "organic shrapnel" is, of course, very specific, incomparable, "these, like, pellets of flesh." But the notion might nonetheless be expanded to describe the way in which something other, something from another, comes not simply to complement its host or to act as its counterpoint but to interrupt, infect, contradict, or contraband it. Organic shrapnel, then, as an invasion of the other, the violent incorporation of a foreign body, a kind of trauma that allows a bit of the living other to live within the self, the terrorist within the victim, one victim within another. Organic shrapnel insinuates itself into our bodies at a distance, from a distance, and it happens without our knowing it—like a secret language or an ideology, a cult identification or the murmurings of a terrorist cell, replicating within our tissue's cells. DeLillo writes in *Mao II* during the Moonie mass-wedding scene in Yankee

Stadium: "All things, the sum of the knowable, everything true, it all comes down to a few simple formulas copied and memorized and passed on. And here is the drama of mechanical routine played out with living figures" (*M* 7). Repetition leads to a kind of habituation, to inscription or incorporation, that is, to doubling or contrabanding. DeLillo continues, speaking here of the Reverend Moon, the Father of the 6500 happy couples, "They know him at the molecular level. He lives in them like chains of matter that determine who they are" (*M* 6). "He is part of the structure of their protein" (*M* 9).

Apparently inorganic things, names and phrases, chants and rituals, all those codes we spoke of earlier, enter into us and become us, the inorganic becoming organic or the organic revealing itself to be something other than what we thought it to be. Words and images enter us and become part of us, the other lodged within, like organic shrapnel—images from film and TV, but even perceptions, now, themselves contrabanded by film, the perception, for example, of a Morandi still life where the two towers, now fallen, rise up out of the painting in order to enter our living flesh, becoming fused and confused with those other images, perpetually replayed, that have been seared in our memories. Here is how the narrator describes Lianne in an art gallery looking at the Morandi still lives.

> She could not stop looking. There was something hidden in the painting. ... She was passing beyond pleasure into some kind of assimilation. She was trying to absorb what she saw, take it home, wrap it around her, sleep in it. There was so much to see. Turn it into living tissue, who you are. (*FM* 210)

For all DeLillo's emphasis on repetition, on the reproduction of the work of art, there seems to be something that resists repetition and exceeds the moment proper to art. It is not to be found in the work itself, however, if that still means anything, that is, in the work's unique and irreproducible aura, but in the spectator, the observer, the witness who is marked by the work. What exceeds the reproducibility of a medium seems to be the unique body that records or recoils and absorbs, that reproduces the uniquely irreproducible. Lianne as the witness of the falling man's fall: "There were no photographs of that fall. She was the photograph, the photosensitive surface. The nameless body coming down, this was hers to record and absorb" (*FM* 223). Unbeknownst to her, Lianne records, registers, absorbs the image, contrabands it, like organic shrapnel.

All this is not to suggest that DeLillo II, the techno-DeLillo, is suddenly morphing into DeLillo III, the bio-version, even if these references to tissue and organic matter do seem to be more prominent in later novels. It does suggest that DeLillo has found in the organic a new site for literary contraband, DNA, for example, as a way to describe not only the passing down of a genetic code from one generation to the next but the way language gets replicated or replicates itself from one person to another (see *FM* 20). DNA, which, we recall from *Falling Man*, was used to identify the victims of 9/11, Rumsey, for example, whose mother had to take samples to "an armory ... for a DNA match" (*FM* 204), is thus now being used to think what I have been calling the double band or double strand of the contraband, the way in which two narratives wrap around one another in order to complement or undermine but also reproduce one another. Like organic shrapnel, DNA names at once a thing, a code, and the way language functions by inscribing, embedding, or incorporating itself so as to repeat itself in others. Notice how, in the return of organic shrapnel later in *Falling Man*, it is not so much the *thing* but the *words* that return, as if they, the very words *organic shrapnel*, had entered Keith Neudecker unbeknownst to him, as if they had become lodged within him days earlier, earlier in the narrative, left there to grow and to fester before resurfacing at some later point in time:

> He thought of something out of nowhere, a phrase, *organic shrapnel*. Felt familiar but meant nothing to him. Then he saw a car double-parked across the street and thought of something else and then something else again. (*FM* 66)

Organic shrapnel would thus be both an example of DeLillo's contraband and another name for it. For what are memories or narratives in DeLillo's writing but a kind of organic shrapnel, and what is trauma but shrapnel so deeply embedded that it cannot even be located, identified, and so removed. Such are the memories—fragile or else all-too-powerful—of the survivors of 9/11, those actually in the towers that day, memories that are "inside them now" (*FM* 55-58), clinging and maybe even growing, blooming, like organic shrapnel. The narrator says of Keith and Florence in *Falling Man*:

> He understood that they could talk about these things only with each other, in minute and dullest detail, but it would never be dull or too detailed because it was inside them now and because he needed to hear what he'd lost in the tracings of memory. (*FM* 90-91)

What is literature, DeLillo's literature, then, but a way of engendering in us, a way of contrabanding and smuggling within us, for good or ill, like a curse or a blessing, little bits of language, fragments, ear-worms, parts of a genetic code, sometimes complex, sometimes stunningly simple.

Inside and out, it's sometimes tempting to think that one DeLillo novel is talking to another. In *The Body Artist* Lauren reflects on her own practice of artistic creation, the way stories come to her or the way she inserts herself into them in order to move or to gesture from out of them: she "tended lately to place herself, to insert herself into certain stories in the newspaper. Some kind of daydream variation" (*BA* 14). This provides us with a way to understand both the narrative that is to follow, the sudden appearance of Mr. Tuttle in the house after Rey's death, and DeLillo's contrapuntal writing: "She read a story in the paper about a child abandoned in some godforsaken" (*BA* 16). This is a description of Lauren, the central character of *The Body Artist*, but it is also a description of the work of the author and the work of imagination, the construction of a contraband voice: "How an incident described in the paper seemed to rise out of the inky lines of print and gather her into it" (*BA* 18)—"a voice that flowed from a story in the paper" (*BA* 16). We seem to be describing here at once the work of the body artist and that of the writer—or the reader, because the damn thing is super contagious:

> Or you become someone else, one of the people in the story, doing dialogue of your own devising. You become a man at times, living between the lines, doing another version of the story. (*BA* 20)

Just a couple of pages later there is a reference, again from the newspaper, to someone being tortured half-way around the world, and it does not just echo *Mao II* but actually seems to seep in from it. For that's what it means to have a corpus, a body of work: what happens between newspaper and reader can happen between an earlier reading and a present one. In novels as in newspapers

> there are endless identical lines of print with people living somewhere in the words and the strange contained reality of paper and ink seeps through the house for a week and when you look at a page and distinguish one line from another it begins to gather you into it and there are people being tortured halfway around the world, who speak another language, and you have conversations with them more or less uncontrollably until you become aware you are doing it and then you stop, seeing whatever is in front of you at the time, like half a glass of juice in your husband's hand. (*BA* 19)

It is hard not to think here of Bill Gray, the author, who begins to think—and to write—about the hostage in Beirut, Bill Gray who lets "the words lead him into that basement room. / Find the places where you converge with him. / Read his poems again" (*M* 160). This is precisely where DeLillo himself goes in the novel (see *M* 107–112).

Literature, then, as literary shrapnel, not just stories that are remembered or images that are registered but language that is absorbed. For there are, in DeLillo, in addition to all the narratives, all the scenarios and sketches (in *White Noise* for example), all the riffs and rants, from the opening pages of *Americana* onward (*A* 19, 67–68), accents, at once imitated and described, especially from New York—"Shat ap. Facking cacksacker" (*P* 181), "Siddown, shaddap" (*U* 39), ways of pronouncing or mispronouncing things—a girl who "said deteriated for deteriorated. When she said okay it sounded like okai" (*U* 81), a cabdriver in Beirut who "pronounces the second *b* in bomb" (*M* 228), or someone—not yet the US president but it sounds like him—who took "nuclear" and "pronounced it nucular" (*U* 316). Or take the even more worrisome example of a nurse's aide who had the habit of mispronouncing body parts, saying, for example, "fib-*yu*-la, with the accent on the middle syllable" (*AZ* 241), and "ab-*do*-men," because "wasn't it supposed to be *ab*-do-men?" (*AZ* 300), and "re-*ti*-na," with that middle syllable not only accented this time but detached (*AZ* 349). There are accents, pronunciations, and then, of course, voices, voices distinct from that of the narrator's, whether first person or third, voices embedded in the narrative, sometimes for pages, the voice of Marguerite, for example, Lee Harvey's mother, speaking in his defense before various officials throughout *Libra*. In addition to all the plots and all the stray details, all the comparisons and metaphors, and all the serious talk about less than serious things and vice versa, there are accents and voices and then, especially, sentences, the primary unit of measure in DeLillo's writing. There are long sentences, difficult and sometimes convoluted, clinging almost always to much simpler sentences, sentences finely honed like weapons, charged with stunning insight and resonance, sentences that stick, like organic shrapnel, sentences like "Let it express itself" (*C* 186), "It's a gesture" (*GJ* 73; see *C* 123), or even something so simple as "I believe that" (*RD* 231).

Counterband narratives at the level of plot, chapters, paragraphs, and sentences, therefore, but then also counterband writing at the level of the signifier, a lexicon or a vocabulary—military jargon, for example, the idioms of war and destruction, or the language of medical technology or cyber-capital. But then also everyday language and everyday expressions—things like "a New York cut": "'I want to buy some New York cuts,' he said, gesturing toward the butcher. / The phrase seemed familiar, but what did it mean?" (*WN* 169) Or else, and this one was new to me, "making gravy": "She heard the women talk about making gravy ... It meant, Don't you dare come home late" (*U* 698; see 699). Everyday language, then, either integrated as such into the narrative or else recalled as being everyday: "Please report any suspicious behavior or unattended packages. That was the wording, wasn't it?" (*FM* 127) And then there are formulations that have been rattling around in there since grade school: "The square of the hypotenuse is equal to the sum of the squares of the two sides. ... The battle of Bunker Hill was really fought on Breed's Hill. ... Tippecanoe and Tyler too. ... Anthracite and bituminous ... Isosceles and scalene" (*WN* 176). The things we hear are thus often no more than clichés, and yet we carry them around inside us and cannot help repeating them as a sort of everyday poetry, a secular prayer to help us make sense of the world: "A boy is dragged a hundred yards, it is always a hundred yards, by a car that keeps on going" (*U* 823; "AE" 100). "Wandering hands, Lee thought. An old term, an old thing they said in junior high, what a girl said about a boy. He's got wandering hands" (*L* 341). These are the phrases one hears or used to hear everyday, everyday phrases, often accompanied in DeLillo by reflections on that fact. And one doesn't have to be all that old to make such reflections. Fourteen is already old enough to know about the ways of the world when it comes to everyday phrases:

> "Most of these fires in old buildings start in the electrical wiring," Heinrich said. "Faulty wiring. That's one phrase you can't hang around for long without hearing."
> "Most people don't burn to death," I said. "They die of smoke inhalation."
> "That's the other phrase," he said. (*WN* 239)

These phrases embody a past, an entire language and culture, sometimes even the fading memory of a people: "It's called an Indian burn when you put your hands around someone's wrist and twist in opposite directions. Another old term, a thing from grade school maybe" (*L* 341). "It's called an Indian burn, remember?" (*U* 48) Here's one more, also Indian-related: "I could tell you about Indian summer in Badger, but maybe it's just enough to say the words, and they're the two words my mother always said were the most beautiful in the language when put one after the other. Indian summer" (*AZ* 165–166).

We thus say things because those are the things people say: for example, "a dear sweet man": "It's something people say. One of those expressions that sound like someone else is talking. A dear sweet man" ("HS" 152). It's trite, hackneyed, tired, even somewhat ridiculous, and yet it can also be heard as "the uninventable poetry, inside the pain, of what people say" (*M* 216). These are the kinds of things we people say.

8

Words for Words

The word for water is water.

U 193

Let the words be the facts.

"MD" 122

Names

To bear a name is both terrible and necessary.

RS 19

They keep changing the names. … The names we grew up with. The countries, the images. Persia for one. We grew up with Persia. … Rhodesia of course. Rhodesia said something. … Every time another people's republic emerges from the dust, I have the feeling someone has tampered with my childhood.

N 239–240

How do you connect things? Learn their names.

N 328

Whence DeLillo's interest in words, in names, his desire—which can be found throughout his works—to find the right word or name and then the right or appropriate relationship between the word or name and the thing. What interests DeLillo, perhaps before all else, is the way language shadows or overshadows, encounters or counterfeits, the things to which it is supposed to refer. One of the curious effects of Dylar in *White Noise* is that one cannot "distinguish words from things, so that if someone said 'speeding bullet,' [one] would fall to the floor and take cover" (*WN* 193). Knowing, then, that the drug causes "the user to confuse words with the things they referred to" (*WN* 310), Jack says the words "falling plane" in his confrontation with Mink and gets the desired reaction: "He looked at me, gripping the arms of the chair, the first signs of panic building in his eyes" (*WN* 309). The double-banded relation between word and thing can thus sometimes get in the way of leading a simple, seamless life, even eating a simple meal: "I could not chew and swallow without thinking of *chew* and *swallow*" (*ZK* 89; see *WN* 126). It is the opposite of what we see in *Americana*, a world in which "words and meanings were at odds," where "words did not say what was being said nor even its reverse" (*A* 36).

We have already seen DeLillo's interest in secret names, hidden names, noms de plume and noms de guerre. Here is one theory about names from *Ratner's Star*: "Names are the animal badges we wear, given not only for practical necessity but to serve as a subscript to the inner person, a primitive index of the soul" (*RS* 396). The name is, as it were, the contraband of the self, and this contraband can itself be contrabanded, that is, repeated, concealed, masked, imitated, transformed: "That's the power of names. People act in response to their names. There's a tiny sector of the human brain where the naming mechanism is located" (*GJ* 250; see *RD* 230). Billy Twillig was born William Denis Terwilliger, Jr., "Jr." because his father didn't think he would live and so didn't want to waste a name (*RS* 74). Klara Sax was initially "Klara Sachs without the *x*" (*U* 374; see 482), but after her divorce from Albert, "she changed her name from Bronzini back to Sachs but made a point of spelling it with an *x*" (*U* 483). In *Underworld* Lenny Bruce does a riff on the names in the Kennedy White House: *Adlai* Stevenson, *Dean* Rusk, *McGeorge* Bundy, *Roswell* Gilpatric, *Averell* Harriman, concluding: "You want names. I'll give you names. My name is Leonard Alfred Schneider" (*U* 592). No whiff of the Ivy League in that name ...

There are "confirmation names" (*U* 759), forgotten names, "a girl named something or other" (*U* 673), and then people named or renamed, whether by themselves or others. Sullivan renames Richard Spector "Kyrie Eleison," a name that is also a chant or a prayer—like Allah (*A* 217; see *M* 181, "HS" 175, *P* 211). Others have fake or phony names, contraband names, Martin Ridnour, for example, aka Ernst Hechinger, or mistaken names, Bill Lawton for Bin Laden, as well as pen names, Bill Gray for Willard Skansey Jr., a name that Scott, Bill's assistant, vows never to reveal because "it would bring him closer than ever to Bill, keeping the secret of his name" (*M* 185; see *U* 15–16). There are stage names, like Rey Robles, the name that Alejandro Alquezar took after "a minor character he played in an obscure film noir" (*BA* 27–28), the stage name being thus taken from a name that has already been staged.

There is an enchantment in names, especially when these names are hidden or forbidden. It was the power of names, of secret names, that seems to have put Oswald on the path to becoming who he became. As a kid visiting the library, "he found names in the catalogue that made him pause with a strange contained excitement. Names that were like whispers he'd been hearing for years, men of history and revolution" (*L* 34), names like Marx and Trotsky, and particularly this latter, with whom he had an unknown, secret connection: "Trotsky in the Bronx" (*L* 34).

Like Trotsky, then, Oswald would need another name, a secret name. For "Trotsky was not his real name" (*L* 34), "Trotsky's name was Bronstein" (*L* 236), a name he took "from a jailer in Odessa and carried it into the pages of a thousand books" (*L* 327). Similarly, "Lenin's name was not really Lenin. Stalin's name was Dzhugashvili" (*L* 34; see 40, 155). Not even Jack Ruby was Jack Ruby, as everyone but Oswald would eventually learn, but "Jacob Rubenstein," and he apparently "adopted the middle name Leon"—interesting little factoid—"to honor the memory of a friend, Leon Cooke, shot to death in a labor dispute" (*L* 301). One can thus try to grow into the name one has been given—"His name was Leo Zhelezniak. It took half a lifetime before he began to fit into the name" ("*S*" 186)—or else, like Lee Harvey Oswald, try to change one's name, to disguise or *decline* it, into O. H. Lee, or the more cryptically diacritical "D. F. Drictal" (*L* 301, 371), or the well-hidden Hidell:

> Take the double-*e* from Lee.
> Hide the double-*l* in Hidell.
> Hidell means hide the *L*.
> Don't tell. (*L* 90)

The name is the secret but also the code: "Die and hell in Hidell" (*L* 440). Of course, retired CIA agent Win Everett was also doing all he could to lend a hand in this. His plan was to find or invent a gunman who would "emerge and vanish in a maze of false names" (*L* 145). As for the name the world has come to know him by, Lee Harvey Oswald, "he didn't recognize himself in the full intonation of the name. The only time he used his middle name was to write it on a form that had a space for that purpose" (*L* 416). It sounded historic already to everyone and especially to him. And yet he must have known he had it coming, for earlier in his life he had witnessed this phenomenon of two names suddenly becoming three as a sign of notoriety:

> It occurred to Oswald that everyone called the prisoner by his full name. ... Once you did something notorious, they tagged you with an extra name, a middle name that was ordinarily never used. You were officially marked, a chapter in the imagination of the state. Francis Gary Powers. In just these few days the name had taken on a resonance, a sense of fateful event. It already sounded historic. (*L* 198)

But that would not be the end of his proper improper names; he would get at least one more after death: "They lowered [him] to the red clay of Texas, burying him for security reasons under another name, the last alias of Lee Harvey Oswald. It was William Bobo" (*L* 454). *Libra* in fact ends with Oswald's mother thinking about her son's name, the name that *she* had once given him and that was now known to the world:

> Lee Harvey Oswald. Saying it like a secret they'd keep forever. ... Lee Harvey Oswald. No matter what happened, how hard they schemed against her, this was the one thing they could not take away—the true and lasting power of his name. It belonged to her now, and to history. (*L* 456)

A name can be like a mantra, a totem, a shibboleth, or a talisman. Take Matt Shay's name in the mouth of his wife Janet: "Janet called him Matthew. This was her way of separating him from family history, the whole dense endeavor of Mattiness" (*U* 454). Or Emma Breslow in the mouth of Jeffrey Lockhart: "I thought of walking to her school and asking someone if I might see Emma Breslow. I spoke the full name inwardly" (*ZK* 226). Or Jeff's name, Jeffrey's name, in the mouth of Artis:

> I was Jeff to everyone but Artis. That extra syllable, in her tender voice, made me self-aware, or aware of a second self, more agreeable and dependable, a man who walks with his shoulders squared, pure fiction. (*ZK* 18)

As for place names, the narrator of *Zero K* looks at a map of the former Soviet Union and thinks of the "decades of upheaval flattened into place-names" (*ZK* 188). For example, "Chelyabinsk, right here, where the meteor had struck, and the Convergence itself buried somewhere on the map in the old U.S.S.R." (*ZK* 188). And then there are place-names like Idaho, "the word, so voweled and obscure" ("MD" 134), or Valparaiso (*V* 29, 43), in Indiana and in Chile, which raises the question, "Don't all places collapse into their names? And if the name is the same, why should the pronunciation be different?" (*V* 73) It's a problem not just because two very different places can be named "Valparaiso" but because both places are already called "places" (*DR* 76).

There is a power in names, a power one gains in having a name of one's own, especially when it is unknown to others, and a power one gains over others by knowing their name. In *The Names* the cult members of the group *Ta Onómata* (The Names) follow an ancient ritual of carving "the initials of the victim ... into the blade of the crude iron tool used to kill him" (*N* 150; see 158, 207, 250): "You will want to hurt your enemy ... to destroy his name" (*N* 150; see 250). It's an ancient desire and yet also one from just yesterday. James Axton reflects: "I thought of the dead man's initials cut into the weapon. Old westerns. If one of those bullets has your name on it, Cody, there's not a goldarned thing you can do about it" (*N* 153).

There is a power in names because names are one of the ways of giving order to the world. Take football, for example, where "each play must have a name" (*EZ* 118), and where the coach, as the "maker of plays," is "the name-giver" (*EZ* 135). In *Ratner's Star*, Siba Isten-Esru, the "name shaman" (*RS* 266), whose "vocation" or "serious amusement"—in addition to her area of expertise, "crystal structure"—is "the study of names," gives a long demonstration of how to read names, first her own and then Billy Twillig's (*RS* 152–155). Of this latter, she says: "My first reaction is strictly a sense impression. Twinkle and twig. I see and touch star and stick." But then her reading gets more involved: "There are two distinct parts to your name and they comprise the essence of my analysis. *Twi*—two. *Lig*—to bind, as in 'ligate' and 'ligature.' Is it your destiny then to bind together two distinct entities? To join the unjoinable? ... *Twi* means not only 'two' but 'half,' while *lig* can mean 'constrict' as well as 'bind'" (*RS* 154–155). It's like reading a name from *Finnegans Wake* or like an exploration of the ambivalent origins of primal words; and it's all to be found in a passage from "Ratner's Star," where there is "star" in "Ratner's" and "rats" in "star."

It is thus not just proper names, the names of people or places, that interest DeLillo but names in general. In *The Names* James Axton seems to find a kind of solace in knowing as many of these names as possible: "This was limestone, those were fig trees, that was a barrel-vaulted chamber. The names. I felt strangely, self-consciously alone" (*N* 196).

These are the kinds of things DeLillo's characters like to know and use, the names of trees, "Norway maple," for example ("MD" 125), but especially plants. As Cleo Birdwell recalls in *Amazons*: "My mother made sure I knew the names of plants and flowers growing around the yard and climbing up the house. Lilac bushes, forsythia, wisteria, hydrangea, and the one I could never remember, which is spirea" (*AZ* 162). A couple of decades later, Lauren in *The Body Artist* picks up the lesson in horticulture with Mr. Tuttle: "She named bog plants for him, spelling out the words" (*BA* 115; see *U* 453). Ross Lockhart in *Zero K* also liked to recall "animals and birds they'd seen close-range, and he named them, and plant species, and he named them" (*ZK* 50). He is right at home, then, in the fake garden of the Convergence, where fake trees and plants are labeled with their Latin names (*ZK* 122). Same thing, and maybe even more so, in *Love-Lies-Bleeding*:

Late the first night, he got going on the subject of plants. He loved the names of desert plants. He went into whirling ecstasies. Reciting, you know, the name, type, genus, species. ... He went into little raptures, reciting the names. I can't remember a single one, not one, maybe one. ... And it's all one running creation. This is the thing he kept saying. The names as well. For those who know them. (*LL* 33–35; see 453)

Among those names are "Larkspur," "Barrel cactus," "Indian paintbrush," and, of course, "Love-lies-bleeding," which Lia and Alex once saw in India, near "the cave temples of Ajanta, unforgettable—sculptured, painted caves" (*LL* 37)—like Alex's own, final project. And Alex not only knows these names but has his own theory of them: "He said they didn't create the names of plants. They discovered them, like explorers, like Magellan discovering whatever he discovered" (*LL* 39). The name "Love-lies-bleeding" was thus waiting out there to be discovered, just like "the Strait of Magellan."

We saw earlier the importance that DeLillo's characters attach to the names of weapons, guns and knives. It turns out that the names of flowers and knives might not be all that different, as this exchange between Lia and Sean in *Love-Lies-Bleeding* suggests:

"We were on a bus, and we were nearly there, and we saw a field of amaranthus, a type of amaranthus, and he told me the common name. Love-lies-bleeding. Slender red flowers. Spiky flowers."
"Who was the poet who thought of the name?"
"So beautiful. Cuts like a knife." (*LL* 37–38)

Owen Brademas in *The Names* has a similar theory about names—a theory about the saving power of memory and the necessity of retaining the past through names, even if this memory is never completely pure of fiction:

Owen believed that memory was the faculty of absolution. Men developed memories to ease their disquiet over things they did as men. The deep past is the only innocence and therefore necessary to retain. The boy in the sorghum fields, the boy learning the names of animals and plants. He could recall exactly. He would work the details of that particular day. (*N* 304)

We thus need to learn names; we need an apprenticeship in names in order to write, to be sure, but also in order to see the world more fully. Here is James Axton in the same novel teaching his nine-year-old aspiring novelist son Tap (not far from Type) about the power of names, teaching him to pay attention to the names of things and, through those names, to the things themselves. Axton is questioning a passage in his son's novel in which the hero goes out "in a blizzard wearing his rubbery Ingersoll":

> "I think you meant Mackintosh. He went out in a blizzard wearing his rubbery Mackintosh."
> "I thought a Mackintosh was a boot. He wouldn't go out with one Mackintosh. He'd wear Mackintoshes."
> "He'd wear Wellingtons. A Wellington is a boot."
> "Then what's a Mackintosh?"
> "A raincoat."
> "A raincoat. Then what's an Ingersoll?"
> "A watch."
> "A watch," he said, and I could see him store these names and the objects they belonged to, for safe keeping." (*N* 9–10; see 134)

(Ingersoll, Wellington, Mackintosh: learning such names puts a whole new spin on DeLillo's use of brand names like Johnnie Walker and, especially, Panasonic—which, of course, makes more than just typewriters: "I'll give you an idea how out of touch I've gotten. I didn't even *know* about the Panasonic five-foot screen" (*AZ* 256). Brands are corporate names, to be sure, but they are also, and first of all, names, first names of a sort, and it is perhaps no coincidence that the first of DeLillo's name-givers, that is, the first writer, even if he was failed writer, was, in *Americana*, already branded Brand.)

It is this same lesson that Father Paulus even more famously and more fully gives Nick Shay in *Underworld*—the same Father Paulus who once taught epistemology at Fordham and gave Nick a copy of *The Cloud of Unknowing*, a book about God and His secret name. He first explains the need for the lesson:

> Sometimes I think the education we dispense is better suited to a fifty-year-old who feels he missed the point the first time around. Too many abstract ideas. Eternal verities left and right. You'd be better served looking at your shoe and naming the parts. You in particular, Shay, coming from the place you come from. (*U* 540)

After this general statement about pedagogy, we get the example—the shoe that's right there on Nick's foot. Father Paulus gets Nick to name all the parts he knows and then teaches him those he doesn't: "Name the parts. Go ahead." Nick names "laces," "sole and heel," and then seems to be coming up short: "There's not much to name, is there? A front and a top." But when prompted, first by sarcasm, his tongue gets untied: "You're so eloquent I may have to pause to regain my composure. You've named the lace. What's the flap under the lace?" "The tongue ... I knew the name. I just didn't see the thing" (*U* 540). Here's where we get from Father Paulus the principle behind it all: "You didn't see the thing because you don't know how to look. And you don't know how to look because you don't know the names" (*U* 540). In other words, Nick didn't know the word for the tongue of the shoe because he didn't have the language, the name, the tongue to say it. And the tongue is just the beginning. There's a whole little world between the tongue and the eyelet. The lesson continues with the "cuff," the "counter," the "quarter," the "welt," and so on:

> "How everyday things lie hidden. Because we don't know what they're called. What's the frontal area that covers the instep?" "I don't know." "You don't know. It's called the vamp. ... The perforations at either side of, and above, the tongue." "I can't think of the word. Eyelet." "Maybe I'll let you live after all." (*U* 541)

As Father Paulus says after putting Nick through a few more paces: "We're doing the physics of language, Shay" (*U* 542). And Father Paulus's lesson works like a charm or like an enchantment. It is Paulus who unseals the new language or at least Nick's newfound interest in language: "I wanted to look up words. I wanted to look up velleity and quotidian and memorize the fuckers for all time, spell them, learn them, pronounce them syllable by syllable—vocalize, phonate, utter the sounds, say the words for all they're worth. / This is the only way in the world you can escape the things that made you" (*U* 543). Indeed Nick seems to have learned his lesson well. Later in narrative time—though earlier in the novel—Nick and a colleague are discussing a photograph of Charlie Parker, and they try to identify the shoes he is wearing in the photo. At first Nick thinks they're "old-fashioned two-tone shoes" (*U* 327), but then he gets it, "they're called spectator shoes" (*U* 337). He wouldn't have remembered those shoes if he didn't have the name, and he wouldn't have even seen those shoes in the first place if he didn't have the name that fits them.

Like James Axton, Nick himself not only learns the lesson but tries to pass it on to the next generation: "I used to tell my kids when they were small. A hawser is a rope that's used to moor a ship. Or, The hump in the floor between rooms, I used to say. This is called the saddle. ... A hawser is the thing you tie around a bollard" (*U* 102–103). "I used to say to the kids. I used to hold up an object and say, The little ridged section at the bottom of the toothpaste tube. This is called the crimp" (*U* 105). There are in DeLillo no shortage of similar injunctions to pay attention to and to learn the names of the things we see so that we can really see those things in the first place (see *EZ* 30, 89, 162, *RS* 195, 351, *N* 284, *U* 227, *ZK* 96). In *White Noise* Jack Gladney gives Babette a little vocabulary lesson even when he is confronting her about her use of Dylar. When Babette says, "I thought I was going through a phase, some kind of watermark period in my life," Jack suggests that she meant to say not "watermark"—a word she might have used if she were talking about typing paper—but "landmark" "or watershed" (*WN* 191).

Jeffrey Lockhart from *Zero K* seems to have gone to the same school of names: "The doors here were painted in gradations of muted blue and I tried to name the shades. Sea, sky, butterfly, indigo" (*ZK* 23). Names help us to see things, even taste them: "'It's called morning *plov*.' I took another bite and tried to associate the taste with the name. … The food was beginning to taste like what it was, now that he'd identified it for me. Mutton. Morning *plov*" (*ZK* 39, 41). In *Cosmopolis* Eric Packer, like Jeffrey in *Zero K*, cannot help himself from naming what he sees: "He entered the enclosed space of the courtyard, mentally naming what was in it" (*C* 25). Much later, he sees someone and thinks: "She had light brown hair, or brownish blond. Maybe it was fawn-colored. What is fawn? A grayish yellow-brown to a moderate reddish brown. Or sorrel. Sorrel sounded better" (*C* 174)—not to be confused with the herb: "We also ate sour grass, which might have been sorrel" (*AZ* 164).

There are also, sometimes—and we must always recall that this is literature, part of DeLillo's writing—attempts to recall a name. Something at a wake, for example: "This was something called the viewing, she believed" ("BM" 105), or attempts to come up with the right name for something, not just the names of weapons but, say, the names of a nun's vestments, "the old things with the arcane names, the wimple, cincture and guimpe" (*U* 238; see 232, 571; see "AE" 74). In *Zero K* the narrator speaks of "the Monk in his old rutted cloak, his scapular" (*ZK* 92), "the Monk in his sweatshirt hood, his cowl" (*ZK* 95). "It's called a trench coat, she said" (*ZK* 107). The writer is the ultimate name-giver, the one who gives names to people, places, and things—indeed, to every last thing in a book—though there are others, as we have seen, who share in this craft and find delight in finding the right name for things: "The sliver of soap, the washcloth bunched. Soap is called a sliver in this configuration" (*BA* 68; see *U* 114).

Sometimes stories revolve in large part around the remembering of a name. When, in *Zero K*, Jeffrey Lockhart's plane runs into a sandstorm, he tries "to think of the word, in Arabic, that refers to such phenomena. This is what I do to defend myself against some spectacle of nature. Think of a word. / *Haboob*, I thought" (*ZK* 230). In "Hammer and Sickle" it's the Vietnamese name of a garment that the narrator tries to recall: turns out that the name is attached to the memory of his wife from long ago, to her "slowly shedding her clothing, a tunic and loose trousers, an *ao dai*" ("HS" 178).

Then there are new things for which names have just been invented, "Dacron, Orlon, Lycra Spandex" (*WN* 52), or foreign things, "*Anorak* is an Inuit word" ("MD" 120). Or "two women in chadors. ... I knew the word. Chadors. Or burqas. Or whatever the other names. This was all I needed to know" (*ZK* 52). It's actually a name that another DeLillo character had already tried to remember once: "Black-veiled women, the women in full-length veils, Karen tried to think of the word, chadors, women wrapped in chadors" (*M* 192).

Clothes, plants, weapons, but then also tools—like Murray Siskind's landlord and fix-it man: "He's very good with all those little tools and fixtures and devices that people in cities never know the names of. The names of these things are only known in outlying communities, small towns and rural areas" (*WN* 33). They are the kinds of names Jack wouldn't know but his father-in-law would:

> There were times when he seemed to attack me with terms like ratchet drill and whipsaw. He saw my shakiness in such matters as a sign of some deeper incompetence or stupidity. These were the things that built the world. Not to know or care about them was a betrayal of fundamental principles, a betrayal of gender, of species. (*WN* 245)

There are, then, languages within language, counter-languages, if you will, the names of weapons or tools or articles of clothing or vehicles: "Parked nearby were school buses, motorcycles, smallish vans called ambulettes" (*WN* 149; see *U* 457). The narrator is not just using a word like "ambulettes" to describe smallish vans but recalling that smallish vans are "called" ambulettes; in other words, he is pointing out how the name contrabands the thing.

There is a power in names, though there is perhaps an even greater power in the nameless or the unnameable. Having earlier evoked "the beauty and horror of wordless things" (*GJ* 52), Bucky Wunderlick in *Great Jones Street* temporarily loses the capacity to speak because of the super-drug at the center of the novel. In time, though, the drug wears off and *mouth* is the first word to come to mind, just as, in *Underworld*, *tongue* was the first word to come to the tongue-tied Nick:

> I walked more slowly, as though in fear of objects, all things with names unknown to me. ... I was unreasonably happy, subsisting in blessed circumstance, thinking of myself as a kind of living chant. I made

interesting and original sounds. ... *Mouth* was the first word to reach me, dropping from one speech mechanism to the other. ... Soon all was normal, a return to prior modes. (*GJ* 264)

Names are thus forgotten in limit situations, in moments of crisis, after a death, for example, or in ecstasy. After Jack's death in *Players*, Pam "declared everything nameless. Everything was compressed into a block. She fought the tendency to supply properties to this block. That would lead to names" (*P* 199). In *Mao II* losing names is actually the object of the Moonies: "They chant for one language, one word, for the time when names are lost" (*M* 16). But then there are nameless dangers—just about the worst kind (see *RS* 91)—and certain diseases, like Alzheimer's, that threaten the total loss of names: "This was an occasion that haunted Lianne, the breathless moment when things fall away, streets, names, all sense of direction and location, every fixed grid of memory" (*FM* 156). The path to taking pleasure in names or to being fascinated by them seems to go by way of their threatened loss, that is, by their withdrawal, their forgetting, their contradiction, precisely.

Words

"We might as well begin then."
"Begin what?" I said.
"The dialogue. The exchange of words. The phrases and sentences."
EZ 231

Every word fills a void. We only have to talk, Mr. Wyatt, to keep the world turning. The world at the tips of our fingers, the tip of our tongue.
DR 47

Here is the word "horse." You all know what a horse looks like. This is what the word looks like. Is there anyone who sees a resemblance?
DR 80

Ratner's Star is a novel about the relationship between things and their names, about language and numbers and names, families and peoples, for example, who have no name (*RS* 103), but then also about "the secret power of the alphabet, the unnameable name, the literal contraction of the superdivinity, fear of sperm demons," and other things even more difficult to define (*RS* 215; see 333). We are introduced in the novel to J. Graham Hummer, "widely known as the instigator of the MIT language riots," which started years back when Hummer tried "to assert that what there is in common between a particular fact and the sentence that asserts this fact can itself be put into a sentence" (*RS* 31, 33). In other words, he asserted the possibility of a meta-language, a perfectly contraband language, if you will, a language that expresses in language the relationship between things and words. *Ratner's Star* is thus a novel about words, about language, about the possibility of a mathematical "grammar" (*RS* 287), the possibility of constructing a completely "formal language, void of content" (*RS* 340), "a universal logical structure able to speak about itself in metalogical terms" (*RS* 349).

It is tempting to think that contraband language or the contraband that is language detaches language from the world. But the point of the contraband is that language is entwined with the world, the contraband always there not just to affirm but to help constitute the world, the wordness of words there to give definition to the thingness of things.

In *The Names*, the cult, *Ta Onómata*, seems to be seeking similar insights into the relationship between language and the world, something less rational than our usual sense of these things and yet something that strikes a chord: "Something in our method finds a home in your unconscious mind" (*N* 205). Owen Brademas understands that by attempting to work at this "preverbal level" (*N* 205)—a bit like speaking in tongues—the cult threatens all the order and structure that languages lend the world:

> These killings mock us. They mock our need to structure and classify, to build a system against the terror in our souls. They make the system equal to the terror. The means to contend with death has become death. Did I always know this? It took the desert to make it clear to me. (*N* 308)

The power of language, of names, of words. It's not what the word says but the saying of the word that counts, an insight that seems easier to appreciate the farther we are away from home, that is, the farther we are away from ourselves and the assurances of our language:

> The word in India has enormous power. Not what people mean but what they say. Intended meaning is beside the point. The word itself is all that matters. The Hindu woman tries to avoid speaking her husband's name. Every utterance of his name brings him closer to death. You know this. I'm not telling you something you don't know, or am I? (*N* 294)

This power of words becomes greater and greater, it seems, the closer we get to death or to the limits of meaning or intelligibility. In *Great Jones*

Street the drug being peddled by the Happy Valley Commune is designed to "attack a particular region in the left hemisphere of the brain. That's the verbal hemisphere, it seems. Where the words are kept" (*GJ* 228). Bucky Wunderlick is told after taking the drug that he will be "perfectly healthy" but "won't be able to make words. ... Sounds yes. Sounds galore. But no words. No songs." When asked whether he has "Anything to say? ... Any last words?" Bucky says: "Pee-pee-maw-maw" (*GJ* 255–256). What does this mean? Well, earlier in the novel, Bucky is asked about the "origin and meaning" of this odd, childlike phrase, and he responds:

> Childhood incantation. ... As a little kid in the street I used to hear older kids saying it. ... Pee-pee-maw-maw. Chants like that can be traced to the dawn of civilization. Like games kids play can be traced a thousand years back to kids in India. Same with incantations. ... The beast is loose / Least is best / Pee-pee-maw-maw. (*GJ* 106–107, 118)

Pee-pee-maw-maw—at once the origin and the breakdown of language, the most modern as the most primitive or archaic. Bucky is reduced to producing only sounds, comparable, perhaps, to speaking in tongues, close to an aboriginal pa-pa-ma-ma (see *GJ* 263).

Pee-pee-maw-maw: when college professor Jack Gladney thinks of his own death and Babette's, he is reduced to similar childish babble: "A two-syllable infantile cry, *ba-ba*, issued from the deeps of my soul" (*WN* 104). It's also not far from the state of language achieved by Wilder during his hours-long crying fit, his inhuman human wailing, a "huge lament ... wave on wave ... a sound so large and pure ... an ancient dirge all the more impressive for its resolute monotony" (*WN* 78). This is the language of extreme states, that found in childhood, or under the effect of drugs (the contraband with which we began), or before one's first cup of coffee in the morning: "Mumbling in my coffee mug. ... I'm at the language level of the origin of species" (*V* 66). It's all language, therefore, save the silence—about which DeLillo also has a lot to say (see, for example, *EZ* 30–31, 33, *GJ* 246, *LL* 11, *WN* 97, *C* 5, *FM* 157, *PO* 94).

If the radiance of things seems to coincide with their becoming themselves, that is, with the overlapping of band and contraband, its equivalent in language seems to be the moment when language serves no other purpose than its own expression, that is, when the saying of language overlaps with or contrabands the said. James Axton in *The Names* seems to suggest that this is what he experienced in everyday language in Greece:

> This is a way of speaking that takes such pure joy in its own openness and ardor that we begin to feel these people are discussing language itself.

What pleasure in the simplest greeting. It's as though one friend says to another, "How good it is to say 'How are you?'" The other replying, "When I answer 'I am well and how are you,' what I really mean is that I'm delighted to have a chance to say these familiar things—they bridge the lonely distances." (*N* 53)

Mr. Tuttle in *The Body Artist* is an object lesson in this power of words to refer only to themselves or to their own possibility. While it is never exactly clear what Mr. Tuttle is saying or trying to say, the words he uses nonetheless make sense; they are not meaningless sounds or gibberish; there is even a sort of poetry in them. "He hasn't learned the language" (*BA* 99), thinks Lauren, and yet his language is all the even more extraordinary as a result: "She didn't know what to call this. She called it singing" (*BA* 74). This becomes crystal clear in a single phrase from Mr. Tuttle, a simple phrase that is repeated in various forms in other DeLillo works: "The word for moonlight is moonlight," says Mr. Tuttle: "This made her happy. It was logically complex and oddly moving and circularly beautiful and true—or maybe not so circular but straight as straight can be" (*BA* 82). Here he is, Mr. Tuttle, in his unsettling voice, "reedy and thin and trapped in tenses and inflections, in singsong conjugations" (*BA* 63), "shadow-inching through a sentence, showing a word in its facets and aspects, words like moons in particular phases" (*BA* 48), and the next thing you know he has happened upon a fundamental truth: "The word for moonlight is moonlight." Like "the word for snow is snow," the name of an unpublished play by DeLillo, or, in *Underworld*, after melting, "the word for water is water" (*U* 193), the phrase is, obviously, a tautology, a redundancy, self-referring and self-justifying. And yet, already in DeLillo, it is not as obvious as all that since "moonlight" can mean more than one thing, as Babette's father testifies: "Shingling here, rustproofing there. I moonlight, except there's nothing I'm moonlighting from. Moonlight is all that's out there" (*WN* 245). But, even more, "the word for moonlight is moonlight" reveals the contrabanding of thing and word, moonlight and *moonlight*, the first seemingly present well before the second and yet recognizable as such only through the second.

Mr. Tuttle is one of several DeLillo characters who might be thought of as "counter-characters," characters, often children or artists, who resist or perturb all totalizing or normalizing narratives, who test the limits of language. Artis Martineau is another such character, in *Zero K*, pushing herself and thus us to the limits of language as she slowly fades into her state of suspension in the Convergence and her language, her "inner monologue," "the open prose of a third-person voice that is also her voice," becomes "a form of chant in a single low tone" (*ZK* 272). In the end, there are only the words, detached somehow from the one who knows them; it's like words free-floating after the end of the person or the end of the world: "She knows these words. She is all words but she doesn't know how to get out of words into being someone, being the person who knows the words" (ZK 157).

Defining Words

They were clinging to the surface, weren't they, both of them? Earth in all its meanings, third planet from the sun, realm of mortal existence, every definition in between.

ZK 242

I was defining myself. That's what my father said. He said people who have to define themselves belong in the dictionary.

"HS" 169

"Define rock." I was thinking of myself at his age, determined to find the more or less precise meaning of a word, to draw other words out of the designated word in order to locate the core. ... "Officially let's say a rock is a large hard mass of mineral substance laying on the ground or embedded in the soil." I was impressed.

ZK 216

Writers write with words; words and names are what writers use to make their sentences, their stories. There is nothing more obvious than that. It is thus never an indifferent gesture when a writer's characters talk about language in general or express a preference for certain words or phrases, certain *defining* words, as it were. In DeLillo, this happens much more frequently than in most writers and in a variety of ways. Already in *Americana* David Bell expresses an odd penchant in high school for everyday phrases like "suiting up" (A 158), preferring the phrase, it seems, over the thing—actually suiting up—and even over the thing for which one would suit up. This attraction to words can go so far that one can change one's hair color simply because one likes the sound of the words: "I used to be a frosted blond. You know why? I liked the sound of it" (DR 84). And while some preferred phrases are somewhat predictable—phrases like "make me come" (LL 62) or "we kept on hoping she'd present me with a child. What a wonderful verbal concept. To be presented with a child" (DR 29)—others are more idiosyncratic, like "fluctuating planes. I liked this phrase" (WN 243), or "lancet window"

(*ZK* 116), or "*pendant light*" (*ZK* 269), or "rife," "what's more dramatic … What more rife? I like that word" (*V* 67), or "*gravlax*," "You fell in love with the word *gravlax*" (*LL* 62), or "hammer and sickle," "The girls like saying it. Hammer and sickle" ("HS" 165). Or else, unexpectedly, good household words like "breezeway" and "crisper": "One of Erica's favorite words in the language was breezeway. … Another word she loved was crisper. The Kelvinator had a nice roomy crisper. … He came in from the breezeway" (*U* 516). Jeffrey in *Zero K* says: "'We don't forget. People like us.' I liked saying that. People like us" (*ZK* 19). Or the word *phantasm*: "When I was in my early teens I came across the word *phantasm*. A great word, I thought, and I wanted to be phantasmal, someone who slips in and out of physical reality" ("HS" 149; see 160). And this too is what the novelist does, because words are not just strokes on a page or sounds in the air but conveyers of memory. When Lauren Hartke thinks of her mother, for example, she is apt to think not of her face or character but of her favorite words, remote memories: "The room faced east and would be roiled in morning light, in webby sediment and streams of sunlit dust and in the word *motes*, which her mother liked to use" (*BA* 123–124).

DeLillo himself seems to have certain favorite words, like acanthus (*BA* 113) or amaranthus, the love-lies-bleeding (*LL* 37, *RS* 202), or—to give a more extended example—"newel": "She touched the oak grain of the newel when she reached the landing" (*BA* 33); "she climbed the stairs, touching the top of the newel when she reached the landing" (*BA* 113); "she would mount the stairs, touching the top of the newel at the landing, and walk down the hall into his time" (*BA* 115; see also *L* 74). It's like a renewal, each time she goes up, each time she reaches the landing. It's just a little architectural detail, like a "pineapple finial" (*WN* 4), but it's obviously also more than that. It's the *name* she is touching, and thus we along with her, each time she would mount the stairs. You can start with the "finial" but then move on to the "oak balustrade," the "plank floor," and so on—the best names or the best words in the house: "The best things in this house were the plank floor in the kitchen and the oak balustrade on the staircase. Just saying the words. Thinking the words" (*BA* 93). Sometimes even literature is less about the names and words in literary works than about the names and words that surround or describe them: "I wanted to read Gombrowicz in Polish. I didn't know a word of Polish. … I wanted to read him in the original. The phrase appealed to me. Read him in the original" (*ZK* 105).

There are thus names that return, sometimes repeatedly, names DeLillo likes, names that return or that recall one another, names like Shay and Gray, Gary and Garry—these latter being almost always on the younger side, because "you never see an old man named Gary. … You never see a kid with a grandfather named Gary" (*DR* 64, 66). And then there are names that seem to belong together in a series, Lynn, Lyle (*P*), Lynette (*DR*), Pammy (*P*), Babette (*WN*), and so on. And then there's a kid from the Bronx in *Libra* named "Nicky Black": "The name was always used in full, never just Nicky or Black" (*L* 8). Nicky Black, then, a combination, it seems, of Nick Shay, Mr. Gray, and Bill Gray, all of them together making up an "Arrangement in Gray and Black" (a Whistler painting, okay, but also the title of Part 6 of *Underworld*, see *U* 659).

Now to know a word one has to know more than the word itself, its letters and its sound, one has to know its meaning, its relationship to other words and, perhaps, the thing it names in the world. One must know, in short, its *definition*. Near the beginning of his lecture to Nick on the importance of knowing the names of all the parts of a shoe, Father Paulus asks about a particular word: "Have you come across the word velleity? A nice Thomistic ring to it." When Nick says he knows nothing about it, Father Paulus goes ahead and defines it: "Volition at its lowest ebb. A small thing, a wish, a tendency" (*U* 539). This penchant for definitions is echoed elsewhere in DeLillo's novels, but nowhere more emphatically than in *Zero K*, where we read, in the voice of Jeffrey, the son of Ross Lockhart:

"Define *person*, I tell myself. Define *human*, define *animal*" (*ZK* 103). "I watch her use the roller to remove lint from her cloth coat. Define *coat*, I tell myself. Define *time*, define *space*" (*ZK* 109; see *N* 180). "I tried to define the word *roller* without sneaking a look in the dictionary. ... A rotating cylindrical device that collects bits of fiber sticking to the surface of a garment. ... I'd been doing this for a while, attempting to define a word for an object or even a concept. Define *loyalty*, define *truth*. I had to stop before it killed me." (*ZK* 55)

We could imagine Socrates in a Platonic dialogue asking his interlocutors to define such things as *loyalty* or *truth*, but probably not *roller* or *lint* or *hunger*, *Bessarabian*, *penetralia*, or *pellucid*, *tennis racket* or *falafel* (*ZK* 59, 199, 107).

We also have in *Zero K* a little lesson in the labyrinth of words that a dictionary is. The narrator recalls how a single word he did not know, "fishwife," led him to "shrew," which itself led to "shrewmouse," which takes him back to "shrew," and then "insectivorous" and "insectous," "vora" and then "vorous," and you can see how lost one can get (*ZK* 25). Words are thus used by every author, but they are commented on only by a contraband author. For example, "nanobots—a child's word" (*ZK* 146) or "orphanage—Sounds like a word out of the sixteenth century. The orphan boy becomes a prince" (*ZK* 219). Only in a contraband author are there reflections on the origins of the words being used in writing, words like—and this one happens to have a word for writing within it—"polygraph": "A nice technical sound to it, a specialist's sound, but still traditional, decipherable, from the Greek" (*L* 362).

Eric Packer comments throughout *Cosmopolis* on words that seem to him outdated, "anachronistic," words that, like specters or ghosts, are living on well after the animating intentions that first formed them. Hence "the anachronistic quality of the word skyscraper" (*C* 9), ditto for *office*, "outdated now" (*C* 15), and "automated teller machines" (*C* 54), even the word *phone*: "It was time to retire the word phone" (*C* 88; see also 43, 71, 162, 164). Indeed today "even the word computer ... sounds backwards and dumb" (*C* 104). (It is probably no coincidence that *Cosmopolis* is dedicated to Paul Auster, author of the *New York Trilogy*, a collection whose first tale, "City of Glass," is about the obsolescence of language.)

There are phrases, then, and then words, simple words, words without verbs sometimes, words lined up like nouns or names on a list, words like "sleep, earth, creature" (*P* 139), or "'earth, creature, touch.' ... 'Birds, fly, look.' ... 'Make sound, talk'" (*P* 164). After a long, detailed description of the effects of nuclear war, both immediate and for generations to come in the form of chromosomal mutation, we get this description, as if the world had to be rediscovered or recreated or renamed after its annihilation: "The sun. The desert. The sky. The silence. The flat stones. The insects. The wind and the clouds. The moon. The stars. The west and east. The song, the color, the smell of the earth" (*EZ* 87).

It is striking how often DeLillo seems mesmerized, and wants to mesmerize us, by simple names, elemental names. It is as if their appearance on the page were the event itself, the event of elemental word-things. Bill Gray says in *Mao II*: "Our theme is four. Earth, air, fire and water" (*M* 71). Or Lianne in *Falling Man*, through the narrator: "Look around us, out there, up there, ocean, sky, night" (*FM* 232). After 9/11, these words sound very different, as "the witness wonders what has happened to the meaning of things, to tree, street, stone, wind, simple words lost in the falling ash" (*FM* 103). Inadequate words all after 9/11, and yet still oddly powerful. Simple words like: "All dust. Cars, houses, people" (*FM* 174).

So absolutely simple and primitive and then so absolutely contemporary and complex. It is hard not to think here of Mr. Tuttle, whose first words, in response to Lauren asking him how long he had been there, are "it is not able" (*BA* 43), followed by such phrases as "the trees are some of them" (*BA* 44), and "I know how much this house. Alone by the sea" (*BA* 48). Or later, "chair, table, wall, hall, all for the moment, in the moment" (*BA* 74).

Simple words, elementary words, like "moonlight." Simple English words, American words, somehow reinvented, DeLillo inflected, words that DeLillo will have signed, that he will have uniquely marked by his writing, words like *loomed*, as in the looming of death or the looming of the World Trade Towers: "Out the south windows the Trade towers stood cut against the night, intensely massed and near. This is the word 'loomed' in all its prolonged and impending force" (*M* 87). "Looms" looms over just about all of DeLillo's works: there are houses that "loomed over the street" ("MD" 126), and people "looming" (*L* 345; see 49 and *U* 608), and "looming figures" like Hitler and Freud (*WN* 289). In Athens, the Acropolis "looms. ... so powerfully there" (*N* 5). At a crucial moment in *White Noise* Jack Gladney himself—having earlier attended an academic ceremony where he "stood against the wall, attempting to loom, arms folded under the black gown" (*WN* 70)—tracks down his wife's Dylar dealer to a seedy motel and then "loomed in the doorway, conscious of looming," seeing himself "from Mink's viewpoint, magnified, threatening" (*WN* 311; see 312). And then there is Keith Neudecker, gone from his son's life for some time before 9/11, returning home in the aftermath of the attacks to "loom over the household" (*FM* 101). If one wished to prove pseudoscientifically but nonetheless convincingly that Don DeLillo really was the author, or one of the authors, of the pseudonymously penned *Amazons*, an analysis of how "loom" looms over the entire novel would surely suffice. We read there of how "bankruptcy loomed" over one of the players in a high-stakes game of strip Monopoly (*AZ* 280), of a sexual partner who, as the other partner says, must "kind of enjoy just looming up there above me" (*AZ* 71), of catastrophe constantly "looming around the bend" (*AZ* 246), and of a waiter, "a hostile presence" who "loomed like the shadow of a giant wing" over his rather inebriated diner: "Too soon for DTs, I thought. It was a waiter with champagne" (*AZ* 319; see also 190, 236, 293, 322).

Foreboding—that too is a DeLillo word: "This time the foreboding shook her strongly" (*U* 251; see *U* 167, "HM" 35, *WN* 161, *L* 261, 393), and *festering*: "But this was not history we were witnessing. It was some secret festering thing, some dreamed emotion that accompanies the dreamer out of sleep" (*WN* 128).

So there is *looming*, which is almost always a *looming over*—at once band and contraband—and *foreboding*, the contrabanding of present and future, or *festering*, a combination of past and present, and then a series of contrabanded words that suggest a concealment or a bringing out of concealment, a cover-up or a revelation (*L* 30), words like *folding* and *unfolding*, as in people "folded in hope" (*BA* 114), or people with their guard up, "keeping it folded close" (*U* 373), or the "deep fold in the grain of things" (*FM* 105), and then, on the other side of the fold, games in which "strategies unfolded" (*FM* 117), or an "evening slowly unfolding" ("S" 204; see *RD* 73), an "event unfolding" (*L* 225), or a moment that is forgotten, "never to be thought of except when it's in the process of unfolding" (*ZK* 19), "an unfolding of something half hidden and dazzling" (*FM* 92; see *U* 806 and *WN* 78).

Unfolding, then, but then also unraveling, the way someone can try to "unravel the event" (*N* 21), or let the event itself do the unraveling, to watch, for instance, the way, "point by point an event unravels / Invariant in its sequence" (*RS* 174). Things unfold or unravel or, indeed, *unwind*, as in "an image unwinding" (*RD* 223) or "a memory unwinding" (*RD* 191), a body or mind "unwinding, unspooling," as it thinks of "details buried for years" (*ZK* 16–17, 4). The mind thus can unwind, not such a bad thing, but then it can also *unravel*, being reduced to "gibberish," to "the sound of a mind unraveling" (*L* 127; see *N* 50).

Folding and unfolding, winding and unwinding, raveling and unraveling—all words, in short, with *implications*, "in the sense that major things are implied in minor moments" (*V* 46; see *RD* 133), or things with "vast implications" (*RS* 171), or "latent implications," like Lauren "tasting the breeze for latent implications" (*BA* 9), or "hidden implications" (*WN* 95), as in the eyes of one of Jack's daughters, which "seemed to contain two forms of life, the subject matter and its hidden implications" (*WN* 95). There are always implications, then, implications and "involvements" (*WN* 301), the price to pay, the recompense, for being "enmeshed" in the texture of things (*WN* 151).

Everything has a *texture*, then, if one is patient enough to unfold or unravel its implications, that is to say, its contrabands: "It was the time of year, the time of day, for a small insistent sadness to pass into the texture of things" (*WN* 56). One is thus always looking or listening in DeLillo, looking or listening along with DeLillo, "for some disturbance of tone, a nuance or flaw in the texture" (*L* 69; see 18), attempting "to find deeper textures" (*N* 6; see 196), the texture of "a faded brick building," for example, that seems to mirror the "texture of a life" ("BM" 112; see "IA" 69, *RS* 116, 253, 381, *C* 104). There are little things, like the way someone folds a napkin, "the unseeable texture of a life" (*ZK* 104; see *RS* 357; see 329), unseeable and yet, sometimes, indelibly registered, deep in the "weave," moments that may return in "precise textures" (*N* 225), or else will have "seeped into the texture of the world" (*N* 297). The famous Giants-Dodgers of 1951, for example, with "the textured histories of the teams" (*U* 14), along with a baseball "wobbling on the textured surface" (*U* 48), or a street that "began to acquire a medieval texture" (*U* 494), or a "piano work that had the texture of something old and gentled over" (*U* 173; see 82), or being "home alone, surrounded by all the things and textures that make you familiar, once again, to yourself" (*U* 482).

There is even, seriously, a word like "serious" in DeLillo, which is never used lightly, not with reports coming in about Kennedy, "seriously wounded"

(*L* 402), or worries about being or not being "a *serious* man" (*RS* 290; see *N* 300, *U* 416, 538): "I used to think I was a serious man. The work I did, the effort and dedication" (*ZK* 31). There are "serious people" (*RS* 290, *N* 92) everywhere in DeLillo, "serious men" down in the New York Subway, "rocking in the copper light" (*L* 13), or else ex-CIA operatives after the Bay of Pigs, "serious men deprived of an outlet" (*L* 63; see 330), or "serious people" working out of the Middle East, itself a serious place (*N* 92, 98), and people who know how to prepare themselves for "a serious evening" (*N* 234), or who know how to spend "serious time" on a thing (*L* 6, 112, 177, 334). Occasionally, there are even serious objects: "All right, pencils. Wood and lead. Pencils are serious. Wood and graphite. Materials from the earth. We respect this about a pencil" (*FM* 200). Or George the Waiter, George Manza, who one day shot up heroin in front of Nick and "cut him down to size," giving Nick "a lesson in serious things" (*U* 727).

There are words like *collapse* as well, "faces in collapse" after the attacks on 9/11 (*FM* 4), or the Kennedy motorcade "in collapse" after the shots (*L* 403–404), or, in "Creation," a single face that "went slowly dead. All the selves collapsing inward" ("C" 22). Or "shatteringly," an off-kilter word used as an adverb, as when Lauren suspects that Mr. Tuttle "experiences another kind of reality where he is here and there, before and after, and he moves from one to the other shatteringly, in a state of collapse, minus an identity, a language, a way to enjoy the savor of the honey-coated toast she watches him eat" (*BA* 64–65). And maybe all these words are being used correctly or incorrectly, I don't know, but I do know that no one else uses them quite like that. They sound right, then they don't, and then they do again.

It can happen in a moment, the result of a singular event, and it can become a state of affairs, as in all those "encrumpled bodies" in tents in Tompkins Square (*M* 152), all those people "shambling" or "in shambles." Rey and Lauren, for example, who, just after getting up, together in the kitchen, "shambled past each other to get things out of cabinets and drawers" (*BA* 7). "A shambling man" (*U* 753) is, it seems, someone "with a looseness about him, something offhand and shambling" ("BM" 110; see "MD" 131, *L* 337, *N* 39, 146), "a tallish, shambling fellow," for example, with "put-upon eyes," because "people with put-upon eyes usually shamble. It gives them time to figure out how wary they should be of a given situation" (*AZ* 348; see 83). But then how not to think of Rumsey after the attacks on the towers, of Rumsey "in shambles now" (*FM* 243; see *U* 447).

Then there's the slightly uncommon or incongruous use of a perfectly common and appropriate word, of a noun like *spill*, as in "the spill of electric light" (*BA* 101), or, in a description of poker, nouns like "toss and scatter," "mass and stack," or a noun like *instant*, oddly applied: "I saw a dark shape come out of the scrub near the road, an instant with a speed and weight to it" (*N* 191). Or adjectives like *wet* turned into nouns: A glass drops and Lauren sees the "speckled wet begin to spread on the plank floor" (*BA* 93).

And then there are words that are not made up but sound as if they were, words like *glop*, as in "a slick syrupy glop. This was the texture of his life" (*M* 135)—there's that texture again—or *smear*, as in "the smear of an abandoned car" (*GJ* 18), "small dull smears of meditative panic" (*PO* 17), or a mother's "smeared speech" (*FM* 193), smear, then, for a sight or a sound that is slurred, but then also *schemer* and *schmeered* (*U* 471), "the whole schmeer" (*P* 124), not to mention *slop*, "the moist slop of their pectorals in contact" (*P* 190), or "kitchen slop" (*ZK* 53), or *slurry*, as when Lauren scraped the back of her tongue, "a slurry of food, mucus and bacteria" (*BA* 97, see *N* 55), or *shimmy*, as in "a kind of shimmy in the way the water falls from the showerhead" (*PO* 13), or *slug* as a verb, intransitive but mobile, as when the UN hostage in Beirut "spat up blood" and "watched the pink thing slug into the drain" (*M* 107), among so many other words in "s," to pick on just the s-words. Or words like *blur*, which, though even more common, get reinvented in the form of Mr. Tuttle. "He was not skittish under her touch, or only routinely so, and she thought that nothing could seem unusual to him, or startling, or stirring, measured against the fact, the blur, whatever it was—the breathless shock of his being here" (*BA* 69).

Then there are all the words that get flagged by spell- or grammar-check because of an added *un-*, *dis-*, or *de-* (as if DeLillo were itself a negation), words like *disregardless*, used as an adjective, as in "I like old movies on television where a man lights a woman's cigarette. ... I'm normally so totally disregardless" (*PO* 46). Or *unstratify*, as when one tries to "unstratify the culture" (*U* 571), or to try to get at what is "unlayered maybe, if that means anything" (*BA* 121), or *unready*, as in "he's a little unready" for marriage (*U* 471), or as in—the negation of a negation—a "not unoccurring" smell (*U* 361; see *BA* 77), or something *unshoulderable* (*U* 191), or, in *Libra*, "a tininess, an unnoticeability (if such a word exists)" (*L* 123), or *unremarkable*, as in lab tests whose "findings were unremarkable" (*FM* 206). "You told me these were routine tests. 'Unremarkable' was the word you used" (*DR* 37–38). Or this one, right up DeLillo's alley: "It is well within your experience to invent a fantasy of events as you think they transpired or are transpiring. This not un-up your alley" (*U* 202). Or, finally—a performative contradiction all unto itself—the word *unwordable*, as in "all the unwordable rubble" (*P* 22). Unwordable, then, like the first word of a new negative theology.

Simple Words

I use words, absolutely.

P 20

What?

BA 9

There are thus all those words that DeLillo has made his, partly his, and then those very common words, simple, everyday words, that he has inimitably signed, most definitely marked and sent off anew, words like, to be exact, "definitely": "I'll get you a copy, definitely" (*FM* 149). "I see you with a cat, definitely. There ought to be a cat slipping along the walls" (*FM* 107). But even more than definitely, *absolutely*, as in "Of course. This room. Absolutely" (*EZ* 238). "'Just the two of us,' he said. 'If that's all right.' 'Sure, absolutely, why not'" (*P* 193). Or again, "That's what kids do, absolutely, but I have to admit I'm beginning to wonder" (*FM* 16). "Can I bring my tarot cards with me?" "Of course you can. Absolutely. It's a picnic (*EZ* 68; see *A* 167, 313, *GJ* 132, 196, *RD* 21, *BA* 118; *P* 92, 108, *WN* 29, 261, 288; *N* 47, 165). "Sure, together, absolutely" (*RS* 271; see 63, 110, *U* 78, 479, *ZK* 51). And it can even come at a time when nothing sounds absolute:

"Did you get a haircut?"
He sat thinking, then reached back to run his thumb over the back of his neck. A haircut was a hurried few moments in a well-scheduled day, submitted to in order to be forgotten.
"I think so, absolutely." ("*S*" 185)

Absolutely, then, but then even a phrase like "all right," a mark of that retrospective recognition we have been talking about throughout. Recall Packer realizing what's going on around his limo by watching TV inside it: "It was a protest all right" (*C* 89). In *End Zone*, Gary has a similar moment of recognition, just after a concussion: "There was music. She was standing behind a chair now, listening to a Bach cantata. It was Bach all right" (*EZ* 126). Later in the novel, there is a similar confirmation of another injury: "It's a clean fracture. Right below the elbow. I saw the x ray. It's broke clean. They broke it all right. No question about it" (*EZ* 145). Then there's *Great Jones Street*, "We've got a limousine all right" (*GJ* 151), and *Running Dog*, "She was eye-catching all right" (*RD* 4), and *Mao II*, "Mao Zedong. She liked that name all right" (*M* 62, 178). Or, as people leave by way of the Dodger clubhouse after that famous game in which Ralph Branca gave up the winning home run to Bobby Thomson, "there's Branca all right, the first thing you see, stretched facedown on a flight of six steps, feet touching the floor" (*U* 59). Or this one, as Nick on that fateful day goes to the basement room, scared but also intrigued by what he might find there, and "George was in the room all right, playing solitaire" (*U* 778). Or, finally, this one, from *The Body Artist*, as Lauren learns after Rey's death about all the money he owes. "He had debts cascading on other debts. This made her feel good. It was Rey all right" (*BA* 94). That's how you recognize Rey and that's how you recognize DeLillo. You read a phrase like that and you think, "That's DeLillo all right."

So there's that, but then there are idiomatic phrases like "there's that" or "at least there was that": "He was taller than she was. At least there was that" (*PO* 106). And then everyday words, the simplest possible, like "what," as in "What?" Gary says in *The Day Room*: "I walked in the door and thought what for" (*DR* 65). And then just after: "Now that we're finally here, I'm thinking so what" (*DR* 68). Or else, elsewhere, "I haven't thought of that since I was, what" (*U* 197). Or, "You've lived here, what?" "Just under four months" ("BM" 113). Or, "I want to say something but what" (*TBA* 8).

Then there are combined or hyphenated whats, like "whatnot" (*M* 175), as in "Does he have religious affiliation and whatnot?" (*L* 10), or "what with" (*RD* 144, *BA* 120) and "what-have-you" (*RD* 95), not to mention "What's-her-name" (*L* 265, *U* 176) or "what's-her-face?": "He felt like calling up what's-her-face, the photographer, and talking to her machine" (*M* 197). "I'm reasonably sure that's what's-his-name over there who used to be married to the paper bag woman" (*U* 485; see 664), "what's-his-name with the orange pickup" (*U* 128; see 359). "Look at these people. It's like I-don't-know-what" (*U* 54). And then this about Nick, "This boy has got I-don't-know-what written all over him. You know exactly what I mean" (*U* 756). And we do.

Distinctly American idioms all, now forever DeLillo-inflected, from now on distinctly DeLillo, whatever that means. And that's another one—"Whatever that means"—where the reference to language is crucial. Think, for example, of Eric Packer who, after having seen himself recoil from the blast on the TV screen inside his stretch limo, "recoiled for real," "whatever that might possibly mean" (*C* 95). Or Keith Neudecker, walking through New York just minutes after the fall of the towers, Keith, for whom "there was something critically missing from the things around him. They were unfinished, whatever that means. They were unseen, whatever that means, shop windows, loading platforms, paint-sprayed walls. Maybe this is what things look like when there is no one here to see them" (*FM* 5). Later, Florence says to Keith: "Because there's something about you, in the way you hold a space. I'm not sure what that means" (*FM* 88). Or again, "Keith stopped shaving for a time, whatever that means" (*FM* 67), where it's uncertain whether we are talking about the act of not shaving or the phrase that designates it. Or think of the anonymous viewer of *24 Hour Psycho* at the MOMA who "wanted complete immersion, whatever that means" (*PO* 115). Or Lauren in *The Body Artist*, who told herself stories that "did not seem hers exactly. She was in them so heedlessly they seemed to come from a deeper source, whatever that might mean" (*BA* 115). Or Nick Shay who says to Klara Sax some forty years after their brief affair: "I thought I owed us this visit. Whatever that means" (*U* 73).

One of the implications of linguistic shrapnel seems to be that we get hit by these things, that they get embedded, reemerging or resurfacing one fine day, unfolding or unraveling, unwinding, expressing themselves, becoming a gesture, and only then do we know or only then can we even try to know what they mean.

Letters

The birds broke off the feeder in a wing-whir that was all b's and r's, the letter b followed by a series of vibrato r's. But that wasn't it at all. That wasn't anything like it.

BA 17

Think what would happen if we didn't fill the grids. People. Pause and think. How empty it would be. Suddenly nothing. Would be dark. Would be bleak. All the words that end in the letter k. What is out there? Who are we?

V 96–97

She made the noise again. A long wet whinnying letter k.

U 81

In *Ratner's Star* Shazar Lazarus Ratner himself advises Billy Twillig: "Don't look down your nose at esoterica. If you know the right combination of letters, you can make anything. This is the secret power of the alphabet" (*RS* 222). In *The Names* a scholar in Jerusalem echoes this thought: "If you will know the correct order of letters, you make a world, you make creation. This is why they will hide the order. If you will know the combination, you make all life and death" (*N* 152). After reflecting upon language in general and words and names in particular, DeLillo's characters also often reflect upon letters, simple letters. They sometimes even reflect upon the way in which characters, as we call them, are letters. As Owen Brademas recalls, "'Character' comes from a Greek word. It means 'to brand or to sharpen.' Or 'pointed stake' if it's a noun. ... This is probably because 'character' in English not only means someone in a story but a mark or symbol." "Like a letter of the alphabet" (*N* 10).

The whole intrigue of *The Names* revolves, in fact, around murders committed by a cult "interested in the alphabet," "the alphabet itself ... letters, written symbols, fixed in sequence" (*N* 30; see 210). Like Owen Brademas, they are even interested in the "shapes" of letters, in the "material" used to form them, in the history of writing (*N* 35–36), in anagrams and palindromes, names and place-names (*N* 76, 139). With references to Sanskrit, Aramaic, Arabic, Greek and Latin characters (*N* 155, 167, 170, 291), and even comparisons between them—"If Greek or Latin characters are paving stones, Arabic is rain" (*N* 137)—letters become the principal character, as it were, of *The Names*. Later in the novel, the narrator runs his hand across a marble surface with black Koranic letters, only later to learn that they were "the ninety-nine names of God" (*N* 272; see 283). James Axton, James "Ax-stone," as someone calls him, almost understands, but not quite:

> What was it about the letter-shapes that struck his soul with the force of a tribal mystery? The looped bands, scything curves, the sense of a sacred architecture. What did he almost understand? The mystery of alphabets, the contact with death and oneself, one's other self, all made stonebound with a mallet and chisel. (*N* 284)

There's something about letters and their relation to sound: "Each sound has one sign only. This is the genius of the alphabet. Simple, inevitable. No wonder it happened in the desert" (*N* 295).

After the word or the name, then, there's the letter—a letter like *k*, for example, from *Amerikana* (just kidding—that's more Kafka) to *Zero K*. The two boys in "Midnight in Dostoevsky" try to imagine the name of the mysterious man they have been tracking like spies or like novelists: "Great name possibilities. Pavel, Mikhail, Aleksei, Viktor with a *k*" ("MD" 137). In *Falling Man* Lianne thinks of the dog downstairs, "Marko, she thought, with a *k*, whatever that might signify" (*FM* 119; see 120). When Jack Gladney gives himself an "extra initial" to add to his authority as a Hitler scholar, "a tag" he would wear "like a borrowed suit" (*WN* 16), it appears to be none other than the initial *K* (and maybe *A* as well) that he adds to his name in order to become J. A. K. Gladney: "I am the false character that follows the name around" (*WN* 17). There seems to be something special about that *k*—beginning with the final letter of New York, New York, to which Nick Shay, for example, has come back for the Great Northest Blackout, followed by Keith Neudecker, witness and victim of the attacks on the World Trade Towers on that dark day in 2001. And then, of course, there's *Zero K* and its narrator Jeffrey Lockhart. All these letters, uniquely signed, initialed, from *Americana* (with an *A*) to *Point Omega* (with an Ω) to *Zero K* (with a *Z*).

Punctuation

"When will the book be done?" "I'm fixing the punctuation." "Punctuation's interesting. I make a point to observe how a writer uses commas."

M 127

Or the other Nancy, what's-her-name, briefly, between incidental sex acts, in Portland that time, Oregon, without a last name. The city had a last name, the woman did not.

FM 19

After the name, the word, and the letter, what's left but the unconventional uses of articles, definite and indefinite, as when someone sits "in a dining room at the Chesterfield, eating the sole" (*M* 125), the one on the menu, of course, the one that was just ordered (I'll have the sole), but also the one that, in the ordinary course of things, would not have been garnished with a definite article, that is, that would have been served sole. And if there are sometimes added words, there are also omitted ones: "Want something?" "Mineral water be nice," she said (*U* 114). Or words—a simple preposition, for example—wonderfully deferred: "'I brushed my teeth with my finger after the Ali-Foreman fight in Zaire,' Murray said, 'That's the southernmost point I've ever brushed my teeth with my finger at'" (*WN* 67). What makes this so funny is not only the trivia being pursued, and in a faculty dining room no less, but that final preposition, ungrammatical and yet somehow unavoidable, somehow just right.

There is the prolepsis of our everyday language: "I had a local chain of stores, dry cleaning, which I sold after my wife passed away because I didn't need it anymore, the aggravation" (*U* 180). And interruptions in the normal course of a sentence, that is, interruptions that are maybe normal in the course of everyday conversation but not so normal in writing: "He loved her, she lives in Vermont now, very much" (*U* 228); "Well, I had a little scuffle in the elevator. It's noticeable? At my hotel" (*U* 340). Or little interruptions in writerly conventions: "George the Waiter was sitting in a small storage room he used as a home, he said, away from home" (*U* 721)—the commas coming to take "home" away from "home." Or, "finally it broke, all hell" (*GJ* 15)—the comma coming to break the sentence at "broke."

Sentences, then, made like donuts, as Bill Gray says, with phrases and words and then, the holes within the donuts, punctuation, periods and commas, like little pieces of shrapnel, commas to break up sentences, to scan them, give them breathing room: "For one whole day it was here until they removed it out of my sight and took it to the medical examiner, with his blood and what else, I won't even describe, okay, for evidence" (*BA* 59). There are commas that slow down thought or that make normal thought seem like an afterthought, retroflective in its contraband: "She thought of the Japanese woman, a beautiful and problematic thing, if she is Japanese at all, watering her garden when the sky shows rain" (*BA* 36).

All these forms of prolepsis and analepsis, of supposition and apposition, all these ways of looking forward or doubling back in language: "Now he was the smoke, Rey was, the thing in the air, vaporous" (*BA* 33). These are the things that give "texture" to prose, to be sure, though they are also pretty amusing, sources of inestimable pleasure: "He came back out, carrying a can of beer and a soft drink, also in a can" (*RD* 186). There's something about that "also in a can" that just kills you. Or, finally, this one, where the retrospective identification of the subject of a sentence, that is, the delay in identifying the subject, in this case a *name*, at once describes and performs what I have been calling Don DeLillo's contraband: "They talked a while and changed the subject and he turned off the recorder and she turned it back on and maybe he'd had one, yes, a name, but he'd forgotten it or lost it and could not get it back" (*BA* 54). Mr. Tuttle may have forgotten his name, there's that, but in this sentence the name *name* is itself withheld, delayed, embedded in Lauren's head, allowed to come out, to express itself, only later, like organic shrapnel, in the narration. Mr. Tuttle may have forgotten his name, or lost it, and we may forget this passage, but I guarantee that we will be forever marked by this syntax, this cadence, this delay, this temporality, this contraband writing. Not so much plots or plotlines, stories or story lines, then, at least not for me, but words and phrases, tones and intonations, a certain way of punctuating a phrase and, thus, a certain way of speaking and of breathing. Because he is in our tissue now, Don DeLillo is, in our literature and our language, a voice smuggled in from the outside that now makes us, some of us, who we are or who we will be, whatever that means.

Countersignature

Today's little task is pretty simple, a sort of signature that could be used as both beginning and end.

A 240–241

I myself appear briefly at the very end, reflected in a mirror as I hold the camera.

A 347

"In our privatest mind," he said, "there is only chaos and blur. We invented logic to beat back our creatural selves. We assert or deny. We follow M with N."

"MD" 139

Mike the Book had a flourish he did with his hand. It was broad and Roman, a flat hand moving parallel to the earth as a gesture of burial or a way of writing finis to something significant.

U 770

finis,

M. N.

Acknowledgments

I'm afraid to talk to writers about their work. It's so easy to say something stupid.

M 37

We are making a daring entrance into the city of Chicago in a howling blizzard at four or five in the morning and there is no camaraderie in our vehicle.

AZ 190

I thought of calling Bellevue next but decided finally in favor of St. Vincent's, gentle, humane and dedicated, St. Vincent's, merciful and compassionate. I insisted on speaking to a nun. I wanted someone who believed in St. Vincent himself, in his ideals, in his sacrifices, whatever these may have been. ... someone who believed in the sacredness of dying and the veneration of the dead. No nun, no deal. This is what I told them.

GJ 92–93

Mr. Bronzini called it a sabbatical. One of those words of his, to be spelled, explained and acted out.

U 715

Without the generous, unexpected, and, I had to admit at the time, completely undeserved invitation from Karim Daanoune to speak at a conference devoted to the work of Don DeLillo in Paris in February 2016, I would never have dreamed of doing this book. While I had been an avid, enthusiastic reader of DeLillo for many years, truth be told, for decades, I had at that point written precious little on his work, especially when compared to experts such as Peter Boxall, Linda Kauffman, Mark Osteen, Jacqueline Zubeck, Karim Daanoune himself, and others at that Paris event. But I gratefully accepted that invitation despite these reservations and despite the fact that Don DeLillo himself would be there and that, as Brita Nilsson says in *Mao II* about meeting Bill Gray, it would have been so easy to say something stupid in front of him. Let me thank here then, first and foremost, Karim Daanoune for that unique opportunity and then Don DeLillo, who, if he heard me say something stupid about what I called at the time "Don DeLillo's Contraband," was kind enough not to call me on it.

Acknowledgments

If the original motivation for this book was that Paris conference in 2016, it was a research sabbatical from DePaul University in spring 2017 and a two-year stint as a fellow in the DePaul Humanities Center that allowed me to turn that original conference paper into this more complete work. I am grateful to DePaul University (named, for those who don't know, after St. Vincent de Paul) for that sabbatical and fellowship and then for the opportunity to teach a seminar on DeLillo's *Underworld* in spring 2018 with thirteen (!) exceptional students. Thanks also to my colleagues at DePaul, and particularly Elizabeth Rottenberg, who encouraged me to teach that seminar on DeLillo and who has been a receptive and critical ear throughout the entire time I was writing this work. She, as much as anyone, has convinced me that friendship all comes down to the simplest of things, like the "things that happen and what we say about them" (*N* 312). I am grateful as well to Matthew Pacholec, who read an early draft of this work and offered many helpful suggestions, to Randy Honold and Russ Ford, fellow DeLillo travelers at DePaul and Elmhurst College, and to Peter Steeves, who, as Director of the DePaul Humanities Center, offered not only support but much excellent advice on a penultimate version of this work.

This work would also not be what it is without the guidance and encouragement of two old friends, both DeLillo aficionados in their own right, Nicholas Royle at Sussex and Jeffrey Nealon at Penn State. I owe much of my own thinking about DeLillo to their published works, as well as to my many conversations with Nick in Seaford and my many years of "discussions," let's call them, with Jeff and our common friend Joe Sullivan at the Old Town Ale House, Simon's, and Ravens in Chicago, and, most recently, Duffy's in Forest Park. I would also be remiss not to thank here the remarkable staff at Bloomsbury, and particularly Katherine De Chant, for her consummate professionalism, her valued assistance, and her unwavering support of this project.

My thanks, finally, and yet again, to Pascale-Anne and Jean-Stéphane, who bring me every day the genius of the everyday, "the sand-grain manyness of things that can't be counted" (*U* 60). Only that, in the end, still has the power to make me believe—not to go all religious on you here—come what may and "world without end, amen" (*U* 824–825).

www.ingramcontent.com/pod-product-compliance
Lightning Source LLC
Chambersburg PA
CBHW070312230426
43663CB00011B/2092